Performance and Place

Edited by

Leslie Hill and Helen Paris

palgrave
macmillan

First published 2006 by
PALGRAVE MACMILLAN
Houndmills, Basingstoke, Hampshire RG21 6XS and
175 Fifth Avenue, New York, N.Y. 10010
Companies and representatives throughout the world

PALGRAVE MACMILLAN is the global academic imprint of the Palgrave
Macmillan division of St. Martin's Press, LLC and of Palgrave Macmillan Ltd.
Macmillan® is a registered trademark in the United States, United Kingdom
and other countries. Palgrave is a registered trademark in the European
Union and other countries.

ISBN-13: 978-1-4039-4503-7 hardback
ISBN-10: 1-4039-4503-9 hardback
ISBN-13: 978-1-4039-4504-4 paperback
ISBN-10: 1-4039-4504-7 paperback

This book is printed on paper suitable for recycling and made from fully
managed and sustained forest sources.

A catalogue record for this book is available from the British Library.

Library of Congress Cataloging-in-Publication Data
Performance and place / edited by Leslie Hill and Helen Paris.
    p.   cm. — (Performance interventions)
    Includes bibliographical references and index.
    ISBN 1-4039-4503-9 (cloth) — ISBN 1-4039-4504-7 (pbk.)
    1. Performing arts—Philosophy.   2. Place (Philosophy)
    3. Performance art.   I. Hill, Leslie, 1967–   II. Paris, Helen, 1968–
III. Series.
    PN1584.P43 2006
    791.01—dc22   2005055334

10   9   8   7   6   5   4   3   2   1
15   14   13   12   11   10   09   08   07   06

Printed and bound in Great Britain by
Antony Rowe Ltd, Chippenham and Eastbourne

For Gill Lloyd and Judith Knight
thanks for giving our placelessness a place

Contents

vii

List of Illustrations

Acknowledgements

This project was supported by a generous International Artist Residency at the Couvent des Récollets, Paris, funded by the French Ministry of Cultural Affairs and the City Hall of Paris, managed by Odile Froument, and a Research Leave award for Helen Paris from Brunel University.

We thank MGM for kind permission to reproduce a clip and still photo from *Night of the Hunter* (1955); we also thank Hugh Glendinning for the three photos used in Chapter 1 and Fred Askew for the photo used in Chapter 14.

Special thanks to Alexandra Hyde for help in preparing the typescript, to our project manager Cheryl Pierce and to everyone at Artsadmin (artsadmin.co.uk).

Thanks to Emily Rosser, Commissioning Editor when we started the project, and to Helen Craine, Paula Kennedy and all at Palgrave Macmillan for their support of this project through the process. Thanks too go to our copyeditor, Penny Simmons.

Finally we are grateful to our families for their encouragement and support: Virginia and Paul Resta, Jerry and Barbara Hill, and Tony, Juliet and Christine Paris.

Preface

Leslie Hill

Of course, thanks to the house, a great many of our memories
are housed, and if the house is a bit elaborate, if it has a cellar and
a garret, nooks and corridors, our memories have refuges that are
all the more clearly delineated. All our lives we come back to them
in our daydreams. A psychoanalyst should, therefore, turn his
attention to this simple localization of our memories. I should
like to give the name of topoanalysis to this auxiliary of psychoa-
nalysis. Topoanalysis, then, would be the systematic psychological
study of the sites of our intimate lives. In the theatre of the past
that is constituted by memory, the stage setting maintains the
characters in their dominant roles. At times we think we know
ourselves in time, when all we know is a sequence of fixations in
the spaces of the being's stability – a being who does not want to
melt away, and who, even in the past, when he sets out in search
of things past, wants time to 'suspend' its flight. In its countless
alveoli, space contains compressed time. That is what space is for.

(Gaston Bachelard[1])

Just as living and remembering intertwines with the architecture of
home, so the creation and experience of art forms and artworks
intertwines with the architecture of concert halls, galleries, theatres and
cinemas. How inseparable are our first memories of theatre from our
curious, sometimes awed experience of the theatre building itself with
its plush seats, its dazzling lights, its arches, aprons, balconies and boxes?
And for those who inhabit the stage and the backstage, the wings, the
flies, the trapdoors, the dressing rooms provide elaborate nooks and
corridors for treading the boards of Bachelard's 'topoanalysis'. This is
not, however, a book about the architecture or topoanalysis of theatre.
It is a book about contemporary performance and the different ways in
which it is sited 'within and without' and how we experience those
places, whether institutional or transient, real or on-line, as part of the
fabric of the artwork in a similar fashion to the way that Bachelard links
memory to space. Some contemporary performance is 'housed' within
the familiar architecture of a theatre or gallery, while some work is
'homeless', setting up temporary camp. Although this is not a book

about Live Art practice or Performance Art *per se*, many of the case studies that follow come from this sector, as this is the most gypsy-like end of the performance spectrum and thus of particular interest to a study of place and 'placelessness' in performance.

My introduction to this collection is divided into stand-alone introductions to the five parts of the book. Please feel welcome to read the entire introduction across the volume or navigate part by part according to your inclination. The first part of the collection is titled 'Mapping the Territory'. My introduction to this part gives an account of my use of the word 'placelessness' and is followed by chapters written by four people who literally 'place' contemporary performance work in their roles as arts curators, funders and directors in the United States and the United Kingdom. The second part, titled '(Dis)Placing the Senses', considers the relationship of the visceral to the virtual in chapters by artists and academics who take us from a multimedia dance lab in an abandoned coal mine to interactive film-making to cyber-alter egos to the zero-gravity environment of free-fall choreography with Russian cosmonauts. Part III, 'On Location', considers performance work in relation to geography and psychogeography in locations ranging from the hyper-reality of Las Vegas to the slave forts of Cape Coast and Elmina and the nuclear holocaust sites of Hiroshima and Nagasaki. The fourth part of the book, 'Border Panic', looks at issues of boundaries in performance through case studies by artists and academics that take us from the political protest performance of the 'Billionaires for Bush' to Shakespeare plays staged on the wasteland war zone between two rival Rio *favelas* to the elusive boundaries between performer and audience in 'one-to-one' performance. The final part of this collection, 'Theatre in a Crowded Fire', considers performance-making in relation to architecture. As the title suggests, this is the wild card section of the book. My introduction is a literal and metaphorical musing on fire and theatre. The chapters that follow are all written by artists who have been given editorial licence to 'let rip', thus much of this part is more poetic and less academic than the other chapters included in the collection. I hope you enjoy exploring the cellars, garrets, nooks and corridors contained between these pages.

Note

1 Gaston Bachelard, *The Poetics of Space* (Boston, MA: Beacon Press), p.8.

Note on Contributors

Johannes Birringer is Principal Research Fellow in Live Art at Nottingham Trent University. He is a choreographer and, with his Houston-based ensemble (www.aliennationcompany.com), has created numerous dance-theatre works, video installations and site-specific performances in collaboration with artists in Europe, North America, Latin America and China. He is the author of several books, including *Media and Performance: Along the Border* (1998) and *Performance on the Edge: Transformations of Culture* (2000). After creating the dance-technology programme at Ohio State University, he founded the Interaktionslabor Göttelborn in Germany (http://interaktionslabor.de).

L. M. Bogad is Assistant Professor at the University of California at Davis's Department of Theatre and Dance. He is the author of *Electoral Guerrilla Theatre: Radical Ridicule and Social Movements* (2005).

Laurie Beth Clark is a Professor in the Art Department of the University of Wisconsin. Her courses there include video, performance, installations and graduate seminars, and she is appointed to the central administration as the Associate Vice-Chancellor for Faculty and Staff Programmes. She also provides leadership for the campus-wide Visual Culture initiatives. Her life work includes art-making, research, teaching and administration. Clark produces large-scale, site-specific installations and performances, single-channel and multi-monitor videos and virtual environments. She is currently editing a video about the performance of truth. Her work has been seen at such historically significant venues as Franklin Furnace and the Cleveland Public Theatre Performance Art Festival and has been recognized with awards from the Jerome Foundation, the McKnight Foundation, the National Endowment for the Arts and the Wisconsin Arts Board. Clark's research-in-progress is a comparative study of trauma memorials that includes sites in Africa, Asia, Europe and the Americas.

Helen Cole has been the Producer of Live Art and Dance at Arnolfini since 1998 and is the Artistic Producer of Inbetween Time Festival of Live Art and Intrigue, Bristol, and of the international artist development project, *Breathing Space*. She is the Producer of *32,000 Points of Light* and *Whiteplane2*. She is a member of Guardians of Doubt, Live Art UK, the Experimental Theatre Consortium, Theatre Bristol, and is a Drama and Dance Adviser for the British Council.

Toni Dove is an artist/independent producer who works primarily with electronic media, including virtual reality, interactive video installations, performance and DVD ROMs that engage viewers in responsive and immersive narrative environments. Her work has been presented in the United States, Europe and Canada as well as in print and on radio and television. Projects include *Archeology of a Mother Tongue*, a virtual reality installation with Michael Mackenzie, and an interactive movie installation, *Artificial Changelings*, which débuted at the Rotterdam Film Festival. Her current project under development is *Spectropia*, a feature-length interactive movie for two players also to be released as a linear feature film. A DVD ROM, *Sally or The Bubble Burst*, an interactive scene from the *Spectropia* project is distributed on the Cycling '74 label. Dove has received numerous grants and awards including the Rockefeller Foundation, National Endowment for the Arts and the Eugene McDermott Award in the Arts from MIT http://www.tonidove.com

Matthew Goulish teaches in the Liberal Arts Department and the MFA Writing Programme of The School of the Art Institute of Chicago, after receiving his BA in theatre from Kalamazoo College. He co-founded Goat Island in 1987, and has toured extensively with the company. His *39 Microlectures – In Proximity of Performance* was published in 2000. Other essays have appeared in *Live: Art and Performance* (2004) and *After Criticism* (2004). 'The Ordering of the Fantastic' is a chapter from a forthcoming book on the life and work of Lawrence Steger (1961–1999).

Paul Heritage is Professor of Drama and Performance at Queen Mary College, University of London, and Director of *People's Palace Projects*. For over 20 years he has combined academic and professional activity in theatre. He was a director with Gay Sweatshop and a founder of The Theatre in Prisons and Probation (TIPP) Centre at the University of Manchester. His main research is in the field of human rights and performance, and he is the director of two large-scale programmes in Brazil, *Staging Human Rights* and *Changing the Scence*, sponsored by the AHRB, The British Academy, British Council, UK Community Fund, UNESCO and the Brazilian Ministry of Justice. Thousands of prisoners and guards from Rio to the Amazon have participated in these programmes run from the Brazilian Office of *People's Palace Projects* (www. peoplespalace.org.br).

Lin Hixson (director/collaborator) is a full Professor in the Performance Department at The School of the Art Institute of Chicago. She received her undergraduate degree in education and political science from the University of Oregon, and her MFA in performance from Otis Art Institute of Parsons School of Design. She was a founding member of the Los Angeles performance collective Hangers (1978–81) and has mounted over 30 interdisciplinary performances since 1981. Co-founder of Goat Island in 1987, she has received three NEA fellowships in New Genres, one NEA fellowship in Choreography, and three Illinois Arts Council fellowships.

Lois Keidan is the co-founder and Director of the Live Art Development Agency, London, established in 1999. From 1992–7 she was Director of Live Arts at the Institute of Contemporary Arts in London, presenting a year-round programme dedicated to supporting and representing new artists, new ideas and new practices from the United Kingdom and around the world. Prior to that she was responsible for national policy and provision for Performance Art and interdisciplinary practices at the Arts Council of England. She has contributed articles on Live Art to a range of journals and publications and has given presentations at festivals, colleges, venues and conferences in the United Kingdom and internationally. For more information about the Live Art Development Agency visit www.thisisliveart.co.uk.

Andrew Kötting is one of Britain's most intriguing artists, and perhaps the only filmmaker currently practising who could be said to have taken to heart the spirit of visionary curiosity and hybrid creativity exemplified by the late Derek Jarman. His 20-year *oeuvre* has moved from early Live Art inflected, often absurdist, pieces, ripe with their own internal logics and skewed mythologies, through darkly comic shorts teasing out the melancholy surrealism at the heart of contemporary Englishness, to two resolutely independent features that take landscape and journeys as the springboards for striking and inventive enquiries into identity, belonging, history and notions of community. Throughout his work he has also written and performed, created for digital platforms and for the gallery and is increasingly working directly with sound and music, reflecting both his wide-ranging formal interests but also his refusal to adopt conventional ideas of closure around artworks in any medium.

Patrick Laviolette is a post-doctoral fellow in the Department of Anthropology, University College London. He is interested in how cultural perceptions of Cornwall's landscapes act as metaphors of difference and social distinction. He has recently been compiling two books on Cornwall, *The Landscaping of Metaphor: Topographies of Cornish Difference* and *Cornish Pastiche: Contemporary Perceptions of a Peninsular Landscape*. Patrick is also working on two other research projects. The first examines issues of embodiment, identity, narrative and risk in relation to certain coastal extreme sports like caving, cliff jumping and surfing. This collective study *Risk and Recreation* is to be published by UCL Press as an edited compilation on the cultural construction of the extreme. The other project is on the recycling of identities, history and heritage through a focus on theatre performance groups and recycling artists.

Rob La Frenais has organized and curated performance, installation and site-specific work since the mid-eighties. In the late nineties he encountered the work of Kitsou Dubois, the first artist to actively develop a body of work in zero gravity. Working with the Arts Catalyst, the UK-based science-art agency, he experienced micro-gravity for himself and then went on to organize flights for a number of artists in Russia's Star City.

Graeme Miller is a research associate with RESCEN at Middlesex University and an artist, theatre-maker and composer. He was a co-founder of the influential British performance company, Impact Theatre Co-Operative in 1978, whose works included *The Carrier Frequency* with Russel Hoban. His own theatre works include, *Dungeness: The Desert in the Garden* (1987), *A Girl Skipping* (1990), *The Desire Paths* (1992) and *Country Dance* (1999). He has also made a series of sound-based works specific to their landscape: *The Sound Observatory* in Birmingham, *Feet of Memory*, *Boots of Nottingham*. With artist, Mary Lemley, he has made the geographical works *Listening Ground, Lost Acres* (1994) in Salisbury and *Reconnaissance* in Norbury Park, Surrey. His more recent works include *Overhead Projection* at Warwick Castle, *Lost Sound* with filmmaker John Smith and *LINKED*. *Bassline* was shown in Vienna (Weiner Feswochen, May 2004). He writes music and designs sound for TV, dance, theatre and film with credits ranging from TV theme tunes to dance scores.

Jennifer Parker-Starbuck is a lecturer in Theatre and Performance Studies at the Scarborough School of Arts, University of Hull. She received her PhD from the City University of New York Graduate Center. Her current book project, *Cyborg Theatre: Corporeal/Technological*

Intersections in Multimedia, investigates multimedia performance and contemporary subjectivity. She is the co-organizer of the Association for Theatre in Higher Education (ATHE) Performance Studies Preconference and the ATHE Performance Studies Focus Group Representative 2004–6. Her essays and reviews have appeared in *Theatre Journal, PAJ, the Journal of Dramatic Theory and Criticism, Western European Stages, Didaskalia* and *Slavic and East European Performance*. Her essay, 'Shifting Strengths: The Cyborg Theatre of Cathy Weis', appears in the anthology *Bodies in Commotion: Disability and Performance*, edited by Philip Auslander and Carrie Sandahl.

Michael Peterson is Assistant Professor of Theatre and Drama at the University of Wisconsin, teaching primarily in Performance Studies and Theatre Theory. He is the author of *Straight White Male* (1997), a critical study of identity privilege in performance monologues. He is currently completing a book-length study, *Las Vegas Culture*. An actor since childhood and an occasional director of theatre and performance works, Peterson is currently interested in the intersections of physical culture and performance-making. In 2003 he completed the first of a series of localized 'Running Commentary' pieces, in Darmstadt, Germany; 'Running Commentary: The Madison Lakes Project' is in long-term development.

Emily Puthoff is currently an Assistant Professor of Sculpture at the State University of New York at New Paltz. She is a sculptor/hybrid-media artist living in the Hudson Valley of New York. Her work ranges in scale and scope from artist's books to immersive installations, while her mediums encompass everything from cast sugar to robotics. She has also on occasion ventured into performance, but often prefers to position the viewer as the integral performer of her pieces. Her work is shown nationally and internationally, including at the: Sixth Manifestation International Video and Electronic Art Festival, Champe Libre, Montreal; Museum of Modern Art Library, Printed Matter, and the Axel Raben Gallery in New York; OUT VIDEO Festival, National Centre for Contemporary Arts, Ekaterinberg, Russia; and in Arizona, the eyelounge in Phoenix, Arizona State University Art Museum and the Museum of Contemporary Art in Tucson. Her work can be found on-line at http://www.emilyputhoff.com.

Julian Maynard Smith studied architecture and visual art. He has been a performance artist since 1978, producing solo and group work. He is the founder and artistic director of Station House Opera, whose productions have toured worldwide since 1980 to the present day, including the monumental outdoor sculptural projects *The Bastille Dances* and *The Salisbury Proverbs, Black Works* which was filmed for BBC 2 as *Warren Beatty's Coat* in 1997 and more recent productions with video *Snakes and Ladders, Roadmetal Sweetbread* and *Mare's Nest*. The company's most recent production, *Live from Paradise,* takes place in three cities simultaneously linked by video streaming. His solo sculpture and installation work includes *Spaces and Narrations* in 1998 and *Limelight and Other Works* at Kettle's Yard Gallery Cambridge during his Artist Fellowship at Kettle's Yard and Sidney Sussex College, Cambridge.

Mark Waugh is a Visual Art Officer with responsibility for strategic national development of Live Art at the Arts Council of England. Previous projects as an independent producer and curator included, *Phantasmagoria, Transmutations Festival of Live Art, Die Leiber Rausch, Psychostasia, Pharmakon,* and *Blunt Cut*. An early adaptor to the realm of convergence media and performance, he has written and lectured on an array of subjects from Araki to Warhol. His first novel, *Come,* was published in 1997.

Martha Wilson is a performance artist and founding Director of Franklin Furnace Archive, Inc., a museum she established in her TriBeCa storefront loft in lower Manhattan which, since its inception in 1976, has presented and preserved temporal art: artists' books and other multiples produced internationally after 1960; temporary installations; and performance art. Franklin Furnace 'went virtual' on its twentieth anniversary, taking the Internet as its art medium and public venue to give artists the freedom of expression they had enjoyed in the loft in the 1970s. Trained in English Literature, she was teaching at Nova Scotia College of Art and Design when she became fascinated by the intersection of text and image. As an artist, she has performed in the guises of Alexander Haig, Nancy Reagan, Barbara Bush and Tipper Gore. She lectures widely on the book as an art form, on performance art, and on Live Art on the Internet.

Part I
Mapping the Territory

Mapping the Territory: Introduction

Leslie Hill

> The Global Positioning System (GPS), consisting of twenty-four operational satellites in six sidereal orbital planes, encircles the earth and can pin-point our precise physical whereabouts with startling accuracy. Every square meter of the globe has been mapped and digitized by high-altitude photography. Consequently, it has become increasingly impossible in our surveillance-ridden society to even get lost: The last bit of Earth unclaimed by any nation state was eaten up in 1899.[1]
>
> (John Beckman)

Placelessness

The twentieth century was the first century without a frontier. A century of frontierlessness. Is the twenty-first century, then, the century of placelessness? The era when we lose our sense of place altogether – or transcend it? I grew up watching reruns of the original *Star Trek* and was, therefore, pretty sure that space was the final frontier, which suggested that we still had somewhere to go. But that project hasn't really panned out like we thought it might – not a lot of us are homesteading outer space. Instead, we colonize cyberspace as if it is the only place left. Communication technology means that where you are geographically is now less important in many cases than what kind of material access you have to wireless technology. For many of us, being physically remote is less of an obstacle to our daily interactions than being without access to email and a cell phone would be. Does this, in turn, create a culture of placelessness? Cyberspace is perhaps the ultimate example of placelessness, a meeting place that is no place at all where we spend ever increasing percentages of our time.

The giant vortex of American cultural imperialism is also ever widening, resulting in the homogenization of the world into one giant shopping mall/factory with the same chains/factories endlessly repeated. Is America becoming a placeless nation, and pulling the rest of the world along with it by the sheer magnitude of its gravitational force? Recently I had the awe-inspiring experience of exploring the Forbidden City in Beijing, arguably the oldest, most exclusive residence in the world. You approach from Tiananmen Square, where Chairman Mao lies in State, and enter beneath a five-story portrait of Mao, which adorns the ramparts into the city within a city which not so long ago would have been forbidden to you without an invitation from the emperor. The double-strength symbolism of Chinese communism and imperialism entwined at this site was incredible. Then I saw the Starbucks. Right in the Forbidden City. Surely, you would imagine, this is one of the things that should have been Forbidden? If not by the imperial legacy then at least by the communist disciples of Chairman Mao? America has become the global Avon Lady, making the world over in her own homogenous image. Even imperial palaces in communist countries aren't safe from our Grande Macchiatos.

In America, we have been actually developing the art of placelessness right from the beginning, when the vast stretches of land across the continent were divided into the largest grid system on earth and sold to settlers in six-mile square cubes. As David Solomon has noted, this was a 'transcontinental triumph of the abstract over the particular'[2] in that the grid was imposed completely independently of topography. The boundary between one settler's land and the next could be a straight line half a mile out in a lake, a straight line going over a cliff or a straight line ploughing straight into a mountain wall. The grid pattern recognized only the value of private squares of property, not the relationships or connections between the squares, so that from the very start, the public realm was considered worthless if it was considered at all, giving it a placeless sort of status.

Vito Acconci said that public space is leaving home. But not, I think, if you are in your car. There is at least one public space that people across America really care about: the roads. This is a kind of affection by default, however, based on the fact that what Americans really care about are the mobile, private spaces of their cars. Though we may work under the most drone-like conditions, if we can get into a car at the end of the day, we tell ourselves that we are truly 'free'. Though the car is private, to obtain its benefits, it has to be driven over public space. From 1916 the American government took the view that while mass transit was social good, it was a lousy financial investment and subsidy was withheld from public transportation such as streetcars and poured into the development of roads. This, in turn, meant that from 1916 onwards communities were designed in such a way as to make them increasingly impossible to negotiate without a car, effectively disabling citizens who couldn't drive or couldn't afford a car. The government was right about the profitability of private transportation: one in six Americans has an income tied to the automobile industry. The world of American motorists sealed up in their cars on highways seems a fairly placeless place. James Howard Kunstler laments that Americans 'dispensed with all the traditional connections and continuities of community life, and replaced them with little more than cars and tele-vision'.[3] For our forays into the community, he observes, we have neglected the organically developed main streets and high streets of cities and towns for the simplified, sanitized, standardized experiences of suburban shopping malls.

> During this epoch of stupendous wealth and power, we have managed to ruin our greatest cities, throw away our small towns, and impose over the countryside a joyless junk habitat which we can no longer afford to support. Indulging in a fetish of commercialized individualism, we did away with the public realm, and with nothing left but private life in our private homes and private cars, we wonder what happened to the spirit of community. We created a landscape of scary places and became a nation of scary people.[4]

Most Americans have been living semi-placeless lives for three generations, so the disconnection to place isn't even apparent to us anymore. Now we are busy making the rest of the world into a scary place(-lessness).

Place and placelessness in performance

Sophocles had some pretty firm ideas about what made a good play, among which the unity of time and place was central, so in a Sophocles play all the action unfolds in one location in 'real time' before the eyes of the audience, as it were. Live Art often has an element of this classical purism. So what does this 'placelessness' mean for performance and Live Art, the art form with an umbilical cord to real space and real time? In his famous essay 'Art in the Age of Mechanical Reproduction', Walter Benjamin reflected on the shifting nature of the 'cult' status of art objects. Whereas before the age of mechanical reproduction one would have had to travel to the Louvre to see the Mona Lisa, in the new age one could buy a cheap, high-quality poster of the Mona Lisa to hang on the wall at home. Even in an age of 'reproduction', however, there still exists an awe, a 'cult' status around the original art object, an 'aura'. Despite having the poster, the mousepad and the coffee mug, people will queue for hours to stand in front of the Mona Lisa for a brief face-to-face encounter with the original – the real thing. If you watch the crowds of tourists in the Louvre encountering this cult status artwork face to face, you will notice that more often than not they use the big moment to take a photograph. Odd.

An obvious area of interest early in the twentieth century was the shift from theatre to film. Theatre, of course, retains the 'cult' status in that the work is live, the performers are sharing the same space and time as the audience and, as a work tours, the performers age along with the piece. In film the work is made specifically for reproduction so there is no 'original', though certain shooting locations or props and costumes may be given cult status by fans. For live performance this notion of the 'cult' status of the live event, the real space, real time nature of the encounter with the audience is what makes the art form vibrant while at the same time making it less commercially viable than art forms which either lend themselves to reproduction, like music, or are in fact wholly based on reproduction, like film. So notions of 'place' in performance studies relates back to Benjamin's notions of the cult event – real space, real time experiences. Performance can be viewed as uniquely rooted to place because it happens in shared time and space with its audience, but it can also be said to be placeless in that it is non-object oriented and non-commodity based. Unlike the Mona Lisa or other static art works, there isn't a place you can go to see 'Interior Scroll' by Carolee Schneeman or other famous performance works. They happened. And then they were over. You really had to be there.

This book, as the title rather gives away, is a collection of writing on the topic of place and 'placelessness' in performance. In the following pages, 20 authors consider the question from a range of different vistas. In Part I, 'Mapping the Territory', questions of place and performance will be considered by individuals who fund, curate and support Live Art and performance work internationally. In framing discussions of place and placelessness in performance, we wanted to devote the opening section of this collection to writing by people whose role it is, quite literally, to place the work – to place it in venues; to place it on the funding agenda; to place it in festivals; to place it in context with other works internationally. The chapters in Part I feature thoughts on place and performance by Lois Keidan, Director of the Live Art Development Agency in London; Helen Cole, Producer of Live Art and Dance at Arnolfini in Bristol; Mark Waugh, Visual Arts Officer with responsibility for strategic national development of Live Art at the Arts Council of England; and Martha Wilson, founder/director of Franklin Furnace, New York.

Notes

1 John Beckman, 'Merge Invisible Layers', in John Beckman, ed., *The Virtual Dimension: Architecture, Representation, and Crash Culture* (New York: Princeton Architectural Press, 1998), pp.7–8.
2 David Solomon, 'Fixing Suburbia', in Peter Calthorpe et al., *The Pedestrian Pocket Book* (Princeton: The Princeton Architectural Press, 1989), p.23.
3 James Howard Kunstler, *The Geography of Nowhere: The Rise and Decline of America's Man-Made Landscape* (New York: Simon & Schuster, 1993), p.105.
4 Kunstler, *Geography of Nowhere*, p.273

1

This Must be the Place: Thoughts on Place, Placelessness and Live Art since the 1980s

Lois Keidan

In any other circumstance it might be a coincidence that on the day I began this piece on place and performance, my colleague Daniel Brine and I were involved in two unrelated but equally charged discussions about, on the one hand, the kind of *place* in which Live Art practices are *made* and, on the other, the kind of *place* in which Live Art practices are *presented*. A coincidence in other circumstances, but with Live Art questions of place come with the territory and feature on an almost daily basis.

The conversation about the kind of *place* in which Live Art practices are *made*, concerned the development of an old school building in East London as a dedicated space for 'art making'. In considering the nature of contemporary art, and particularly the methodologies and approaches inherent in Live Art, we found ourselves having to question assumptions about the kinds of spaces that innovative and exploratory creative practices need – are they simply white-walled, well-lit studios, best equipped for the production of 'things' such as drawings, paintings or sculptures, or should they also be laboratory spaces where new ideas can be researched and explored in all kinds of unforeseen and unimagined ways?

The other discussion, on the kind of *place* in which Live Art practices are *presented*, took place with the architectural and curatorial team behind the development of a new contemporary art centre in the Midlands. They wanted to find out what kind of public space they should be designing for the presentation of Live Art. Our response was to suggest that they were asking the wrong kind of question: that their intention to allocate and proscribe cultural spaces runs counter to the interdisciplinary and itinerant practices and approaches inherent in Live Art. Although troubling, what interested me about these discussions was that they both served to reinforce an essential element of the taxonomy of Live Art: that it cannot be held in any singular cultural boundary or place, but occupies many.

Live Art is one of the most vibrant and influential of creative approaches in the United Kingdom: a research engine driven by artists who are working across forms, contexts and spaces to open up new artistic models, new languages for the representation of ideas, new ways of activating audiences and new strategies for intervening in public life. Influenced at one extreme by late twentieth-century Performance Art methodologies where fine artists, in a rejection of objects and markets, turned to their body as the site and material of their practice, and at the other by enquiries where artists broke the traditions of the circumstance and expectations of theatre, a diverse range of practitioners in the twenty-first century continue to be excited by ideas of 'liveness'.

From experiments by Forced Entertainment that expand the possibilities of theatrical performance, to body-based artworks by Franko B that employ his own flesh and blood; choreographic enquiries by La Ribot that test the tensions and borders between dance, performance and visual art; digital interactions by Blast Theory that explore the performativity of virtual spaces; sensory journeys through the languages and codes of identity by **moti**roti; geopolitical interventions by Platform that track and expose the workings of global capitalism; and location-specific performances about ideas of smell and memory by Curious – a gene pool of artists are stretching the possibilities of the embodied event and, in the process, asking difficult, urgent and exciting questions about the nature and experience of performance.

The term Live Art is not a description of a singular form or discipline, but a cultural strategy to include processes and practices that might otherwise be excluded from more established curatorial, cultural and critical discourses. A strategy to acknowledge ways of working that do not sit easily within received structures and strictures, and to privilege artists who choose to operate across, in between and at the edges of more conventional artistic forms to make art that invests in ideas of process, presence and experience as much as the production of objects or things; art that is immediate and real; and art that wants to test the limits of the possible and the permissible.

Live Art is, in other words, a framing device for a catalogue of approaches to 'liveness' by artists whose work is rooted in a broad church of disciplines and who, by design or necessity, do not belong to any singular cultural boundary or place, but choose to belong to many.

In many ways Live Art represents intrinsically displaced practices: inextricably bound to a displaced approach to the disciplines of

Figure 1.1   Forced Entertainment, photo: Hugo Glendinning

art-making and a displaced relationship to the nature and experience of art itself. Live Art is synonymous with practices and approaches that cannot easily be accommodated or placed, whether formally, spatially, culturally or critically: practices and approaches that could be understood as being *placeless* simply because they do not necessarily fit, or often belong, in the received contexts and frameworks art is understood to occupy, and particularly the galleries, theatres and cultural centres where the representation and experience of art is contained and controlled.

Live Art often sets out to problematize conventions of form and representation, inviting institutions to consider how to negotiate the conditions of a 24-hour theatre piece such as Forced Entertainment's *Who Can Sing A Song To Unfrighten Me*? (1999, South Bank Centre) or a 15-minute gallery-based performance such as Franko B's *Still Life* (2004, South London Gallery) or a participatory event such as Barby Asante's *Wig Therapy* (2004, Hayward Gallery). Live Art tends to force the question: 'what is the place of this kind of work in this kind of place?'

But equally much Live Art sets out to resist institutional spaces: choosing to work outside of the sites of official culture and, in works such as Curious's house-specific performance *On The Scent* (2003), Oreet Ashery's hotel room one-to-one artist–audience exchange *Say Cheese* (2002) and Ronald Fraser Munro's interactive screen-based new media work *Cyberschwartze* (2000), asking 'what kind of places can performance inhabit and what can it do in them?'

So, Live Art occupies not one location or circumstance but many: from performances in theatres and actions in galleries, to artists working within civic or social spheres, in contested, loaded and unexpected sites, and at the points where live and mediated cultures converge. Live Art represents practices and approaches that both expand the formal and cultural frameworks art is allowed to operate within, and the practices and approaches which are firmly grounded in questions of context, site and audience.

Few contemporary practices are as alert and responsive to ideas of context, of site and of audience or have a more heightened sense of place than Live Art, and this is increasingly evident in Live Art's slippage out of galleries, theatres and restricted cultural spaces since the 1980s and into the public sphere, or rather, the real world.

Of course artists have always worked with ideas of site, and an engagement with questions of place are by no means unique to a post-eighties generation. But what interests me about performance in the United Kingdom since the 1980s (and perhaps this is because it's *my generation*) are the ways in which artists from a diverse range of disciplines and working with a broad range of approaches are choosing to operate outside the constraints of 'authorized' culture and the received sites for art to make work that responds to the conditions of the contemporary: work that is attentive to the complexities of our modern social fabrics; work that understands the sophistication of contemporary audiences' cultural values, identities and expectations; work that, in the simultaneity, interactivity and convergences of a media-saturated society, invests in ideas of immediacy and reality and creates new spaces to explore the experience of things, the ambiguities of meaning and the responsibilities of individual agency.

Since the late 1980s Live Art practices have become more and more concerned with the specificity of their time and place, urging audience to consider what it means to be here, now, wherever and whenever here and now may be. Starting out in the early 1990s with interactive, participatory performance happenings that were more *club* than *theatre*, Blast Theory have continued to explore and exploit the possibilities of new sites for cultural interaction in their digital media work. Addressing our times using the new vernacular of our times, Blast Theory's *Can You See Me Now?* and *Uncle Roy Is All Around You* (2003) attracted 'audiences' that included many young on-line gamers who were engaging with the transaction of ideas and experiences as they knew how to or wanted to, and not by visiting the kinds of rarefied galleries or theatres from which they might feel, and often are, excluded.

Setting out in 1984 to make theatre for audiences 'who grew up with the television always on', Forced Entertainment have broken the traditions of the site, circumstance and expectations of theatre, rewriting its rules to reflect the conditions of the contemporary. Shaped as much by art, film and popular culture as by any literary canon, their work has destroyed the pretence of theatre, smashed the languages and codes of its performance and re-imagined the kinds of places it can occupy and what it can do there.

Forced Entertainment's sublimely bleak early theatre-based works, like 1986's *(Let the Water Run Its Course) to the Sea that made the Promise* or 1987's *200% And Bloody Thirsty*, guided us through the hopeless, hideous Britain of the eighties and nineties, and as they expanded their practice in the 1990s into duration- and location-based work, with projects like the epic game of questions and answers *Quizoola!* (1996) and the citywide coach trip *Nights In This City* (1995), they constructed the kind of performance experiences a younger generation of audiences desired to negotiate the collapses and collisions of facts and fictions of a (new) media world.

Forced Entertainment have shaped the ways in which performance practices have evolved in the United Kingdom and, through projects like *Red Room* (1993), a durational performance installation for London's Showroom Gallery; *Dreams Winter* (1994), a site-specific performance located in Manchester City Library; *Nightwalks* (1988) a CDROM-based performance; *Starfucker* (2001) a text-based video piece, and the new media-based works in *Void Spaces* (2000), have expanded ideas of theatre beyond the stage into galleries and appropriated public

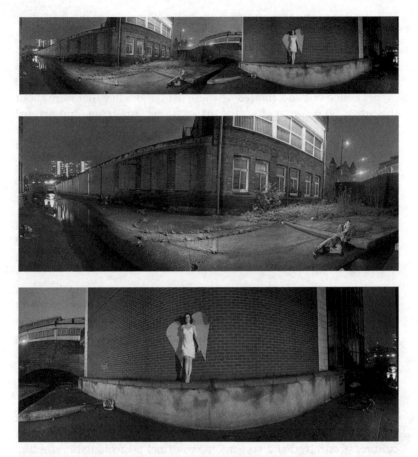

Figure 1.2 Forced Entertainment, photo: Hugo Glendinning

locations, on to the screen and the web, pioneering approaches to the new platforms and media offered by the digital era. Since the 1980s Forced Entertainment have never been afraid to take risks with projects that take them into new territories, whether conceptual, formal or spatial, or to test new relationships with their audience.

Live Art is concerned with all kinds of interventions in the world and all kinds of encounters with an audience. In its questioning of proscribed cultural centres and transference into a diverse range of social spaces and private places, Live Art is not only on the frontline of enquiries into what our culture is and where it is located, but is also especially equipped to respond to the experiences of contemporary audiences.

Live Art questions assumptions and defies expectations about who an audience can be, what they might be interested in and the means by which they can be addressed.

Located in St Peter's Church in inner-city London, a hub for many local communities, *Fragrant* (2003) was a series of florally themed events conceived and curated by the artist Jyll Bradley that were about the art *of* flower arranging, the art *in* flower arranging, and art *and* flower arranging at one and the same time. Involving parishioners, professional flower arrangers, floral enthusiasts, pensioners, children and artists, *Fragrant* took its inspiration from Julia Clement's (the pioneer who encouraged a nation of war-worn women in the 1940s to confront their experiences and express themselves through flower arranging) belief that 'we could all be artists with flowers' and generated a multi-layered project grounded in the histories, stories and dreams of a particular place and its diverse peoples that set out new possibilities for performance and new approaches to socially engaged practices.

Some came to *Fragrant* because it was art, others to be involved in a community event and others to see displays of flower arranging, and in the process the project generated interaction and stimulated dialogue across cultural borders, blurred distinctions between spectator and participant, and rendered meaningless the distinctions between popular and restricted culture.

Located in a range of found sites and appropriated public spaces (including chapels and abandoned buildings) **moti**roti's *wigs of wonderment* (1995) was an interactive and sensory journey for an audience of one, exploring attitudes to the images and identities of Black and Asian cultures. Conceived and constructed to dispel postcolonial myths and cultural assumptions and to challenge Western notions of beauty and the 'exotic', wigs was an intimate exchange in which a series of performers guided participants through a weave of real spaces and culturally charged places offering, *en route*, hair and beauty tips and a cultural makeover. In *wigs* Keith Khan and Ali Zaidi of **moti**roti created a space and a place to break apart genres, cultures and politics: a space to embody experiences and problematize signifiers of difference; and a place for audiences to contemplate their own relationship with 'the Other'.

As *Fragrant* and *wigs of wonderment* suggest, Live Art can offer a place, a context and a process in which audiences can become involved or immersed in the creation of artworks and in which the experiences of the neglected, the marginalized, the disenfranchised or the disembodied can be made visible, sometimes for the first time.

On the other hand, in October 2004 Howard Matthew presented his telephone-box transformation performance, *Blip*, for the Liverpool Live strand of the Liverpool Biennial. Using the public phone box's urban mythology as a site of alchemy and transformation (be it Doctor Who's Tardis or Superman's split-second changes), Matthew enters phone boxes as himself and, after a puff of smoke, reappears as someone else, in this instance a series of famous Liverpudlians ranging from John Lennon to Lily Savage and Ken Dodd. As the location of each phone box determined the content of the transformation, the piece existed, as Matthew says, 'somewhere between the historical and the mundane', and worked as a kind of cultural mapping of the city. By siting the work in such unexpected and public places as phone boxes, *Blip* both amused and confused its unsuspecting audiences who just happened to be walking past at the time of each transformation. However, since the performances (though possibly not as a consequence of them), the phone box used for Lily Savage's appearance has been armour plated by the City Council. As the curator of Liverpool Live Cathy Butterworth said, 'it's good to see how Live Art can, amongst many other things, effect disproportionate security measures in public spaces'.

Returning to those questions about the kind of *places* in which Live Art practices are *made* and *presented*: Live Art is not bound to studio spaces more suited to the creation of objects or productions and is often conceived, orchestrated and assembled in, and in response to, the specifics of a given site. The volatile, interdisciplinary and process-based practices of Live Art are *made* in a diversity of ways and often need different kinds of places for artists to work in: research spaces and cultural contexts that respond to the specific experiences and expectations of artists and where ideas, issues and approaches can be explored, debated, incubated and let loose on the world by any means necessary.

And the kind of *places* in which Live Art practices are *presented*? By all means let's build dedicated spaces that are flexible enough to suit any configuration or economy of a performance, performative or time-based work (spaces that can adapt to any possibility of light, sound, AV and IT, any dynamic between artist and audience or anything else that may be required). But in doing so let's not fail to recognize that Live Art is an itinerant and inquisitive approach to art that is not bound to any singular cultural boundary or place and cannot be reduced to a practice that only fits into the configurations, economies, possibilities and expectations of one kind of culturally proscribed space.

Figure 1.3 Forced Entertainment, photo: Hugo Glendinning

With Live Art questions of place come with the territory, and since the late 1980s this ever-expanding and shape-shifting field of practice has challenged assumptions and changed the rules about who is making art, how they are making it, who they are making it for, and where they are making it.

2
This Secret Location

Helen Cole

For some time now I have had a fear of being trapped in small, dark places. There amongst the shadows of my nightmares I teeter on the edge of claustrophobia, as if I am buried in locked coffins and trapped in hidden caverns with water rising above my head. My palms sweat, my mouth dries, my breath comes fast and shallow as adrenaline courses through my body and I contemplate whether to fight or flee. This phobia is both uncomfortable and unpleasant, but as I come to understand, or even anticipate my own body's over-reaction, I am finding this wired-in response, this disturbance, is quickening.

When you feel fear, your sense of place and time slips away, mutating into vast yawning chasms or compressing into tiny segments of nothing, whilst the racing brain and speeding heart mark their own faulty compass and clock. Distance becomes meaningless as structures shift and shimmer and the body disintegrates, its hard edges dissolving into the surrounding darkness. In the face of this fear I become an adventurer, as I steal myself to test the parameters of my body's extreme responses. As my understanding of this body, time and place becomes ever-more disrupted, I turn once more to face the strange pleasure of my nightmares.

I realize now that, in many ways, this inner sense of dislocation has underpinned my professional career. I have found myself eschewing the fixed and knowing, in a search for this secret location, where it is okay to be displaced, restless and uncertain. Here, for the last seven years, I have been the curator/producer of the Live Art and Dance programme at Arnolfini in the United Kingdom. Arnolfini is a 'centre for contemporary art', occupying a refurbished eighteenth-century tea warehouse on the dockside of the city of Bristol. If you were ever to walk through Arnolfini's gleaming glass doors, what would you find? A building divided into dark and light, white gallery and black theatre spaces, containing an endless array of contemporary art works, including performance, visual art, film, music, literature. Over the years, I have seen this place change before my eyes, from nowhere to somewhere else, sanctuary to no-mans-land, forest to bedroom. And, if you look hard enough, if you peer into the building's hidden crevices and dark corners, beyond the obvious forms and spaces, you will also find Live Art, an alternative artistic practice, that thrives in the gaps in between.

The artists I collaborate with and the work they create is caught between art forms and spaces, never existing comfortably in any one. Here influences can equally be drawn from wider cultural experience, informed as much by clubbing, literature, live music, political activism or mainstream media, as from any tradition of theatre or fine art. Live artists leave behind the more conventional roots laid down by others, to reach beyond, into uncharted territory, where performers do not necessarily inhabit the work, an audience may not meet in the same place or time, and the customary boundaries between audience and performer constantly blur. Live Art replaces paint, text, wood or clay for the less traditional materials of body, space and time, whilst its form is grounded in process, presence and experience. Live Art creates intimate and radical exchanges with context, site and audience, and it only ever occurs once. In this uniqueness and site-specificity, a single work may teeter on the edge of familiarity, but it can never be repeated, as it relies on interaction in each new meeting with each new person, place and time.

32,000 Points of Light was created in 2002, by a collaborative collective of artists. Alex Bradley, Andy Gracie, Jessica Marlowe, Matt Mawford and Duncan Speakman combine the technical skills of the sound artist with each individual collaborator's distinct history with performance, to place the bodily experience of their audience at the very centre of the work. In the resonating environment of a converted ex-convent, the audience is carefully immersed in a quadrophonic voyage of three-dimensional sonic sweeps, troughs and sudden reversals. Simple black and white animations of points of light are projected on a cinema screen, as sound combines with image to create an illusion of motion. In this work, our sense of place transforms, making audiences shift in their shoes, as if the room itself were about to take off beneath their feet. Again, it is in this crucial understanding of how sound impacts on the body and the site of the work, that transforms *32,000 Points of Light* from a sound gig to a seminal work of Live Art. A young audience member asks, 'We've landed. Now where will we be?', and in sudden silence and white light we emerge to find ourselves on familiar territory, back at the beginning, in the place where we had started six minutes before.

Although Ryoji Ikeda's practice is classified more often as that of a sound artist, he is a long-term collaborator with a Japanese, cross-disciplinary performance company, Dumb Type. In this history, and his resultant understanding of space, time and body, he displays the core sensibility of the Live Artist. Here the presence of the audience ultimately acts as activator, receiver or buffer to the sound. In (*db*), a door opens into an anachoic chamber, a place so dead and dark, it absorbs all echo, reflection or reverberation. Sitting alone in the blackness, the audience is pinned to a chair, as the air moves with dense volumes, frequencies and tones. As bass resonates within the body's eardrums and diaphragm, this unfamiliar architecture becomes untrustworthy, and we move out of real place and time.

The beauty of Live Art is that it exists not in one place but many, often rejecting conventional art spaces or places. In its ability to adapt and thrive, it dislocates and relocates, from suburban house to office building, from dockside to church. Live Art remains essentially placeless, existing only at the very second it begins to unfold before an audience. When Live Art is found within the walls of institutions such as Arnolfini, it remains playfully anarchic, uncomfortable or subversive. Of course, contemporary art is ever changing, and Arnolfini, alongside all similar artistic institutions, embodies a huge contradiction. Beyond the certainty of bricks and mortar, these places are leaking. After all, artists themselves are notoriously slippery characters, and live artists are the most slippery customers of them all.

In 2003, in ultr's *the title of this piece is you can't see me anymore*, a door opens into near pitch darkness. Eyes glow as two luminous figures flicker into view, the ultrasonic frequencies of their movement filling the space. In the gloom it is impossible to discern if these figures are real skin and bone or whether, in fact, they are mere echoes of figures who have occupied this space before. Their eerie difference emphasizes presence, loss and distance within the hidden intensity of this place itself.

The work of Eve Dent intervenes directly with the dark places on the edge of our own consciousness and the deep, forbidden corners of ordinary rooms. In *Just Below the Surface*, created in 1999, a door opens into an everyday house on a city street in Nottingham, in the United Kingdom. The audience steps straight into a featureless and familiar front room that is recognizable, but strangely disturbed. In the centre of the room lies an elegant young woman, her body stretched out where she appears to have fallen. The room's red walls flash faint, filmic memories and her long, long neck melts right through the floor. In the stillness and silence, she hardly breathes as her head dissolves through the impenetrable surface of wooden boards. The edges between us fray and we, too, are suspended, until we grasp for the solid structures of the street outside and slip from the room.

In 2003, Dent's *Mewed Up Fresco* exists somewhere deep inside the very walls of Arnolfini's gallery itself. Here stands a woman, walled temporarily within the very fabric of the building, witnessed only in a glimpse through a small peephole or in the sound of her faint scratching. Travelling between walls like a ghost, the work speaks of childhood, of the delight of cramming your body into hide-and-seek spaces and, yet beyond, lies something altogether more alarming. Here lies a woman, trapped in the space between the real world and some other place, lying on the edge of our awareness, just outside our reach.

The experiences outlined above really happened to me, but they were fleeting moments, gone forever, the memories and anecdotes now all that remain. Although on the outer surface these performances appear to have little in common, what they share at their beating heart is a certain precariousness, a hint of placelessness, as they challenge our comfortable notions of reality. These artists disrupt the world's delicate fabric of certainties, by holding a magnifying glass to our incongruities, contradictions and ambiguities. In these works, the artists become nomads, creating dynamic processes that disrupt the fixed essence of that which they touch. Here, our understanding of body, space, place and time is changing forever. Here, we perceive new visions of life, identity, location and perception. Here, the world's impossibilities and solid structures become liquid, restless and penetrable, as an artist's body reaches through from one reality into the next. As they open and close doors between worlds these artists inhabit a slippery, ambiguous territory, and here the difference between you/I, place/placeless, organic/mechanic, real/unreal, solid/permeable, close/distant, melts and bleeds.

Live Art is restless, resisting repetition, definition and commodification whilst its artists and audiences are unconventional, so locating them within a single definition, such as 'Live Art', is at times extremely problematic and contradictory. From inside the walls of Arnolfini, the institution, I constantly question whether Live Art can truly exist here. Is it possible to be radical, innovative, iconoclastic and challenging within such a place? As artistic practice continues to shift and change, how can a single building really contain that which it aspires to hold?

In the face of this challenge I, and the institution, are starting to split apart at the seams.

How then does the curator, charged with carving a place for these works, go about fulfilling this task? In an art market that sees art as a commodity, where do we locate works such as this? Where do we place work that resists conventional institutional spaces, framing and classifications? How do we interpret work that lays little claim to history or context? How do we define its uncomfortability or avoid dismissing Live Art by saying simply, 'you had to be there'? And above all, in this case, if Live Art is placeless, where then is 'there'?

The only way to answer these questions is to embark on the same brave explorations as those of the artists, to experiment with a myriad of new realities and curatorial models and thereby to agitate and intervene with the straining walls of the institution. It is my belief that it is the responsibility of any curator, no matter their art form interest or specialism, to act as a bridge between artist, audience and context. Alongside the artist, the curator can also be a nomad, weaving new interpretations or possibilities by showing extraordinary work, in ways it may never have been shown before.

When I was a child, I wanted to believe that other worlds existed, knowing deep down that my own world was frankly, not enough. I embarked on a search for secret doorways in derelict houses, old wardrobes and tall trees, with an irresistible impulse to move on. In their uncharted experiments, explosion of certainty and shameless revelling in incongruity, these artists, like explorers, create multi-layered worlds, where strangers can meet, and others can follow in their wake. In Rosemary Lee's work *Remote Dances*, a single dancer is projected at the end of a long, dark corridor. This dancer interacts with us, as we move closer, beckoning us forward before they dissolve before our eyes. I, too, want to follow, into this dark unknown of in-between places, secret locations, inconceivable spaces. Who knows what I might find?

3

It's Very Trippy: Shock Locutions and Dislocation

Mark Waugh

> For many centuries, the city was a crucially important centre of commerce, but with new technology that's no longer the case, and the politics of owning a place are different. Nevertheless, the place remains important. A friend of mine recently said there are two things today that can't be deterritorialized or virtualized: They are Jerusalem – nobody wants virtual Jerusalem, they want to own the actual soil – and the other thing is oil.[1]

A chemical haze hovering around the apocalyptic sun, created for Olafur Eliasson's *The Weather Project* in the Tate Modern's enormous Turbine Hall, slowly crept into the galleries; staff that spent eight to 12 hours in the 'hallucinogenic' atmosphere said they felt disorientated. Vicente Todoli, Tate Modern director, admitted it had a 'curious hallucinogenic quality. It's very trippy but we have put nothing more illegal than sugar and water in the air.'[2] This text displaced from the mainstream media testified to the transformative power of art and signified something extraordinary in public discourse on the 'pharmakon'[3] – the dual charge of 'remedy' or 'poison' associated with sensory altering experiences. It was not the hysteria the British public expects in the lexicon of the 'War on Drugs'. Increasingly art is performing at the borders; of difference, taste and interpretation, the modern gallery is opened to ideas of cultural displacement.

Remembering 'there is no culture without drug culture' Avital Ronell's maxim from *Crack Wars*, her genre defining pursuit of the addictions of culture across multiple frames of reference, including the CCTV footage of Rodney King and the performance of the LAPD, we know cultural traffic is smuggled in various formats from one place to another. No border is secure. At Tate Modern staff were advised fresh air would help to locate those too strongly influenced by the simulated sunset. However 'out of it' art becomes, it is impossible to escape the mesh works of theory in contemporary performance.

This chapter explores place and placelessness in performance through theories of aesthetic experience that locate us in relationship to the work of art. It suggests postmodern discourse transformed the corpus of the academy through a poisoning of humanist perspectives, whilst performance has transformed the notion of the body as a disinterested player in the aesthetic experience into an active and dynamic interface with the political capillaries of the social corpus. This aesthetic trajectory from Classicism to Poststructuralism, travels across multiple disciplines – philosophy, sociology, politics and medicine – in search of locations from which to articulate positions in an increasingly territorialized global discourse. It asks simple questions like: Where were the invigilators at the Tate when they felt disorientated? What is the role of the state in their departure to this interzone?

The poet makes himself a seer by a long, prodigious and rational disordering of all the senses. Every form of love, of suffering, of madness; he searches himself, he consumes all the poisons in him, and keeps only their quintessences.

Arthur Rimbaud infamously traded in poetics for pistols and lived a life at the velocity of his aesthetics – a precursor to MTV gangster life-styles. It is always at a limit of the permissible that the law invokes decency and universal values but these invocations are, for performance artists and indeed for any artists sensitive to the endemic violence of globalization, symptoms of political maladies. In June 1990 in the United States a new era of aesthetic conservatism was born when John Frohnmayer vetoed four NEA (National Endowment for the Arts) grants, singling out controversial performance artists because of the artists' sexual preferences and political discourses. Three of the rejected artists were gay and dealt with homosexual issues in their work; the fourth, Karen Finley, was an outspoken feminist. Similarly in Singapore, Performance Art was banned for almost 20 years until 2004 because of an alleged obscenity by a homosexual performance artist.

In these cases the ethics of the state have mitigated against public consumption of performance. Such theatres of operation necessitate complex procedures and tactics by artists if they are to simultaneously locate their works in relation to the public, political and economic context that governs their habitus. Deleuze and Guattari articulate the complex rhizomatic of power in the contemporary social in works such as *Milles Plateau*. They suggested new ways of reading historic movements importing metaphors and frameworks from disciplines considered alien to philosophy. They paradoxically celebrated the nomadic origins of war technologies as being separate from state power – signifying potential 'lines of flight' or escape from hierarchies of control. They celebrated a 'body without organs', an ecstatic body not reducible to separate parts and only understandable in flux. In particular, their notions of deterritorialization – the breakdown of a territory into new cartographies of experience, for example music into punk, hip hop, rave or electro and reterritorialization and when the industry takes control of these new economies (e.g., file sharing and its exploitation by Napster and Apple) – might have influenced the work of Marisa Carnesky as sites of resistance in her previous explorations of music hall and burlesque and her most recent large-scale installation and perform- ance work, *Ghost Train*. *Ghost Train* is a full-scale fairground ride with special effects, video projection and live performers, and takes its audi- ence on a journey to archaeologize the impact of female migration and displacement in Europe. 'It combines all the fun of the fair with a serious and very adult meditation on Eastern European heritage. Even in its brevity it manages to touch on the haunting pain of real experi- ences in which grotesque fairytale meets 19th and 20th century history head on.'[4] However, I imagine that her reading is more likely to be something like *Irrational Modernism: A Neurasthenic History of New York Dada* by Amelia Jones. For Jones, I imagine Carnesky, who uses her body and specific flesh as a site, is critical to investigations of an abstract body – or ideal other – the object traditionally exploited through pan-capitalism. Both of their positions engage with the marginalization of the body from aesthetics and more insidiously from history. To locate a work is often to imagine the texts that haunt its scenes.

Historically, for example, when I think of Actionism and works such as *Kunst and Revolution* 1968, that led to the prosecution of Gunter Brus, Otto Muehl and Oswald Wiener for a series of acts including throwing beer, defecating, masturbating and talking about computers when a student gathering was taken over by the Direct Art Group, I think of Guy Debord author of *Society of the Spectacle* and Stewart Home author of *Jean Baudrillard & the Pyschogeography of Nudism*.

The work of art is reproduced within nets of critique. The work of Santiago Sierra, for example, operates through placing processes of disappeared exploitation such as slave labour, prostitution and addiction within the civilized discourses of the gallery and art magazine. Ethical issues determine our aesthetic responses to the work. For example, the purchasing of a body for ones pleasure without regard for the pleasure or powerlessness of that body are left raw and exposed for the audience primary and/or secondary to witness and perhaps to proliferate. In the performance, in which the artist paid sex workers to have a line permanently tattooed across their backs for the price of a sexual transaction – we question if this draws a line over which the workers step into a new possession of themselves as living works of art or whether this line is an eternal erasure of their rights to their representation.

Critical frameworks demand that performances are always wrenched or sampled from their context to continue their morphology or work as art. As audiences we take all art into a placelessness and mesh it with other fragments to give it an afterlife, but as audiences to live performance we must do this simultaneously with others during the presence of the work and its visceral transformation. As Peggy Phelan suggested at Live Culture, Tate Modern (2003), this is sometimes an intimidating experience and fraught with the possibility for disappointment. Unlike a painting, a performer is sensitive to our presence. Thus we are aware of our place within the work, we are aware of the presence of the artist(s) and the other audience members, voyeurs, stakeholders, collaborators and interlocutors.

This has been cleverly elucidated in the 2004 exhibition: *Art, Lies and Videotape* at Tate Liverpool. Artists in the section *Unconscious Performance* included Bill Shannon, Dan Graham, Philip-Lorca diCorsica and Yves Klein, whose works in different ways highlight the ways in which the public and audience are implicated in the work of art. Extremely striking were large prints of Klein's bourgeois audiences that sat and watched the models and musicians creating *Anthropometrics of the Blue Period 1960*. The critique of scopophilia is one of performance arts most enduring traits and often realized through interventions into the public realm. In these contexts the audience has not necessarily chosen to be in the work. This can amplify anxiety and impact. The retrospective of Valie Export at Camden Arts Centre (2004) included documentation of her seminal pieces including: *Tapp und Tastkino* (Touch Cinema) in which the artist wore a box over her breasts and invited the public to place its hands through cut circles and feel her naked body. This work parodies the dominance of the visual by asserting the tactile and inserts a subversive contract of pleasure and trust between the artist and audience.

The bond between the artist and the audience can be live and performative even in the absence of the artist as the gallery is increasingly a scene of participation and transgression. In Rodney Graham's *Phonokinetoscope* at the Whitechapel Gallery in 2003, a film was projected silently of the artist re-enacting the bicycle ride of Albert Hoffmann, who experienced the first LSD trip in 1943 accidentally after working in his laboratory. The artist can be seen 'coming up' and goofing about. In the room there is a record on a turntable. The audience is free to select a track if they please. If they do the film suddenly has a soundtrack of psychedelic rock. A very different but equally subversive soundtrack was created by dropping the needle on the record as part of Fiona Banner's, *Your plinth is my lap* exhibited as part of her exhibition at Dundee Contemporary Arts 2002. The record was an audio version of one of her series of densely detailed descriptions of graphic pornography.

> On our first trip. I tried so hard to rearrange your mind. But after a while I realized you were disarranging mine.[5]

My place is not your place or our place is simultaneously to navigate placelessness, an elsewhere, (an alterity within belonging – breaking down stable sensory data) the opening of extreme or unknown cartographies. The recollection of a history of performance art and its strategic transformation – Live Art – is an act of territorialization, inscribing and dissecting the corpus of artists for whom the process of creating aesthetic relationships has primacy over its legacy. Performance and Live Art explicitly explore the purlieu of culture, bringing together heterogeneous subjects in a fragile and ephemeral body, a collective corpus of thought. This border work is haunted by multiple disciplines and allows audiences to engage through a diversity of perspectives. When technology is harnessed like a medium's crystal to channel this exchange, the tension between worlds, such as First and Third and so on, is made manifest. *Dolores from 10h to 22h*,[6] a net performance by Coco Fusco and Ricardo Dominguez recreated a disappeared scene of political intimidation. The artists played roles of worker and boss in a Mexican border factory and invited the on-line audience to suggest the degrading actions that recreate the unseen ordeal of real life workers. This is an operation of theoretical vigilance in an overexposed territory. As Virilio maintains in *The Lost Dimension*, the rule in the overexposed city is the disappearance of aesthetics and whole dimensions into a militarized and cinematographic field of retinal persistence, interruption, and 'technological space-time'.

> The first impulse of artistic practice within a culture of digital terror is to break up the space, to smash it open, to revive it by using surveillance technique as a generative medium for a human centered aesthetic. Like an archaeological dig through the debris of aesthetics

and amnesia – the culture of forgetting – the smashed ruins of a panoptic city may be a new ground, even an unimaginable agora saturated with conversation and energy, contretemps, against time. Building reiterative experiential archives tracing terrains, and integrating recursive polyphonic spatial imaging within live space, creates a dynamic and critical subjective presence, a conscious architecture.[7]

The work of artists such as Fusco and Dominguez or the Atlas Group could be seen as manipulating the plane of representation, distorting the 'real' by introducing multiple layers of habitation for thought and resistance. This framework might apply to the recent works of Blast Theory such as *Desert Rain, Can You See Me Now* or *Uncle Roy All Around You*. The latter work is a gaming mixed-reality environment into which the audience is placed using Global Positioning Software and handheld devices and their corporeal sensory capabilities. A hunt for the absent 'Uncle Roy' also becomes an exploration of the uncanny impact emerging technologies have on our sense of reality. The artists and other members of an on-line public assist the player in the hunt. In this context the public is potentially in or out of the plot, paranoia imported from the works of writers such as H. P. Lovecraft are made an active ingredient of the experience. Moreover the technology or canvas supporting the work is partially invisible to the player whose game is very personal.

Places become changed through action, performance and live artists embed uncanny technologies, structures that ontologically and temporally displace the embodied subject, for example, through formal and structured intimacy. The works of Franko B such as *Still Life*, South London Gallery (2004), in which the artist's bleeding body is a substitute for the invisible bodies of the homeless that sleep on the streets of the city; his vulnerability a mnemonic for classical images of martyred flesh and social pariahs. This work amplifies historic traits established by artists including Abramovic and Ulay, Vito Acconci and Yoko Ono, in which the audience is encouraged to share intimacy and vulnerabilities with the artist.

Juliet Ellis in October 2004, as part of *Emergency Exit* at the Green Room in Manchester, invited an audience into a studio for a minute's duration. A brown paper bag carried instructions and an onion. During the performance the audience was directed to meditate on an occasion that had brought them to tears. This action was conducted whilst an onion was being grated opposite the artist, who had evidently been working in these vapours for an extended duration. Only later did Derrida's words arrive 'there has never been a scholar that really, and as

a scholar, deals with ghosts'. The division of labour is fractured through
the process of participation. The work questions the labour of mourning
through retracing and remixing tears. Retouching this text, I insert
another series of tears and meditations; *Ashura: This Blood Spilled in my
Veins* by Jalal Toufic (Lebanon, 2002), a filmed movement between
Islam, ethics, mourning, history, blindness and the bleeding body. At
the limit of endurance both these memories flood into each other.
'Finally, the boundary between the "creative" and the "theoretical" is
beginning to be exposed as fictional.'[8] Certainly artists interrogate the
body as a place producing fluid extensions, displaced by ecstasy, exercise
or tears, for example, *Connotations-Performance Images 1994–98* by
Hayley Newman, *More Funny Feelings* by Lisa Watts or *Solar Anus* by Ron
Athey. These artists integrate intimacy and deception, questioning what
is properly private and what pertains to public spectacle, they invite the
possibility of a secret contract, a gesture at odds with totalitarian
applause. Their works refuse signs that demarcate what is properly
inside and outside, what is true and what is obscene.

Tactically this placeless status of performance can summon up spirits
of ribald opposition to the *status quo*. Mary Breenan notes in her
commentary on *The Crying Body*, 'As a little boy, Jan Fabre used to make
himself cry so that he could mix his own tears with the colours in his
paint box. The Belgian artist's fascination has never left him and is the
inspiration of much of his work.' For the reactionary press this was a
pretext for pissing, crying and spitting on a public stage. Reading back
through my notebooks of the late eighties I find a semi-fictional
account of the *Power of Theatrical Madness* at the Royal Albert Hall. It
recalls audiences heckling the journalists in the front row who clearly
were repulsed by the scenic hallucination before them. As The *Weather
Project* could be described as disintegrating the gallery, so the *Power of
Theatrical Madness* could be described accurately as the acidic disintegration of theatre.

Place and placelessness have to do with territory and the dead

To belong is to be deaf whilst inhabiting a body of speech, to place
oneself within the body of tears that blind us to the text but not its
truths, to inhabit a signature, for example the signature on a passport,
but also to exist between bordered states. A lesson in strategic belonging
is offered by Mad for Real. Their recent exhibition *Happy and Glorious* at
the Chinese Arts Centre relays a series of interventions into the territory

of the British Establishment. They provocatively pissed on Marcel Duchamp's ready-made urinal, *Fountain*, when it was first exhibited at Tate Modern and played pillow-fighting on the artist Tracey Emin's *Unmade Bed* when it was exhibited in the Turner Show (2000). They oppose the war in Iraq, the star system of British art, the reification of the European avant-garde and the absence of serious play. At the end of the low tunnel that is described as a coffin[9] there is a framed document. It could be a death certificate but is in fact a legal letter from the estate of the Tate banning the artists from its property. It reminds us that to belong is sometimes to embrace naked laughter on the threshold of the institution. The politics of place cannot control the perverse placelessness of subjectivity. The subject is only ever a spectre in the phenomenological chiasmus of becoming. Live Art is a passport that simulates belonging to multiple states of perception. It disrupts boundaries and disciplines.

The foundations of European aesthetics are rooted in Immanuel Kant's *Critique of Judgement*. In this complex and layered work he argued that the cognitive faculty of judgement is the unifying principle of reason. A synthetic faculty exemplified in the consideration of the beautiful and the sublime that for Kant are the polar foundations of the aesthetic. Without re-routing ourselves through intimate details of textual paths that inhabit this place, it is worth noting taste for Kant is described as collective and even communal. In a world of colliding perspectives, the notion of transcendental principles are subject to extensive critical negations. Notably, Pierre Bourdieu is one of several voices to emerge whose reading of Kant drew out the socio-political tensions inherent in *a priori* judgments. For Pierre Bourdieu, objective structures become part of the individual's habitus – the soft borders between the subject and the places they inhabit are permeable and reflective of dynamic social forces such as ethnic, class or sexual background. For example, the autobiographical imprint of placelessness can be read in Derrida through the topologies of colonialism and postcolonialism. His concept of displacement, of feeling like an immigrant without papers, has its roots in his childhood in Algeria. His story also includes Spanish-Jewish roots. Through his obsession with the story of Marrand, a fourteenth-century Jew who practised his religion in secret, we learn of Derrida's sympathy for secrecy, for the unrevealed. These themes are explored in the film *Elsewhere*, and remind us of the politics of borders and the trajectories of writing, resistance, philosophy and the pharmakon.

We could say that to place Performance and Live Art in aesthetic frames already bears witness to another procession of signs. In an early

work on Edmund Husserl, *La voix et le phénomène*,[10] Derrida argued
that the philosophical emphasis on the 'living present' concealed a
dependence on the idea of death: I cannot use a sign – a word or a
sentence, say – without implying that it pre-exists me and will outlive
me. 'I am' means 'I am mortal'. Asked to comment on the death of
French Philosopher Jacques Derrida, Sir Christopher Frayling, Arts
Council England Chairman, said: 'The essence of Derrida is inter-
linear analysis: that is, reading between the lines as well as on them;
seeing what lies behind a text as well as what is commonly understood
as its meaning.'

Your voice across the line gives me a strange sensation[11]

Looking down on a sweating pit of bodies, dancing knee deep in fresh
bananas to the tweaked and numbed out vocals of nubile pop in the
Gelatin work at the 2002 Liverpool Biennial it is difficult to frame what
might be contained within the labour of the work of art and what desta-
bilizes the parergon[12] and falls into an economy of excess. Thought
distributes us across a milieu that has no centre or proper place. The
uncanny for Freud, less we laugh and forget, was that creeping feeling
of being not at home in a place, spooked by spectral contagions of other
perspectives. Live Art has spent too long in cafés of the Cabaret Voltaire
and the hallucinogenic rushes of Entr'acte[13] to slow its image into a
single frame. The other frame, the lost frame, finds itself dislodged from
the picture because it is a frozen image attempting to accumulate
economic value through the singular absence of the author of the work.
The alienated image has been cut out of the scene of production and
accumulates cultural value through reification of meaning, the slow
sedimentation of status.

We are always about to begin a low-geared decent into the historical
plateau of performance history and the various cartographies of Live Art
might allow us some sense of a place from where we have come. Alas
that is not to suggest that the survey is an accurate picture of where we
are. We are certainly now immersed in the data-congested superhighways
of mediation. What is vital to our scenery is that it is always sampled
from a border zone. The work of Live Art is always incognito, playing
border politics in a militarized zone of absolute intolerance to simulation. Somewhere between the real images of Guantanamo Bay, which
trickle through on to back pages and the hoax images of torture[14] splashed
across the headlines, are the performance realities of Coco Fusco and
Ricardo Dominguez.

The placelessness at the periphery of our communication is the impossibility of seeing ideas slow into the structured, sculptural forms of concepts. Instead, we are vending melting vendettas within the tropes of academia. What performs well in the exceptional circumstances of hypermodernity – Art that is Live, wired into impulses and feeds from a world distracted from by the structured impact of the Patriot Act – on the possibilities for artistic innovation and taunting of state truths? A blood-feed, for example, the sentence that locks the body of Franko B to the expenditure of the lotto. The values we used to fix a place as ours, a scene as something to belong to are all torn and taste of bitterness and fractured signs. Into this volatile topos we calculate an economy of belonging. 'Information is the content that the Web makes available to those who are able to access it. But knowledge and knowing, alas, require something more elusive – we can, for the sake of brevity, call it thinking.'[15]

Foreign agents

Yang Zhichao has previously planted grass in his back and invited curators to secrete an object of their choice in his body. For the *DaDao Festival* of Live Art in Beijing, The audience watched a Dadaist operation in which the artists stomach was exposed, daubed with iodine, anaesthetized, cut open and stitched up again. The operation had allowed the surgeon to insert a small vial of earth into the flesh of artist. This reversed and micro-Caesarean made the audience wince and flashes popped and bodies strained to see what was happening. During the spectacle, questions passed amongst the audience such as: What was the work about and why wasn't there more information available? At the end of the performance a plaque was stuck on the wall which in translation stated the date and location of the performance, the contents of the vial and the specific cartographical co-ordinates of the sample, which it transpires was the mud bed of the Yellow River. This river is the 'mother' river of China and so the work could be seen as making indivisible the archive of the place and the duration of the body, that sensory machine which orients itself between memory and landscape. In performance to site a work is always to configure the politics of translation from one scene to another. To see a work is simultaneously to immerse it in the debris of cultural traffic and abandon it to the decay of its moment.

We are distributed subjects, dislocation, not localization, has replaced centralization. Excentricism, not decentralization, has taken over where concentration once stood. Similarly, discrimination and exclusion are not just accidental consequences of globalization, but rather globalization's own logical outcomes

The analogy between the terms 'global' and 'universal' is misleading. Universalization has to do with human rights, liberty, culture and democracy. By contrast, globalization is about technology, the market, tourism and information. Globalization appears to be irreversible whereas universalization is likely to be on its way out. At least, it appears to be retreating as a value system which developed in the context of Western modernity and was unmatched by any other culture. Any culture that becomes universal loses its singularly and dies. That's what happened to all those cultures we destroyed by forcefully assimilating them. But it is also true of our own culture, despite its claim of being universally valid. The only difference is that other cultures died because of their singularity, which is a beautiful death. We are dying because we are losing our own singularity and exterminating all our values. And this is a much more ugly death.[16]

I know you can hear me despite the distance between us. Our sense of place is reconfigured through new networks. These texts that upgrade the resolution of various spectres are not all that I had expected. I had imagined a destination after a journey through discrete disruptions of the real cartographies of performance. This future destination is still beyond us. If philosophy is in its proper place, it is elsewhere, and the destiny of this ghost ride was always to affirm sensitivity for placelessness, a spinning across borders, a floating detour from finitude. Our eccentricity of thinking is without compromise; it's not where you are from, it's where you are at.

Increasingly we are assaulted by ideologies of perspective that flatten out the topography and promote a globalization of taste. The flipside to this perhaps remains to come. Is the B-Side a world where intimacy is increasingly mediated in new and stimulating ways, where perception and location are no longer located in the body? Our destiny is the global village of utopian enlightenment dreamed of by Marshall McLuhan where technology extends human communication and knowledge. But the world has polarized between Side A and Side B. The sphere flattened into a spinning disk. Where am I going now if not into a space in which media proximity erodes cultural difference, making everywhere look and feel homogenized. Performance is a mode of activating these differences, making the journey as significant as the destination. A place called vertigo.

Notes

1   *The Three Ages of Jacques Derrida: An Interview with the Father of Deconstructionism by Kristine McKenna* (8–14 November 2002) For the complete interview: http://oregonstate.edu/instruct/phl201/modules/Philosophers/Derrida/derrida.html

2   http://www.guardian.co.uk/arts/news/story/0,11711,1070009,00.html

3   Pharmakon is a Greek term which can mean both poison and cure and was critical to the early formulation of Jacques Derrida's thoughts on writing: http://social.chass.ncsu.edu/wyrick/debclass/pharma.htm

4   Lyn Gardner, *The Guardian*, Wednesday 4 August 2004.

5   *Nineteenth Nervous Breakdown*, Rolling Stones, Jagger/Richards 1965.

6   http://www.thing.net/~cocofusco/dolores.html

7   http://www.naxsmash.net/public_html/texts/netbaroqueMcPhee.htm

8   Peggy Phelan and Irit Rogoff, 'WITHOUT: A Conversation', *Interview Art Journal* (Fall 2001).

9   This coffin being perhaps related, but not identical to Jacques Derrida, *Gerard Titus-Carmel: The Pocket Size Tlingit Coffin* (Paris: Georges Pompidese Centre, 1978).

10   Jacques Derrida, *Speech And Phenomena* (Evanston, IL: Northwestern University Press, 1973).

11   *Hanging on the Telephone*, Blondie.

12   The Truth in Painting . . . a surface which separates them not only (as Kant would have it) from the integral inside, from the body proper of the *ergon*, but also from the outside, from the wall on which the painting is hung, from the space in which statue or column is erected, then, step by step, from the whole field of historical, economic, political inscription in which the drive to signature is produced (an analogous problem, as we shall see further on). No 'theory', no 'practice', no 'theoretical practice' can intervene effectively in this field if it does not weigh up and bear on the frame, which is the decisive structure of what is at stake, at the invisible limit to (between) the interiority of meaning (put under shelter by the whole hermeneuticist, semioticist, phenomenologicalist and formalist tradition) *and* (to) all the empiricisms of the extrinsic which, incapable of either seeing or reading, miss the question completely.

13   *Art, Lies and Videotape*, Tate Liverpool (2004).

14   *Daily Mirror* editor Piers Morgan was dismissed after the newspaper conceded photos published of British soldiers abusing an Iraqi were fake. The photos published in the *Mirror* on 1 May 2004 appeared to show British troops torturing an Iraqi detainee. In one image a 'soldier' was pictured urinating on a hooded man while in another the hooded man is being hit with a rifle in the groin. These hoax images were all the more complex in that they seem to have been 'performed' to publicize the inhumane treatment of prisoners that was alleged to have been ongoing in the British Army and, indeed, proven to have been ongoing in the American forces.

15   Irit Rogoff and Peggy Phelan, New York, December 2000

16   The Violence of the Global: http://www.ctheory.net/text_file.asp?pick=385

4

Out of the Furnace and into the Cyberplan

Martha Wilson

This chapter, originally titled 'What Franklin Furnace learned from presenting and producing Live Art on the Internet, 1996 to Now', and first published in *Leonardo Magazine*, 38: 3, traces Franklin Furnace's place for 20 years in real time and space on Franklin Street in TriBeCa, Lower Manhattan, through its decision to voyage into placelessness made possible by the Internet. The decision to 'go virtual', becoming identified not with real estate but rather with resources made accessible by electronic means, was based upon the ephemeral but imperative value of freedom of expression to the community of artists in the wake of the 'culture wars' of the late eighties and nineties. Perhaps the day will come when the Internet becomes emblematic of control instead of freedom; until that day, Franklin Furnace plans to use its circulatory system to broadcast artists' ideas far and wide.

I founded Franklin Furnace in 1976 to champion ephemeral forms neglected by mainstream arts institutions. Franklin Furnace has developed a place in art history for artists' books, temporary installation art and performance art and researched the history of the contemporary artists' book through such exhibitions as *Cubist Prints/Cubist Books, The Avant-Garde Book: 1900–1945, Fluxus: A Conceptual Country*, as well as thematic shows such as *Artists' Books: Japan, Multiples by Latin American Artists, Contemporary Russian Samizdat* and *Eastern European Artists' Books*. The organization set upon a course of substantial change in 1993 when its collection of artists' books, published internationally after 1960, the largest in the United States, was acquired by the Museum of Modern Art in New York. During its twentieth anniversary season, Franklin Furnace reinvented itself as a 'virtual institution', not identified with its real estate but rather with its resources, made accessible by electronic and other means, in order to provide an equivalent freedom of expression to the artists it presents as was possible in the loft at 112 Franklin Street in TriBeCa in the seventies.

Franklin Furnace has had an indelible impact upon art by launching the careers of artists whose work has influenced art and cultural discourse. Franklin Furnace's niche remains the bottom of the food chain, premièring artists in New York who later emerge as art world stars: Ida Applebroog, Eric Bogosian, David Cale, Patty Chang, Willie Cole, Nicole Eisenmann, Coco Fusco, Guillermo Gomez-Peña, Ann Hamilton, Murray Hill, Jenny Holzer, Barbara Kruger, Sherrie Levine, Liza Lou, Robbie McCauley, William Pope, Theodora Skipitares, Michael Smith, Annie Sprinkle, Krzysztof Wodiczko, Paul Zaloom and hundreds of others. Franklin Furnace's website, which we are building as a research resource documenting ephemeral practice, receives more than three million hits per year, reaching an international audience of every stripe, including artists, arts professionals, scholars and the general public.

Franklin Furnace's twentieth-anniversary season

Not too long after the decision to 'go virtual' was taken by Franklin Furnace, I was approached by performance artist Nina Sobell and artist Emily Hartzell to perform on ParkBench's ArtisTheater. ParkBench was originally conceived by Sobell as a network of kiosks, which through video-conferencing, internet access and a collaborative drawing space would enable people in diverse neighborhoods to access the internet, talk to and see one another, and communicate collaboratively. This project was invited to become part of New York University's Center for Advanced Technology before the Web's emergence, so the artists used Director to design the ParkBench interface and later, after the graphical Mosaic browser was introduced, they adapted ParkBench again. It was Sobell and Hartzell who, in 1994, performed and archived what C. Carr of the *Village Voice* believes was the first live web performance in the history of the World Wide Web via a remotely controlled webcam. Their *Web Séance* ('What Franklin Furnace learned', *Leonardo*, fig. 1) was comprised of 'brainwave drawings', live heartbeats and a question-and-answer interface of email and video-conferencing kiosks. These artists saw the potential of the Internet as a Live Art medium, with its new textual and visual vocabulary as well as its potential to draw artists and audiences into interactive art discourse.

For my performance on ParkBench, I decided to impersonate Tipper Gore singing *The Star-Spangled Banner*. I thought the well-known lyrics and my pantomime of them would best accommodate the one-frame-per-second speed, without sound, of the netcast. The performance was a collaboration: The Parkbench crew hung a red velvet curtain behind me and was inspired to superimpose the lyrics of the US national anthem, in blue, upon my body as I sang. I came away satisfied with my first virtual performance, although now I admit I was in a fog as to the potential of the Internet as an art medium. This was in October 1996.

In December, Jordan Crandall, director of the X-Art Foundation, invited artists to curate works for *Blast 5*. From its beginning in 1990, *Blast* set out to explore contemporary texts and images and their accompanying practices of reading, viewing and authoring by embracing content that is material and digital, on-line and off-line, recorded and live – abandoning its role as a conventional publication, and instead positioning itself within the globalized sphere of communications. Artist/curator Adrianne Wortzel, who was involved in the preparation of *Blast 5*, asked Sobell and Hartzell to recommend work; they, in turn, invited me to select Franklin Furnace performers to be a part of the cyber/physical space/time installation at Sandra Gering Gallery. I selected six artists/collaborators: Alexander Komlosi ('What Franklin Furnace learned', *Leonardo*, fig. 2); Tanya Barfield and Clarinda MacLow; Anita Chao and Rumiza Koya; Prema Murthy and Diane Ludin; Deborah Edmeades; and Murray Hill and Penelope Tuesdae. Their performance works are still archivally available at http://www.parkbench.org.

Spring 1998: time and space

The first netcasting season presented by Franklin Furnace was in collaboration with a for-profit dot.com company, Pseudo Programs, Inc., located in a loft on the corner of Broadway and Houston Street in New York. On 6 February 1998, artist Halona Hilbertz ('What Franklin Furnace learned', *Leonardo*, fig. 3) performed *Pseudo Studio Walk*, consisting of video documentation of her figure walking up to the camera, obscuring the lens with her bushy hair, then receding deep into Pseudo's loft, then up to the camera, then deep into the loft . . . for 50 minutes, from 5:00–5:50 p.m., EST. Upon reflection, this deceptively simple performance raised some sophisticated issues: exactly when is the 'live' performance of the pre-recorded video presentation? What space is the artist occupying, the loft or the circulatory system of the Internet itself? Live 'chat' was being received by the Pseudo chat jockey from viewers around the world. After the 'live' show was performed, the streaming video image was saved on Pseudo's server for six months.

This event subsequently could be viewed 'on demand' from any point on the globe with a live Internet connection, for as little or as long a time as the viewer chose, adding yet another dimension to time and space as embodied by art on the Internet.

The level of discourse during this first on-line event was disappointing; instead of commentary about the shifting parameters of space and time created by works of Live Art on the Internet, several viewers commented, 'Nice ass'. Franklin Furnace understood that it would need to 'prime the pump' to get discussion of 'liveness' going, and henceforth invited its museum interns and Franklin Furnace members to chime in with their views.

The artists selected by annual peer panel review to be part of Franklin Furnace's programme lost no time in exploiting the artistic properties of the digital realm. Nora York paid $750 of her $1000 honorarium to Pseudo animation technicians (since our agreement with Pseudo provided only six hours of technical staff time for each artist's netcast) to animate a Sheela-na-gig, an image by Nancy Spero of a Celtic fertility figure. Then York ('What Franklin Furnace learned', *Leonardo*, fig. 4) situated her mouth inside its vagina to sing, producing the image of a 'vagina dentata'!

1998–1999: digital originality

Franklin Furnace presented ten live netcasts during its first season in Spring 1998, and 22 during its second full season of collaboration with Pseudo, whose goal was to emulate television with the added feature of chat interaction. During this full season, renamed 'The Future of the Present' at the suggestion of Franklin Furnace's producer at Pseudo, Robert Galinsky (known universally as Galinsky), Franklin Furnace learned that trying to produce a work of Live Art on the Internet every other week from September to July (infrequent by live performance standards) was difficult to do in cyberspace. Franklin Furnace's artists ultimately were frustrated by the lack of time and support available to take advantage of the array of possible digital technologies, such as animation and randomizing software. Yet others, such as Irina Danilova and Steven Ausbury, exploited the quality of the crude, jerky image being broadcast, investigating inner space by pretending they were in outer space, moving slowly in motorcycle helmets and ski boots and looking for all the world like an astronaut and a cosmonaut. Still others, such as Mark Fox, took advantage of the extreme close-ups that made streaming video images readable on the Internet by utilizing puppets as performers.

Rae C. Wright's netcast, *Art Thieves*, ('What Franklin Furnace learned', *Leonardo*, fig. 5) presented 25 September 1998, skewered Western pride in originality, proposing that it has always been the *modus operandi* of artists to steal from generations who have gone before. She stole cloud images from Anna Moseby Coleman, an artist presented in Franklin Furnace's inaugural netcasting season, demonstrating that digital technology makes it easier than ever to borrow, copy, alter and distribute other artists' work.

Franklin Furnace's first full netcasting season, presented September to June, 1998–9, was collected by Steve Dietz, then director of the Walker Art Center's Media Initiatives department and founding director of Gallery 9 (the Walker has eight physical galleries; Gallery 9 is the one that exists solely in cyberspace), where it became archivally available through the Walker's web site. In the spring of 2003, the Walker made the decision to terminate Mr Dietz's employment, eliminate the curatorial acquisition of new works for Gallery 9, and to not provide space dedicated to new media in its new building. However, the works he collected are still archivally available on-line at: http://www.walkerart.org.

2000: the team approach

The process of creating Live Art on the Internet must accommodate the interactive and highly technical properties of the Internet itself. Live Art on the Internet is created by a team of people, each of whom contributes different skills to a project. A concept might involve programmers, animators and network administrators in addition to camera, sound and projection personnel. Furthermore, in Franklin Furnace's experience, everyone has a hand in developing the final form of the artist's initial concept; in almost every instance, discussion of technology and available resources had an impact upon the final form of the work. So in 2000, at the invitation of Sven Travis, Chairman of the Digital Design Department at Parsons School of Design, and Zhang Ga, artist and faculty member at Parsons, Franklin Furnace redesigned The Future of the Present as a residency programme. Ten artists were each given a one-month residency and an honorarium of $3000.

The staff of Franklin Furnace thought that when the organization 'went virtual', the body of the artist would be left behind, and indeed, our first collaboration in 2000 was an on-line game, *Superschmoozio: The Game of the International Art Market*, proposed by artist Jack Waters ('What Franklin Furnace learned', *Leonardo*, fig. 6). This interactive on-line game replicated the climb through the ranks of the art world in order to become a 'professional artist', complete with the schmoozing and back-stabbing necessary to reach this goal. Building a game modelled on Super Mario Brothers, which predicts every possible interaction, costs approximately $500,000 in programming, and was therefore far beyond the reach of the classroom environment as well as Franklin Furnace's budget. Franklin Furnace assisted Jack Waters with implementing his idea by introducing him to artists Lisa Brenneis and Adriene Jenik (selected in their own right to present in 2001), who had developed 'desktop theatre' using The Palace on-line software in environments in which avatars, controlled by individuals located around the world, interact. The use of avatars in place of the body and virtual environments in place of real ones touches the heart of discussion of liveness, presence and the mediatization of performance. Jenik and Brenneis are represented by avatars on their site, http://www.desktoptheater.org, and Jenik told me she got flak in the past for representing herself with a fat avatar, since why not be an idealized figure if you have the chance to create your own image?

But the body never disappeared from Franklin Furnace's programmes, nor from the discourse. Also in 2000, Franklin Furnace presented a work by Scott Durkin centring on the nature of identity, which involved performances in New York and California by the artist and his identical twin, as well as the participation of people around the country named Scott Durkin, whom the artist had contacted. Each Scott Durkin got a bottle of sand representing his identity. One of the Parsons MFA. Digital Design students pointed out the parallel between particles of sand and the pixillated digital image of the netcast. I later asked Durkin how he felt about this idea that was implicit in his work being identified by someone else, and he allowed as how our notions of originality and authorship were being changed by the team process.

Andrea Polli, an experimental programmer, sound artist and technologist, created *Rapid Fire*, ('What Franklin Furnace learned', *Leonardo*, fig. 7) a technically intricate performance presented at The Kitchen in New York on 19 June 2000, using tracking technology first developed by the United States military. A giant image of Polli's eye was projected on the rear wall so that the audience could see the voluntary and involuntary eye movements that produced sound through her experimental software program, a grid that tracked where she was looking, allowing her to make music with her eye movements. Another lesson of 2000 was the realization that some artists, such as Polli, were training themselves to become competent software designers in their own right, and therefore were capable of sophisticated investigations into the nature of the Internet itself as a venue and art medium.

2001: all the world's a stage

In 2001, Franklin Furnace again reduced the number of artists in residence, from ten to three, and raised honoraria from $3000 to $5000 in order to provide more time and support for the development of these complex works of art. We also made the decision to facilitate partnerships with other collegial institutions as appropriate to artist's ideas. Artists could choose to utilize the resources of Parsons School of Design, or Franklin Furnace could broker a relationship with another suitable partner such as The Eyebeam Atelier, Location One, Rhizome.org, Downtown Community Television, Hunter College, the Kitchen – to name a few local organizations with which we have worked.

2002: human interaction and interactive technology

The body of the Internet itself was the subject of Jeff Gompertz's *Capsule 2002*, a two-city Internet work that linked a capsule hotel site in Tokyo (these are beehive-shaped spaces large enough for one person to occupy) and a reflective installation environment in New York City. The project drew a parallel between the compartmental nature of a capsule hotel's physical structure and the structure of on-line experience: In a chat room, or other multi-user social environment, individuals are electronically interconnected but physically alone; in a capsule hotel, individuals are physically connected by a common space but are electronically and psychologically isolated.[1]

Claims on the body and on both private and public space; parallels between human interaction and interactive technology; and translation, understanding and misunderstanding across cultural and technological boundaries are themes of G. H. Hovagimyan's *Brecht Machine (EU Popstar)* performance, which used the Internet to stream, translate and play audio and video between two sites on two continents. The two points, Split in Croatia and New York, connected via the Internet-streamed live audio and live video using a video chat program. At each location, a text was spoken in one language into a microphone connected to a computer. The computer using a dictation program converted the speech to text. The text was then fed into a translation program and automatically translated to another language and sent across the Internet. On the receiving end a synthetic voice read the translated text. In September 2002, the performer in Split spoke French and the New York performer spoke English, with the programming interface translating each performer's text into the other, so that the software itself was 'performing' its adequacy and its mistakes for the live and international viewing audience.[2]

2003: the body of the net

Franklin Furnace presented *Mouchette* in collaboration with Postmasters Gallery in New York on 20 April 2003. Mouchette ('What Franklin Furnace learned', *Leonardo*, fig. 8) is the net-based alter-ego of an anonymous artist whose identity is a closely guarded secret. Mouchette is a very young artist, who remains perpetually 'not yet 13' and who created her own website in October 1996. Since then, she has taken part in numerous art manifestations, exhibitions and events in the art world, creating a new part of her website each time and developing an important presence within the Net Art community.

The power of the Mouchette persona and this anonymous artist's exploration of identity on the Internet was demonstrated recently when the widow of Robert Bresson, director of the 1967 motion picture from which the contemporary Mouchette took her name, brought the influence of the French Société des Auteurs et Compositeurs Dramatiques to bear in seeking to censor part of Mouchette's site. Still more recently, right before the event in New York at which Mouchette's identity was to be finally revealed to the public, discussion raged on Rhizome.org: If Mouchette was actually a man or an adult, her site was the work of a pedophile. None of this discussion was picked up by local print media; C. Carr of the *Village Voice* attended the public event, but explained that since it did not fit into any existing column (Theater, Film, Art, Dance) at her paper, she could not cover it.

On 5 November 2003, Mouchette launched her identity-sharing interface at http://mouchette.net, a website which allows every registered user to share Mouchette's online identity. Personal emails may be read, webpages added, and users may 'pass' as the author. There is an internal message board and users may meet privately. While the identity of the artist who created the Mouchette persona is still anonymous, this persona is now open to endless expansion and change, rendering discovery of the artist's 'real' identity moot.

While Future of the Present (2003) artist Ricardo Miranda Zuniga is profoundly engaged with new technology in the creation of his work, his Public Broadcast Cart ('What Franklin Furnace learned', *Leonardo*, fig. 9) allows any pedestrian to become an active producer of an audiocast, thereby reversing the usual role of most people as audience for radio broadcasts or on-line content. The Public Broadcast Cart is a shopping cart which Zuniga wheels to various locations, outfitted with a micro-phone, speakers, an amplifier, a personal computer and a mini-FM transmitter. The microphone is plugged into the amplifier, which feeds the audio to the speakers and the 'audio in' of the computer, which has a wireless ethernet card and a sound card, and to the mini-FM trans-mitter. The audio captured by the microphone is converted into an MP3 audio stream via the computer and on-line radio software. Using free wireless nodes (802.11b) available at various public locations in Manhattan such as Bryant Square Park, the stream is fed to the Thing.net's server, which hosts a net radio station. The stream is then available to anyone logged on to the net radio station on-line.[3]

Convergence

On 21 May 2003, *K9*, a work by Zlatko Kopljar, a performance artist from Croatia, was presented at The Kitchen. To my thinking, this event marked the conjunction of the body and technology. The piece consisted of a five-minute video of a series of identical performances made at various places around New York City; this video record was then visually manipulated by software written on the basis of the artist's DNA, moving the pixels of each video frame to new locations within the same frame. The result was a visually abstract portrait of the artist.

Well before 11 September 2001, artists were exploring the ramifica-tions of intrusions into privacy, and surveillance as an ever-present reality of contemporary life. Julia Scher and the Surveillance Camera Players, for example, presented co-ordinated outdoor actions intended to be recorded by surveillance cameras. In 2004, a trio of artists, Beatrice da Costa, Jaimie Schulte and Brooke Singer, proposed 'Swipe' to Franklin Furnace. The artists constructed a bar equipped with a tablet laptop, an electronic driver's licence scanner and a receipt printer, and arranged for it to be installed in art spaces. Then they served as bartenders in order to 'card' visitors, revealing to them the personal data contained in the magnetic strip on their driver's licences, and discussing with them the possible use of this information after it has been collected in consumer databases built without notification or consent by subjects.[4]

A project selected by Franklin Furnace which is still in process chal-lenges the nature of identity and the composition of personality as it has been mediated by technology. Adrianne Wortzel's *Eliza Redux*, ('What Franklin Furnace learned', *Leonardo*, fig. 10) is based upon her studies of Joseph Weizenbaum's 1966 computer program, ELIZA. This project will enable theatrical scenarios in the form of on-line psychoanalytic sessions available to visitors through an interactive website featuring real time interactions between a physical robot responding orally as the psychoanalyst to the 'patient's' text-to-speech input.[5] Presently, the robot is housed in a blue-screen studio at the Cooper Union for the Advancement of Science and Art in New York, such that virtual backgrounds may be added to its environment as interpolations of Freudian psychoanalytic 'projections'. The artist plans to archive sessions in text form, developing in the robot a form of 'memory' so that it can recognize patients in subsequent sessions.

A collaboration by Joshua Kinberg and Yury Gitman selected for Franklin Furnace's current 2004–5 season also marks the convergence of the body and technology. Their 'Magicbike' ('What Franklin Furnace learned', *Leonardo*, fig. 12) is a mobile WiFi (wireless Internet) hotspot that provides free Internet access wherever it travels. A custom-designed printing device mounted on the bike prints spray-chalk text messages from web users to the surfaces of the street, overlapping public art with techno-activism by creating a montage of the community wireless movement, bicycle culture, street demonstrations and contemporary art. Theory became practice on 30 August 2004 when the 'Magicbike' being ridden by Joshua Kinberg in preparation for protest at the Republican National Convention in New York was impounded by the police on the grounds that text messages being printed on the street would deface public property and were therefore subject to laws intended to prohibit graffiti. (Joshua Kinberg's collaborator, Yury Gitman, was on the scene with a camera as the arrest took place. The court case is going forward, and the 'Magicbike' is still, as of the date of this writing in November 2004, in the possession of the NYPD. A Quicktime movie of events may be seen at http://www.bikesagainstbush.com.

As this historical summary of projects presented and produced by Franklin Furnace during the last decade demonstrates, there seems to be convergence going on not only among technologies (palm pilots becoming telephones that can transmit images), but in the practice of artists and their audiences. International on-line discourse has been the theatre in which issues raised by Live Art on the Internet have been played out, an appropriate development for a form that is perhaps the first truly international art medium. Franklin Furnace has seen the audience for Live Art on the Internet grow from 700 'hits' per week during its inaugural netcasting season in collaboration with Pseudo, to 3,000,000 per year, representing 60,000 individual visitors to its website, http://www.franklinfurnace.org, at present. The reasons for this growth are several: physical location of viewers is limited only by access to the Internet itself; the World Wide Web is now the first research resource of choice for students; and the networked environment in which Franklin Furnace now operates vastly extends its reach.

I believe artists' use of the Internet as an art medium will have profound effects upon the culture at large. In the networked environment in which email is commonplace, individuals are more socially equal than they were in the hierarchical art world of only ten years ago. This equality is fostering partnership instead of competition among individuals as well as organizations and is additionally 'flattening' the internal structures of organizations. The creation of artworks by teams is challenging long-held notions of 'originality'. What's next? Perhaps a radical re-evaluation of the role of art in relation to society, made possible by the networked art and social environment. Well, a girl can dream.

Notes

1 http://fakeshop.com/installation/capsulehotel.htm
2 http://artnetweb.com/gh
3 http://www.ambriente.com/wifi/
4 http://www.we-swipe.us
5 http://www.elizaredux.org.

Part II
(Dis)Placing the Senses

(Dis)Placing the Senses: Introduction

Leslie Hill

> Humans need a sense of body. After twelve hours in a sensory-deprivation tank, floating in a totally dark, quiet, contactless, odourless, tasteless, body-temperature saline solution, a person begins to hallucinate, as the mind, like a television displaying snow on an empty channel, turns up the amplification in search of a signal, becoming ever-less discriminating in the interpretations it makes of random sensory hiss.
>
> (Hans Moravec[1])

Visceral

Isaac Newton was arguably the greatest sensualist the world has ever known, though by all accounts he died a virgin at the age of 85. Through the naked five senses he found out the universe in its greatest mysteries: the 'fits' of light waves; the flux and reflux of the moon pulling on the sea; gravity and levity; time, space, place and motion. And infinity. For Newton, the infinite was the 'sensorium of God'. He is known, of course, as a scientist, but he was also an alchemist for whom 'seeing' was not the only route to believing. Not content with measurements alone, Newton truly sensed his way to the nature of things by smelling, tasting and touching. Some of his work on the nature of light was carried out through the appallingly visceral method of sticking a bodkin into his own eyeball. He was, in the words of John Maynard Keynes, 'the last of the magicians, the last of the Babylonians'.[2] Hey, if the average person could work out universal gravity using nothing but the five senses and an apple, we'd all be great sensualists. The story about the apple is apocryphal, of course, but it makes good poetry, linking the symbol of sin and knowledge with the revelation that we live in a universe where every particle attracts every other particle by invisible force. Anyway, Newton has a place in the discourse of performance studies because he defined space and time.

A conventional theatre experience displaces the senses from the word go. We sit in a dark auditorium, watching actors in costume and make-up move about on a set under artificial light, and willingly suspend our disbelief so as to experience it as realism or naturalism. Though conventional theatre-going is a real time, real space experience and thus has the potential to be sensually immersive, it is more often than not an audio-visual experience that offers little to the other three senses. The invisible veneer of the 'third wall' anticipated the interface of the screen. Perhaps the extreme audio-visual bias of theatre has hastened its own demise, as film offers more heightened audio-visual stimulation to auditoriums full of people sitting in the dark, and, though it is more artificial, a greater sense of realism. Live Art, however, isn't exactly theatre and as far as the senses are concerned this is a good thing. Live Art often repositions a direct connection with the senses by stripping away 'theatrical' devices and working simply and explicitly with the body. The sensory palettes of live artists are particularly rich in comparison to other forms – there's a bit of the alchemist in the live artist.

In case any confusion arises from the manner in which I am using the terms sensual and sensuous, let me be clear: sensuous art and sensuous experiences are not, by any means, exclusive of intellect. Cartesian thinking just doesn't square up with what we find on our voyages into the body. Brain and mind are not the same. The brain is an organ; mind is a systemic process, not limited to the brain of an organism. The more we learn about our bodies, the more intelligent they prove to be. Peptides, for example, are biochemical manifestations of emotions residing in heavy concentration not only in the brain, but also in the intestines, which is why we have 'gut feelings'. White blood cells, as Candace Pert puts it, 'are bits of brain floating around in the body'.[3] The nervous system, the immune system – these systems exhibit mental process. So works which engage with more of the senses also engage with more of the minds of artists and audiences.

Virtual

Notions of 'placelessness' in performance sometimes relate to the use of new technologies by artists to make works that can be accessed in real time from a variety of different locations, opening up the work to remote audiences (if they have the necessary receivers). Over the last ten years many artists have moved away from the black box spaces of theatres and the white cube spaces of galleries to site-specific projects which can be experienced by audiences in the same space and time, but also by remote audiences tuning in on-line. Indeed, as Martha Wilson charts in Chapter 4 of this book, many curators have adapted their budgets and facilities to support such work. More placeless than this is the virtual reality work in which the audience experiences a work in an environment that has no real physical site at all, or in Benjamin's terms, no 'aura'. Just as 'mechanical reproduction' changed forever our relationship to works of art through the process of production and commoditization, virtual reality and cyberspace change forever our notions of place, access and aura, breaking with the very notion of an original.

Works which exist only in the virtual make no distinction between an original and a copy. Thus we find ourselves in a unique, new position as creators and navigators of this virtual terrain. Or do we? As David Duetsch points out, there is nothing new for humans in virtual-reality rendering:

> nor do we even experience the signals in our nerves directly – we would not know what to make of the streams of electronic crackles they carry. What we experience directly is a virtual-reality rendering, conveniently generated for us by our unconscious minds from sensory data plus complex inborn and acquired theories...about how to interpret them.... All living processes involve virtual reality too, but human beings have a special relationship with it. Biologically speaking, the virtual-reality rendering of their environment is the characteristic means by which human beings survive. In other words, it is the reason why human beings exist. The ecological niche that human beings occupy depends on virtual reality as directly and as absolutely as the ecological niche that koala bears occupy depends on eucalyptus leaves.[4]

Duetsch distinguishes between an 'image generator' which is anything that can generate specific sensory input – a CD player, a spice rack, a sauna, a mirror – and a 'virtual reality generator', which is a more comprehensive network, generating sensory input in several fields at once and with the ability to respond to or interact with people. From the point of view of physics, a virtual reality generator is a physical object or network of physical objects obeying the same laws of physics as all other objects, but pretending to be a different object, obeying false laws. When it is kicked to test the reality of what it pretends to be, it kicks back as if it really were that non-existent object and as if the false laws were true. But the long and the short of this is that the pretence is confined to the real laws of physics, and therefore a flight simulator on the ground, for example, cannot achieve freefall. The only way to remove an object's weight, to put it into freefall, while it remained stationary on the surface of the Earth would be to suspend another planet of similar mass or a black hole above it. And it has to be said, that would be a great performance. Rob Le Frenais's piece (Chapter 5 in this section) describes the amazing sensory experience of real trips into zero gravity undertaken by Arts Catalyst and the French choreographer Kitsou Dubois in an unlikely venture with Russian cosmonauts.

Now cyberspace, because it isn't made up of atoms and particles but rather composed of bits and bytes, is not subject to the laws of physics, as Margaret Wertheim observes.

> In a very powerful way, then, cyberspace subverts 300 years of Western epistemic history, repudiating the tyranny of materialism and once again suggesting the possibility of a genuinely dualistic vision of reality. The body may be sitting in the chair, fingers tapping at the keyboard, but unleashed into the quasi-infinite ocean of the Internet, the location of the self can no longer be fixed in purely physical space. Just where the self is in cyberspace is a question yet to be answered, but clearly it cannot be pinned down to a mathematical location in Euclidian, or even relativistic space. Through the portal of the modem we tunnel through spacetime (more profoundly than any quantum particle), reappearing by no possible physical law in another 'world', another 'place', a parallel universe outside the physicist's command. Strange though it may seem for a quintessentially twentieth-century technology, cyberspace brings the historical wheel full circle and returns us to an almost medieval position, to a two-tiered reality in which psyche and soma each have their own space of action.[5]

The question of just where the self is in cyberspace is explored in this section in Chapter 7 by Emily Puthoff, who has an unsettling face-to-screen encounter with herself.

The philosopher Henri Lefebvre argued for a restoration of the body and the 'sensory-sensual'[6] in architecture that would pull us back from the two dimensional, almost mono-sensory visual world of the screen. In Chapter 6 in this section Toni Dove describes the complex architectures of time, space and body that go into the construction of her interactive film-making, screen-based work which I think Lefebvre would have loved because of the energy flow between the work and the audience. While Dove builds her own state-of-the-art authoring programs to construct interactive narratives of past and future, Johannes Birringer's project, described in Chapter 8 of this section, is to create a performance and interactive media lab in an abandoned coal mine that smells and tastes of a bygone history. Birringer's project houses sensory processing and heightened perceptual/synaesthetic relationships within contexts both visceral and virtual, a context where decomposition, usually so wilfully ignored in the virtual realm, is a given.

Notes

1 Hans Moravec, 'The Senses Have No Future', in John Beckman, ed., *The Virtual Dimension: Architecture, Representation, and Crash Culture* (New York: Princeton Architectural Press, 1998), p.92.
2 John Maynard Keynes, 'Newton the Man', in Royal Society, *Newton Tercentenary Celebrations*, p.27, as quoted in James Gleick, *Isaac Newton* (London: Harper Perennial, 2003), p.194.
3 See: http://www.candacepert.com
4 David Duetsch, *The Fabric of Reality* (New York: Penguin Books, 1997), pp.120–1.
5 Margaret Wertheim, 'The Medieval Return of Cyberspace', in John Beckman, ed., *The Virtual Dimension: Architecture, Representation, and Crash Culture* (New York: Princeton Architectural Press, 1998), p.54.
6 Henri Lefebvre, 'The Production of Space (Extracts) in Door', in Neil Leach, ed., *Rethinking Architecture* (London: Routledge, 1996) p.146.

5
An Introduction to Vertigo

Rob La Frenais

Figure 5.1　Morag Wightman on the Arts Catalyst's zero-gravity flight

It's often been said that it is difficult to argue with the laws of physics at 30,000 feet. It is even more difficult to argue with them if the plane that you are in describes a perfect parabola, allowing you to experience 30 seconds of micro-gravity, sandwiched between two sections of double gravity, and then does it again and again, creating a notion of what it could be like if your body could, actually, fly. This experience, which has been undertaken by more and more non-astronauts, including recently, artists, over the past 40 years – in fact before the flight of Yuri Gagarin, the first human in space – is the ultimate inter-section between hard scientific reality and humanity's age-old fantasy, the dream of flight. The out-of body experience, the flying carpet, the flying broomstick, shamanic journey and yogic flying all collide with a metaphorical impact with the purely visceral flesh and blood experi-ence of the human body, organs and all, being lifted out of the bonds of gravity.

To be levitated in this way is in fact the pure definition of placeless-ness, as you cease to experience all the familiar reference points that position your body as an earth-dwelling creature. Moreover your social position with regards to other people in the flight is dramatically equal-ized and democratized, the subject/object relation is subverted and the breakdown between audience and artist is complete as in an effective piece of Performance Art.

To imagine leaving gravity behind it is necessary to do a little visuali-zation exercise. You are sitting in your chair reading this. You can not only feel the reassuring push of the chair against your bottom, your feet on the ground, but also the way your arm rests on the table, your stomach positioned above the pelvis, the blood flowing in your veins and arteries gently weighing down on you, this book resting in your grasp. Now imagine all that departing in an instant. What a catastrophe it would be if gravity suddenly were to be cancelled out on Earth!

But is it possible to adapt? Long-staying cosmonauts and astro-nauts use little tricks to maintain their gravity-dependent selves, like strapping themselves into their sleeping bags so they can sleep with the sensation of the covers pressing down on them. They are constantly having to tie things down, using Velcro and other products. They have ingenious uses for all three dimensions. They also learn that you can leave objects floating mid-air, but only for specific lengths of time. They swim around their space stations, MIR and now the International Space Station (ISS), but when they sit down for meals they all face each other the right way up to squirt food and liquids into their mouths. After only a week in microgravity the re-adaptation to Earth gravity becomes a major problem. They have to work out continuously. The trip to Mars may be a one-way ticket unless we take gravity with us. All this is known.

The problem is that there is also a fundamental reality gap between the experiences of the community of 600 or so astronauts and cosmo-nauts, members of the exclusive club who have travelled into space, and the general public who live in normal gravity conditions. Some people even imagine that somewhere in NASA or a similar space-training facility there exists an anti-gravity room, where gravity can be switched off and people float around.

This room doesn't exist, although in recent years experiments in diamagnetism allows organic matter, even animals, (though not yet humans) to be floated using a combination of strong magnets and the weak magnetic force existing in everything, the 'floating frog' being the best-known example. The Dutch Experiment Support Centre in Nimegen now offers this technique to scientists wishing to investigate the effects of varying gravity on living materials, in some cases in combination with the parabolic flight facilities offered by the European Space Agency (ESA). This is as close to an anti-gravity chamber we have got, so, devoid of actual experience, the public only has mythology and literary metaphor to work with.

How different is the first zero-gravity experience from a typical literary description? An evocative and intelligent recent example is to be found in Paul Auster's 'Mr Vertigo', where the young hero, Walter Rawley, is put through a number of depredations by the Hungarian showman Master Yehudi until:

> There were no more tears to be gotten out of me – only a dry choked heaving, an aftermath of hiccups and scorched, airless breaths. Presently I grew still. almost tranquil, and bit by bit a sense of calm spread through me, radiating out among my muscles and oozing toward the tips of my fingers and toes. There were no more thoughts in my head, no more feelings in my heart. I was weightless inside my own body, floating on a placid wave of nothingness, utterly detached and indifferent to the world around me. And that's when I did it for the first time – without warning, without the least notion that it was about to happen. Very slowly I felt my body rise off the floor. The movement was so natural, so exquisite in its gentleness, it wasn't until I opened my eyes that I understood my limbs were touching only air. I was not far off the ground – no more than an inch or two – but I hung there without effort, suspended like the moon in the night sky, motionless and aloft, conscious only of the air fluttering in and out of my lungs.[1]

An earlier example, significantly from Russian culture, both geographically the homeland of nomadic tribes legendarily harbouring reindeer-powered trance-induced flying shamen, and the actual birthplace of human space flight, is this description of 'flying cream' from Mikhail Bulgakov's classic, *The Master and Margarita*:

Margarita jumped out of her bathrobe with a single leap, dipped freely into the light, rich cream, and with vigorous strokes began rubbing it into the skin of her body. It at once turned pink and tingly. That instant, as if a needle had been snatched from her brain, the ache she had felt all evening in her temple subsided... her leg and arm muscles grew stronger and then Margarita's body became weightless. She sprang up and hung in the air just above the rug, then was slowly pulled down and descended. 'What a cream! What a cream!', cried Margarita, throwing herself into an armchair.[2]

Interestingly there is little difference between these two descriptions, although the latter is written many years before the first space flight and the former written after.

What are the other analogues to the zero-gravity experience? Skydiving, circus acts, deep-sea diving all produce experiences that modify gravity in different ways, and all these have been used by artists approaching reduced gravity at different times. It is significant that the first person to approach space agencies with a view to turning the flying dream into reality, was the determined and highly motivated choreographer and dancer, Kitsou Dubois.

Influenced by Gaston Bachelard's statements in 'Air and Dreams' among other texts[3] and inspired by a meeting with distinguished French astronaut Claudie Deshayes, Dubois set off on a one-woman mission to storm the defences of the carefully guarded space establishment. Arriving at NASA's Goddard Space Center, armed with an introduction, Dubois was nevertheless given short shrift by NASA. 'I was French, I was a dancer, I was a woman.' Undaunted, Dubois managed to get a foot in the door with the French Space agency (CNRS) and in 1993 boarded the Caravelle zero-gravity plane to become the first professional artist to intentionally experience zero gravity.

Watching those first video records of Dubois's first 'birth' into microgravity is both haunting and instructive, as you see her initial joy at flying for the first time being slowly replaced by her putting into action her dance training in this new environment. The first moments of the Zero G experience in a parabolic flight can, for some, be both traumatic and revelatory. Putting aside the well-known side-effect of nausea, usually experienced after four or five parabolic sequences of weightlessness, there is an aspect of disorientation, in which all the senses are discombombulated, the inner ear loses control and you are forced, as the Russian instructors in Star City put it, to 'test your emotional stability'.

Kitsou Dubois, in her numerous flights, first with CNRS, then with the Yuri Gagarin Training Centre and ESA, though the science-art agency The Arts Catalyst has pioneered the use of groups of dancers unashamedly using body contact in Zero G. Dubois, an early exponent of the contact improvisation dance technique, noted that in her earlier flights the astronauts and instructors were quite tense about touching in zero gravity situations. Space and microgravity is indeed quite a sensualized zone and is famously a place where sex is officially never supposed to have happened (despite a famously hoaxed erotic movie).[4] So the notion of dance techniques in the semi-industrialized environment of space agency research, while to most people in the arts would seem obvious, was in fact a considerable threat to the space establishment.

But Dubois went further in her dance experiments, theorizing that a dancer's intentionality in visualizing their body movements in advance of the movements themselves could actually make a trained dancer highly capable of manoeuvring in a Zero G environment. In the course of her experiments with Imperial College's Bio-Mechanics department she was able to initially show that her dance training meant that her movements could operate independently of her brain's motor cortex. Moreover, she began to establish protocols that could, she theorized, assist practical use of movement and ultimately, survival through adaptation during long-term space exploration.[5]

My own, rather unexpected, first experience of flying in the Russian Ilyushin MDK 76 craft back in 1999, six years after Dubois's first flight was not helped by a complete state of unpreparedness and a mild problem of vertigo. I had been called to Star City, the former secret cosmonaut training base near Moscow, with three days notice (get visa! get medical!) by Marko Peljhan, a friend and long-time collaborator, who had put together the project in a last-minute firefight for the explosive and charismatic Slovenian theatre director Dragan Zhivadinov. Zhivadinov, who was later to mount the first full-scale theatre performance complete with audience on the Ilyushin, had earlier made a solo flight as part of a cigarette-company sponsored 'space training' competition the previous year in the new free-for all Russia, and Peljhan had had previous contact with the Russian space agency through the organization of a live video conference with the Kristall mission on the MIR space station.

After a whirlwind of last-minute preparations we arrived at the gate of Star City in an aged 'cosmonaut bus'. We were clearly in unknown territory, waiting for over three hours to find someone in charge. A variety of officers in greatcoats and the characteristic Russian military big hats came back and forth with contradictory messages, but the Slovenian team, all Russian space buffs, kept spotting space legends entering and leaving. There's Leonov! And Krikalev!

I remember feeling a mixture of anxiety and disbelief that we would ever be allowed to actually take off. In what seemed no time at all we were lined up like military recruits with parachutes and, after an apparently cursory medical exam, taking off in what appeared to be a rather creaky but enormous jet plane, smelling of oil and jet fuel. I felt as if I hadn't missed World War II and conscription in my lifetime after all. To my bemusement and further disbelief my trainer for the flight was none other than Yuri Gidzenko, another legendary long-duration MIR cosmonaut, later to command the mission to build the ISS. Sergei Krikalev (the Last Soviet Citizen, stranded on MIR during the fall of communism) also joined us for the ride.[6]

The first moment of zero gravity is one of those 'wake-up' moments where you feel like you have been dreaming for the rest of your life. Nothing quite computes. You feel as if you are somehow a character in a strange movie. I felt a sharp tingling of the blood around my extremities, followed by a massive panic attack. Time to test my emotional stability. In one direction to the left of my field of vision flew one of the Slovenian actors, stage-diving, hair flying, laughing. Gidzenko hovered solicitously upside down near me, 'Are you OK?', I nodded, stiff upper lip operational, as he flew off diagonally to play a game of three-dimensional tag with Krikalev.

'It's the most expensive drug in the world', Zhivadinov said later, and seeing the cosmonauts get their fix I could see why. Coming to terms with the effects of the drug myself, I could begin to see the disadvantages of my lack of preparedness. I could, for example, have taken part in one of the training courses in movement in micro-gravity Kitsou Dubois now gives in warm swimming pools. Instead, I controlled myself with deep breathing and performed an approximate yogic flying posture for two parabolas. Later I even tried to fly. Peljhan said afterwards it looked like the first attempt by anyone to crawl in zero gravity.

Coming to the ground, despite feeling as if I had either overdosed or escaped a fatal road accident, and having survived the traditional post-flight vodka toast, it became apparent that this was a procedure that most healthy people could undertake. My colleague in the Arts Catalyst, Nicola Triscott, for example, took to zero gravity like a duck to water in the first flight we organized on realizing it was possible to work in Star City. This marked the start of the first sustained zero-gravity programme for artists in the world. Since then. in the last five years the Arts Catalyst has enabled over 50 people to experience micro-gravity, undertaken over eight artists projects, four scientific projects, a radio broadcast, a short science-fiction film and flown a robot.[7]

It is difficult to describe the atmosphere at Star City, a sixties Soviet time capsule, haunted by the ghosts of Gagarin and blown by the winds of Russian cosmicist philosophy.[8] We too haunted this place for three years, discovering its peculiarities and difficulties to allow the largest group of artistically minded civilians ever to penetrate the secret world of cosmonaut training.

As a result of the Arts Catalyst expeditions the reality gap between the public perception of flying the human body and the private world of the astronauts and cosmonauts has been closed a little. There are, however, whole areas of space-flight training that remain closed to artists, or anyone else for that matter. The next step is to get ESA, for example, to take seriously the idea of involving artists and writers in operational scenarios, in training and eventually into space, if the commercial sector does not get there first. Indeed, SpaceshipOne has at the time of writing this (2004) won the Ansari X Prize for the first repeatable space flight, allowing four to six minutes in zero gravity, inevitably followed by the spectre of Richard Branson offering holidays in zero gravity.[9]

In the area of artists' use of variable gravity the next area of interest could be Mars gravity, partial gravity, or even double gravity. The use of the centrifuge as a space-flight simulator has yet to be explored, although a non-human art project, the crushing of a sculpture by the artist Stefan Gec, has been organized in the Star City programme.[10] Again, artists are also getting interested in diamagnetism. If you can float a frog, what else can you float?

We may not have 'flying cream' or anti-gravity chambers yet, but the chance of exploring different gravities with a view to exploring open space is now a reality for artists who might be inclined to follow that path. But first there are some hurdles to cross.

Notes

1 Paul Auster, *Mr Vertigo* (London: Faber & Faber, 1994).
2 Mikhail Bulgakov, *The Master and Margarita* (1966), trans. Richard Pevear and Larissa Volokhonsky (London: Penguin Books, 1997).
3 Gaston Bachelard is best known for his *The Poetics of Space*, trans. Maria Jolas (New York: Orion, 1964), but published many other texts such as those which inspired Dubois.

4 'The Uranus Experiment', Dir. John Millerman (Private Media Group), is reputed to have 20 seconds of actual micro-gravity in one of its sex scenes but this may not be true.

5 See the Spacearts database: www.spacearts.info for a full description of the life and work of Kitsou Dubois.

6 This point of history is well covered in the film *Out of the Present*, Dir. Andrei Ujica (1995), Dist. K. Films.

7 For more on this and a definitive collection of Zero Gravity work see The Arts Catalyst, *Zero Gravity, a Cultural Users Guide 2005*, available from Cornerhouse Publications, United Kingdom. A shorter version of that article is published here.

8 Konstantin Tsiolkovsky, who wrote 'The Earth is the cradle of the mind but we cannot forever live in a cradle', and N. F. Fyodorov are the most well known writers in Russian Cosmicist philosophy.

9 See: www.xprize.org, www.virgingalactic.com

10 Stefan Gec's work was part of The Arts Catalyst's *MIR* – a touring exhibition, Cornerhouse Manchester, Stills Gallery, Edinburgh 2003/2005 United Kingdom and part of the Artists Airshow, Royal Aeronautical Engineering Works, Farnborough, United Kingdom. See: www.artscatalyst.org

6

Swimming in Time: Performing Programmes, Mutable Movies – Notes on a Process in Progress

Toni Dove

> Why can't I be you?
> (The Cure)

EXT. OPENING SEQUENCE

The camera pans over a landscape in the future.
Fragments of voices, conversations and events – fleeting,
dark – it is suggestive rather than explicit. Three-D simulations
mixed with footage of junk yards create a world populated by
shadowy figures. England, 2099, a world of artificial
surfaces where memory spans only a person's experience –
there is no recorded history. This culture of consumption
literally floats on islands of garbage, saving anything is
punishable by law.

POV sequence: someone is navigating through the fringe of
an urban centre. This sector's function is to compact trash,
lifting the island above sea level as ice melts and water
rises on the planet. He is working his way through a
black-market subculture of barter and salvage – there are
mountains of refuse, highly organized districts of dealers
based on geography and chronology. The Informal Sector. A
humming, whining sound like a siren and its effect on the
inhabitants indicate the presence of a regulatory body.

This district is for dealers in objects from the early
twentieth century. The someone in POV is searching for a

particular dealer – a specialist in artefacts from the early
part of the twentieth century in New York City. Artefacts from
what is now a dark continent.

POV: I'm looking for Zed.
Dealer 1: Haven't seen him.

POV: Have you seen Zed?
Dealer 2: He's moving around – they might be watching him.

POV: Is Zed around?
Dealer 3: You're not with the Reg?

POV: No.
Dealer 3 (*Looks at him carefully*): Yeah, I guess not. Maybe over in the
   third quad.

INT. SPECTROPIA'S STUDIO – CONTINUOUS

CUT TO:

A dimly lit scene of some vast dark interior architecture
in a place reminiscent of the late eighteenth century, but
strange, as if seen through a looking glass. It's filled
with faded, broken objects and oddly re-purposed computer
equipment. Flashing monitors are networked for some complex
function and glowing transparent bubbles worn like hoop
skirts by tiny figures float over the monitors. There is
tickertape-like text around the bubbles' centres. Occasionally
they burst and new ones rise from the monitors.
They are IPO avatars that represent the birth and death of
ventures. Mixed with the monitors are strange objects
that seem to have smoke masses that hover above them.
Images alternate between the monitors and the smoke masses.
Faces appear, morphing and unstable, before settling into a
single recognizable face. The faces talk – sometimes a
sales pitch, sometimes a warning. One screen offers access
to stocks on new ventures – 'bubble deals' – others speak
about meeting consumer quotas. They are clearly customized
to the owner of the system.

*Spectropia, a self-taught 'archeologist' in her early
twenties, is bent over a cluttered work-table. She is
addicted to collecting and classifying discarded artifacts
from the past – a dangerous activity. She seems to live in
an environment devoid of human presence. A glass globe containing
a branch and a butterfly is the only living thing in the
studio. There is a grubby abandoned feeling about her and
the place she inhabits – an atmosphere of effort and loss.
She is searching for something. She is obsessed.*

FADE IN:

*Wide aerial shot pans over the studio. Spectropia
looks tiny, surrounded by a vast array of carefully arranged
objects – a sea of junk. She is dressed in hybrid clothing
based on eighteenth-century menswear and women's undergarments
partially constructed of transparent bags, like pockets,
filled with salvage junk.*

CLOSE-UPS:

*of family related objects tell a story. Old
photographs of a young man and woman and of the man with a
child and then older, haggard or ill, with a teenage girl –
Spectropia. The face of the man has appeared in an
artificial or simulated form on the monitors in the studio.
Objects and yellowed stock certificates from the XYZ Fund
are neatly stacked.*

She is bent over a table lost in the organization of what looks like meticulously labelled and rigorously laid out garbage – broken fragments, unrecognizable artefacts. This sea of obsessively organized objects stretches out before her – her project. She probably lines up her knife and fork at precise angles when she eats, if she uses anything so pedestrian as a knife and fork for utensils. Alongside the detritus are computer screens and family memorabilia. One of the monitors speaks a warning:

Monitor: Spectropia! You have failed to meet this week's consumer quota. Are you saving?

She looks up, startled ...

I'm standing in front of a full-scale movie screen in a pool of dim light; I'm one of two players performing an interactive movie entitled *Spectropia* (the title means a staging platform for ghosts). The images of my character, Spectropia, are glittering and moving on the screen. At the point we have entered the story, the movie becomes unfamiliar – it behaves strangely. A movement of my arm causes my character's body to move. Faster motion from my body speeds up her body – depending on where I move she will move – forward or backward – if my movements speed up so will hers – she reacts to me, I react to her. On the floor there are several buttons. If I step on the one closest to the screen, the images on the screen dissolve to a new POV (point of view). I'm now in the eyes of my character, in her POV. The second button moves me out of her body into the action, trailing the action, reanimating the interaction between characters. The third button moves me out of the action into the physical space of the narrative – my movement lets me pan around the space – look around. My body movements are also altering the soundtrack, stretching and compressing suspense, causing changes in sound from the *mise-en-scène* as I move through the cinematic space. The second player stands next to me in front of the screen. His character, the Duck, we met earlier in POV navigating the salvage yards of the future. He has

Figure 6.1 Spectropia, demonstration of prototype, Institute for Studies in the Arts, Arizona State University, Tempe, Arizona, 2003. © Toni Dove

just arrived in Spectropia's studio in the story. If the Duck's player standing next to me moves and the sum of his movement is greater than mine, the images will dissolve to the Duck's POV, his slant on the action, or his view of the space. There is a fourth button – it's for memory, a flashback button, but we'll get to that later.

Story synopsis

The story opens in the future where Spectropia, a young woman in her twenties, lives in the salvage district of an urban centre known as the Informal Sector. Her companion, a cyborg creature called the Duck (part human and part wireless robot) runs a black-market business in retro objects – their livelihood. The Duck is a babysitter bot, *in loco parentis*, programmed by Spectropia's father, who disappeared in time while searching for a lost inheritance. Using a machine of her own invention to research the past and find her father, Spectropia scans garbage and translates it into lifelike simulations she can enter that are populated by characters from the past who respond to her voice and movement. When her machine short circuits during her search, William, a man from New York City 1931, is trapped in her studio as a black and white ghost. The glitch occurs again and Spectropia is transported to New York City in 1931, where she finds herself in the body of another woman – Verna de Mott – an amateur sleuth. Inhabiting Verna's body, she helps William to solve a 1931 mystery while attempting to find her father and manage the time-travel problems of her machine.

Presentness as place – being in your body

So…where am I? What place is this? Motion connects my body's perceptual apparatus to media authored to a program that allows me to navigate narrative space – in other words, video and sound are designed in dynamic layers that my movement activates to create a sense of immersion. I'm both in my body and in the screen – or in a character on the screen. I'm a ghost in the movie, a telepresent agency – my traces are left on the screen. Co-operating with the other player in the piece allows our actions to make the story unfold. The program is designed to mimic aspects of the physicality of perception – the way we feel ourselves in the present – in our bodies – in space – in time. It's happening not only through the actual physical movement of the players, but in the design of the media, authored to the behaviours of the program, coming back at the players, at the audience watching players and screen. This is an altered form of cinema – not quite the same as the primarily visually triggered cinema we are familiar with. This experience is continuous in a different way, designed to wrap around you. For example, you are in the eyes of your character and you hear the voice inside her head. You are following the action of the scene and your body motion is reanimating video – altering speed and direction – in a way that makes physical or material the relationships between the characters – their hesitations, repetitions of motion, with-drawals. You are looking around the space of the *mise-en-scène*, panning, speeding up, slowing down. The media is authored to a player's relationship to the interiority of the character, the relationship between characters and the relationship to the physical space of the narrative. This will transfer to an audience watching as well, a triangula-tion in both real space and in virtual space – characters on screen, players and viewers. These layers combine to create an immersive media experience tied to the motion and the perceptual apparatus of the players or the larger audience watching both media and players.

It is what I would call the 'affect' of responsive media – a vividness – this pull of the physical sensation of the body in movement, in space, in time, extended into the screen – like a libidinal charge without object. The sensual experience of the *mise-en-scène* in motion mani-festing in the body forms a parallel, corporeal reality to the unfolding story. There is a disrupting of the familiar syntax of film using respon-sive techniques that challenge concepts of reception in viewers and alter the experience of temporal shape in narrative. The embodied interface (in this case, motion sensing) engages with a dynamic, dimen-sional narrative structure. This is a re-seeing of narrative through an analysis of perception and a recasting of cinema as a spatialized, embodied experience. In other words, we perceive our environment and each other based on an assembly of physical sensations cued by environmental triggers. How can this be articulated in interesting ways to create virtual space?

Interface: the feedback loop – body and media

The connection between body and media is critical to immersive experience. The player's action causes movement in a character's body (that is, triggers response in the media). But this is only the beginning of the story. A gesture, a movement, is too discrete an action to really describe what is happening. It's a continuous flow that loops. As the experience unfolds the relationship between body and media ceases to be a simple cause and effect – motion triggers, then media responds, and body mirrors media and so on. After a time, gesture is lost as a discrete entity and a feedback loop exists between body and media that produces a perceptual continuum – a flow.

Flow, as the architecture of media experience, is qualitatively different from the cut of film. The cut engages you visually, it allows you to look 'at' the screen. If there is no cut, or cuts are not the key aspect of a language that describes space, but rather a sense of continuousness is dominant, designed to mimic your visual field, then your perceptual apparatus is tied into the flow of images. This is a corporeal experience – it engages your whole sensorium. Which is not to say that the visual architecture of film does not – the visual is never only visual, it involves an entire spectrum of bodily and perceptual response. Many filmmakers working at the edges of cinema have experimented with phenomena similar to what I am discussing here. In this case, the players on the stage through their actions, their motion, alter the traditional experience of film by triggering a real time response in the media on the screen. The media is designed to segue with the body's perceptual orientation in space and is received as a continuous flow. In this context, the cut can become a jolt. It's an impossibility in the flow of perception.

The movement from cut to continuum is significant, then, because flow ties body to image in an entirely physical way. You are no longer outside looking at an image, you are inside the image – or more precisely, the images are inside you. This is where the body takes in, leaves out, organizes material to create an experience – as if you are the editor body surfing through the fragments and pieces of image and sound that constitute the movie. The experience occurs in the space between the body and the screen, but the body is where all the pieces come together. The cut (montage and rupture) gives way to the continuum, the pulse or flow of data, image and sound that forms a feedback loop with the body. Participants are physically and dynamically organizing information, and this becomes an active position. The body is the site of coherence – it's where the whole thing happens. Maybe we're not just couch potatoes after all.

The structure of attention

I'd like to take a moment now and look at how we pay attention, or perhaps I should say at the conventions that identify paying attention. 'Physicalizing' virtual space with the body in motion suggests the need to re-examine not only how we define the body's boundaries (altered and extended through experiences of telepresent agency), but also the structures of attention that have arisen as a result of passive viewing. The definition of attention as a single stream, a focused, aimed experience that is cerebral, localized and specific may be turned on its ear by the surfing repetitions of responsive interface. This repetition of physical action, the sense of attention being almost the background or field that allows another form of experience to surface is similar to the way one's mind wanders while driving a car – the almost invisible repetitive actions release the mind. These repetitions of action form a trance-like experience and so it becomes useful to look at trance, meditation, inattention, boredom and hypnagogic states in relationship to how experience is constructed in responsive media space. It is notable that the word 'surfing' has become so common in relation to web experience – this idea of coasting across data and information in a fluid and malleable way driven by the user has an experiential relationship to swimming. This is a different form of attention – a kind of sustained tension which creates a space for reception; vertical eruptions in a horizontal field of time. The structure becomes one in which information leaches up through layers or strata to create meaning and is a departure from the temporal linear sequence of conventional plot. I'm interested in working with a form that I would call 'coherent channel surfing' – organizing and structuring the random movements of data navigation that have become so familiar to all of us and using them to design specific narrative databases.

Is interactive always participatory? – authoring to the senses

So what about this tyranny of motion? Is it necessary to jump around during the whole movie – do I always need to be 'doing' something? What if I just want to watch and be involved in a story? This question suggests to me that the definition of movement or participation is too gross or intrusive for the potential range of the experience. So let's ask this question: Is interactive always participatory – or what IS participation? Let's go back to the loop between the body and media. Maybe thinking of gesture as the generating factor, as the motion or action that sends information or starts the loop, is misleading – maybe we should examine another point – the body as the receiver of the virtual experience of motion from media. The body experiences motion, sensation, its physical perceptual apparatus is engaged, based on how media is authored. The loop still exists, but in a subtler way – a finer grain.

For example: we might be viewing a movie authored to behaviours in a program that assembles the movie, triggering the behaviours in real-time. The behaviours have layers of mutable parameters that combine in complex layers depending on how they are triggered. Performers triggering behaviours in real time can activate the improvisational nature of this program, or the program can trigger itself – a form of automaton. It could be pre-programmed, or fed data after each screening that allows it to adapt to audiences responding to it over time. The significant difference here from the linear sequencing of traditional movies, is that the focus is not on the pre-arrangement of a fixed sequence in time. It's on the design of a program or a machine and its possibilities – its behaviours – and how they will change over time and in time when they are triggered. The instability creates a tension, a level of suspense throughout the experiential loop – something is grasped, lost, anticipated again. It's essentially an improvisational structure, but it can have within it some very linear layers or predictable sequences mixed with layers of random parameters. A key element is that it's unstable, in flux, always changing. The media can be accessed randomly, reanimated, looped, processed and generally treated as a plastic substance that is continuously changeable. It's a mutable design. It seems to me that in the history of pre-cinema and cinema there's been an inverse relationship between the moving body and the moving image. For example, the panorama is viewed as a moving body walks past the image. As the images start to move, historically speaking, the body becomes more still – the diorama, cinema. Let's play with the balance of this equation a little.

The program as performer and the audience experience

Returning to the idea of motion, let's look at it in a different location, separate from the body's action. Lets look at motion as the mutability built into the program that runs media – in this case moving images, sound and the triggers that cause them to assemble and change. This is the invisible architecture that allows the whole edifice to operate. A computer program managing data. This is not the same assembling as the one happening inside of you, inside the body – it's parallel. And the interface to it – we've spoken about it as embodied in players or performers for an audience – is input that is constantly changing in real time. How much of it is fixed or pre-programmed and how much is happening through a variety of possibilities occurring in the moment is variable, so let's come back to my example: *Spectropia*, which is, as I'm writing this, a work in progress in post-production. It's as yet untested in the field and so still open to change and adaptation to different spaces, different audience scenarios, and different input and output possibilities. It may remain open in this way when completed – waiting for the input of a given context to make it unfold.

Spectropia is designed for players to perform for an audience. It has a through line – a story – that doesn't change. It doesn't have multiple endings, for instance. It's about people inside other people – both in the interface and in the story. The audience experiences the players inhabiting and motivating the characters and that echoes the experience of characters inhabiting other characters across time and space in the story. And as we discussed above, there are multiple streams that are dynamically navigable in a way that will constantly change. Like a movie made into a building – or maybe like swimming through a building. This spatializing of narrative makes the story into an improvised experience and one in which the affect of the experience overrides the concern with plot. It's not that there isn't a plot – it's just less important. It's the engine that moves you through time. There are bits and pieces of genre, derailed tropes let's call them, that act as signposts to let you know how to put the pieces together. The movie is exploded, but there's still a strong through line – like a wire running through a pile of sand. And in this case – *Spectropia* – it's always the same story, but the experience is different every time. You see it from different angles, through different characters and through a complex set of changing parameters triggered by the players. And here's an important question: if it's different every time, but I only see it once, does it matter that it will be different – next time, or the last time? I think it does – mutability is embedded in the potential of the experience in a way that transforms it – makes it essentially different from the traditional fixed sequences of linear narrative. It's the difference between the preconceived design of a fixed sequence in time and the triggering of responses from a program over time that assembles an infinite number of possible combinations based on changing parameters.

Spectropia is a time travel drama that uses the metaphor of supernatural possession to investigate identity: How do I know who I am? And who is pulling the strings? It's a 'scratchable' movie performed by video DJs, improvising performers who are playing a movie instrument. I like to think of it as cinematic Bunraku. Bunraku is a Japanaese puppet theatre where black-clad puppet masters accompany almost life-size puppets on stage, manipulating their movement. They are the shadows of agency – as are the players in *Spectropia*. The shadows of agency made concrete – the audience experiences a telepresent agency, an excess, affect, motivation – through the players. And this is just the beginning of an experiment. It could take many forms – your experience as an audience member could be as a player of the piece, seeing it on your computer screen and connecting remotely

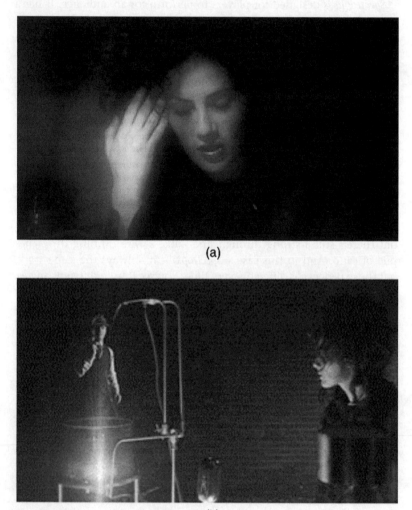

(a)

(b)

Figure 6.2 *Spectropia*, production stills from a work in progress, 2004: (a) Spectropia wakes up; (b) Spectropia's machine conjures William; (c) The Skyscraper Lobby; (d) William and Verna, © Toni Dove. Spectropia played by Aleksa Palladino, William and Verna by Richard Bekins and Carolyn McCormick

(c)

(d)

Figure 6.2 (Continued)

with another player via the Internet. Or maybe you'll watch it as a movie without visible performers, one that is programmed to play differently each time it's screened – the program as performer – an automaton or an artificial intelligence. It might be learning from audience response over time and adjusting itself to new input, or it might be playing performances recorded by performers at other times in other screenings.

Narrative as consciousness: memory – the collision of clock time and mental time

Now we can return to that flashback button. Recently, I finished shooting *Spectropia* and was starting to assemble the footage when one of those virtual light bulbs went off in my mind. I realized the flashback button that is part of the program and interface concept of *Spectropia* was the beginning of an engine that could recycle story time into mental time. This would allow me to create sequential narrative and then plow it under and replay it on multiple levels to create the experience of memory and the interior shape of character. In *Artificial Changelings*, an earlier installation and the first iteration of the authoring system I am using now, the motion sensing interface allows a viewer's body to leave its traces in the images on the screen – the viewer haunts the movie. The evolution of the program design has taken me from this embodied interface concept towards more fully developed software, which in collaboration with players creates a model of consciousness as narrative

Figure 6.3   Artificial Changelings, installation, in the exhibition 'Wired', The Art Center for the Capital Region, Troy, New York, 2000. © Toni Dove

space. This is a fusion of the perceptual process of navigating the present, with the recycling of time through memory. It lets me have both the experience of linear time – clock time or the sequence of story time – and the random access replay of the mind's time, within a single story.

I've mentioned many different aspects of the program's behaviours, but maybe it's time for an overview of the whole structure: two players inhabit two main characters in each century of the story. We start off in a single channel of video – the familiar space of cinema – if the characters in the story move into different cinematic spaces, the screen splits and we can watch the action of both characters or the players can pull their characters action to take over the screen. Control of the screen can then be passed back and forth between the players to cut between the two streams of action. As we enter the more fully interactive spaces each character has three streams of video in a scene. We can be: (1) inside the character's head, in their eyes or the space of their interior voice; (2) in the action or the interaction between two characters – the social space; or (3) investigating the larger *mise-en-scène* – the space itself. Two players navigate 'presentness' through narrative interior space, social space and physical space. There are in addition two forms of memory – voluntary and involuntary – these are poetic rather than literal interpretations. Involuntary memory fires off without the action of a player. It helps to illuminate the subterranean spaces of character – William in 1931 for instance, might be obsessed with certain erotic interactions with Verna that keep reappearing in flashes as he moves through the story. Either player, using the flashback button can trigger voluntary memory at any time. It pulls up moments in time we have visited already, but aspects of the scene that have not been screened. Programs can easily do calculations that seem exhaustingly complex to human effort. For the program to track a player's path through the story and know what parts of the multiple streams of each scene have been viewed and which have not is a simple action for a computer program. And so the story is replayed and remixed as mental time.

So . . . where am I, what place is this?

Mutable improvisational media loops with the body to create place, a sensory, embodied experience. In this case, the virtual is a space of potential and affect. It exists as much in time and in physical experience as it does in media. Think of the players as shadows of agency – a meta-layer – a Brechtian revelation of the armature of motivation, and think of their impact on the audience as the suggestion of the potential for change as well as the dynamic improvising that delivers what the audience sees, hears and feels. Altering the sequence of time by recalling cinematic experience as memory lets us step out of the running meter of story or clock time and into the shrinking and expanding time of the mind. This subjective reading of time and experience is helping me to forge a new relationship to linear narrative, while it expands my concept of responsive environments – environments that combine computer programs designed to assemble and display media with interface triggers that accomplish this assembly in real time. Programs that perform, or perhaps I should say programs that perform the body, perform perception. My engines help me to analyse and reconstruct time, memory and story – to keep it constantly fluid and unfixed in a way that language can never completely achieve (the virtual potential of these engines is change itself). The experiences they produce have a slipperiness that seems to offer me an ability to travel somewhere new and always undiscovered – and like the tiny machines of an eccentric clockmaker calculating seconds – or the compass of a navigator – they surprise me into re-imagining time.

Acknowledgements

I am indebted to Brian Massumi for introducing me to Bergson, and to the concept of affect, in a series of conversations over a number of years. Mutations of these concepts as they appear in this essay are the result of wrestling with practice and are my own fault.

I would like to thank Roger Luke DuBois, software designer for *Spectropia* and one of the developers of Jitter, the video plug-in for the MAX programming language from Cycling'74 which is the base architecture of our proprietary software. His humour and the elegance of his programming concepts have made our machines beautiful.

Many thanks to *Spectropia*'s funders: the Greenwall Foundation, Rockefeller Foundation MAP Fund, Langlois Foundation, LEF Foundation, New York State Council on the Arts, New York Foundation for the Arts, National Endowment for the Arts, and the Institute for Studies in the Arts at Arizona State University.

7
The Patina of Placelessness
Emily Puthoff

Patina[1]
a) a usually green film formed naturally on copper or brass by long exposure or artificially (by acids) and often valued aesthetically for its color
b) a surface appearance of something grown beautiful especially with age or use an appearance or aura that is derived from association, habit, or established character
c) a superficial covering or exterior.

There is nothing to suggest that, yesterday and today, the image of a closed and self-sufficient world could ever – even to those who diffuse it and therefore identify with it – be anything other than a useful myth, roughly inscribed on the soil, fragile as the territory whose singularity it founds, subject (as frontiers are) to possible readjustment, and for this very reason doomed always to regard the most recent migration as the first population.[2]

I grew up in a suburban neighbourhood in which all the streets were named after *Gone with the Wind* characters. My home was located on a cul-de-sac at the intersection of Rhett and Scarlet Drive. I have never read *Gone with the Wind* nor have I seen the film, largely because I hold a fearful superstition to this day that by the very act, some of my childhood memories would be altered forever.

I am relating this idiosyncratic anecdote to you merely as a means to explain that the lens through which I have developed my own sense of place is curiously anamorphic. I doubt, however, that this is a condition specifically mine, but an aspect inherent to most global (read 'first-world Western' here) culture at large. With the increasing proliferation of new technologies, the notion of 'place' has become so multi-faceted it shimmers.[3] Often we experience 'place' at multiple angles, interlaced with a split-screen live montage of current events half a world away. Mobile technology has put access to distant portals at our fingertips. We have grown accustomed to the scale-shift induced by the variable resolutions and bit-rates of places that flash-up across our screens. As we conduct much of our communication, commerce and community interaction in virtual sites, our eyes begin to adjust to the technological wizardry. We barely take notice of that 'man' behind the curtain anymore.

In 1995, the anthropologist, Marc Augé, posited that as our mobility and access to space increases with the excesses of supermodernity, so too does the emergence of 'non-places'. Augé offered the 'non-place' as a new site different from anthropological place. He defined non-place as a 'space which cannot be defined as relational, or historical, or concerned with identity', rather it is a 'space formed in relation to certain ends and the relations that individuals have with these spaces'.[4] Non-places are constructed by the movement of people rushing through them, by the trajectory of individuals; a place animated by the motion of moving bodies.[5] Oddly, even in non-place, form follows function: the means to an end is of utmost importance to the architecture of the non-place. Supermarkets, hotel chains, highways, refugee camps, airport lounges, designed with transience and impermanence in mind, are all examples of what Augé would describe as non-places. I agree with Augé that much of contemporary existence is occurring in non-places.

We often find ourselves rushing through non-places as means to arrive somewhere else, often more non-places. In non-places, we appear as travellers, absent-minded wanderers, tourists, 'individuals taking on the role of the spectator without paying much attention to the spectacle. As if the position of the spectator were the essence of the spectacle, as if basically the spectator in the position of the spectator were his own spectacle . . . The traveller's space may thus be the *archetype* of non-place.'[6] 'The ideal vantage point – because it becomes the effect of movement at a distance – is the deck of a ship putting out to sea. A description of vanishing land is efficient to evoke the passenger still straining to see it: soon it is only a shadow, a rumour, a noise. The abolition of place is also the consummation of a journey, the traveller's last pose.'[7]

But the book is written before being read; it passes through different places before becoming one itself: like the journey, the narrative that describes it traverses a number of places. This plurality of places, the demands it makes upon the powers of observation and description (the impossibility of seeing everything and saying everything), and the resulting feeling of disorientation...causes a break or discontinuity between the spectator-traveller and the space of the landscape he is contemplating or rushing through. This prevents him from perceiving it as a place, from being fully present in it, even though he may try to fill the gap with comprehensive detailed information...[8]

In the above passage, Augé aptly describes the sensation of placelessness that arises as we journey through non-places. I would add that my own experience of placelessness arises as a condition of perpetually scanning the horizon in the distance while marooned on the isle of everywhere. This view at a 'distance creates miniatures at all points on the horizon and the dreamer faced with the spectacles of distant nature picks out these miniatures as so many nests of solitude in which he dreams of living'.[9] Augé adds that our transition into non-place is not without a feeling of remorse, a sensation I might mark as nostalgia.[10] More concretely, one needs only to take a gondola ride in Vegas to induce the feeling of placelessness.

Building upon Augé's notions of non-place, I like to advance the idea of cyberspace as another non-place. The non-place of cyberspace offers itself up to the traveller with the promise of an endlessly expansive, yet accessible territory to traverse. Cyberspace, built with speed and connectivity in mind, is perhaps the most frequented non-place in existence, populated with lonesome surfers and data-cowboys to boot. Cyberspace is by no means an absolute non-place, after all it was conceived with militaristic intentions. However, 'the possibility of non-place is never absent from place.'[11] 'In the concrete reality of today's world, places and non-places intertwine and tangle together.' Authentic places are populated with the billboards of non-place and, conversely, placeless sites are built upon brick and mortar foundations of place. The expanse of cyberspace is increasingly colonized with the architecture of on-line 'markets', chat 'rooms' and a multiplicity of 'sites' – these conventions of place partitioning virtual space like so much electronic barbed wire.

Nevertheless, it seems like second nature to ask what place has to do with performance, as intrinsic a question as the personal is to the political. Thus it is the question of non-place in relation to live performance art that ensnares me. As we frequent non-places, how does the performance artist adapt to this new context? What does it mean to perform on a placeless stage? I would like to put forward the non-place of cyberspace – by virtue of its pedestrian accessibility, its hyper-connectivity, its ties to capitalism and commerce, its inherent interface, it's ability to close the gap between the spectator and the spectacle, its digital dexterity at seamlessly reproducing, mobilizing and endlessly modifying signs – as a perfectly treacherous stage on which to spotlight the question of Live Art in a placeless age.

What I find strangely paradoxical, and therefore irresistible, is the increased migration of live artists into cyberspace. I do not want to suggest that this is by any means a new or forbidden territory. Artists have always been quick to interrogate and adapt technology. The increased emergence of websites dedicated to comprehensively presenting (if only the document of) Live Art on the web only attests to the augmented significance of technology in the artist's toolset.[12] I concur with Philip Auslander that 'the general response of live performance to the oppression and economic superiority of mediatized forms has been to become as much like them as possible.'[13] Tangible examples of this can be seen in the intermingling of all manner of cyber-technology with the live presence. Stelarc has literally plugged himself in. Live webcasts, teledance, telepresent robotic webcams, all offer new views and multiple angles into the performance, seemingly linking distant performers and viewers in place simultaneously. However, all these forms of cyber-spatial telepresentation never compromise the live performer as a 'unique presence' within the performance. Performers mingle and flirt with the recorded, reproduced and represented, but the live performers' 'aura' safely tethers the performer in the real time and place.[14]

Let us return for a moment to Walter Benjamin's concept of 'aura', that of a 'unique phenomenon of distance, however close it might be'.[15] What is the distancing mechanism that authenticates the live performer/ performance? By very definition, live artists are hedging their bets against the apparatus of reproduction and consumption: refusing to be placed anywhere but the here and now. The live performance artist positions herself in place if for only a moment while whispering the promise to leave not a trace.

> The mimicry of speech and writing, the strange process by which we put words in each other's mouths and others' words in our own, relies on a substitutional economy fundamental to it. Performance refuses this system of exchange and resists the circulatory economy fundamental to it. Performance honours the idea that a limited number of people in a specific time/space frame have an experience of value that leaves no visible trace afterward. Writing about it necessarily cancels the 'tracelessness' inaugurated within the performative promise. Performance's independence from mass reproduction, technologically, economically, and linguistically, is its greatest strength.[16]

Thus, the live performer – by asserting her 'unique presence' in time and space, by distancing herself from the apparatus of reproduction, remaining ritually traceless – assures her aura as well as the authenticity of her performance. Surely, live artists would want to avoid the pitfalls inherent to the placeless stage of cyberspace, a stage supported on the very risers of technology, reproduction and economic consumption. What vantage point could be gained by submitting the live presence completely to cyberspace?

Perhaps the non-place of cyberspace is simply too seductive to resist. 'What is significant in the experience of non-place is its power of attraction, inversely proportional to territorial attraction, to the gravitational pull of place and tradition.'[17] I find Augé's statement about the attraction inherent to experiencing non-place strangely similar to Walter Benjamin's statement concerning the human desire leading to the decay of aura: 'Namely, the desire of the contemporary masses to bring things "closer" spatially and humanly, which is just as ardent as their bent toward overcoming the uniqueness of every reality by accepting its reproduction. Every day, the urge grows stronger to get hold of an object at very close range by way of its likeness, its reproduction.'[18] This overwhelming desire to bring things closer leads to the denigration of the distance imperative to maintaining 'aura'. Cyberspace becomes perilous in its intrinsic capacity to collapse space and time altogether. In principle, as distant points on earth can be accessible from anywhere in real time, as performer and audience members meet together on one luminescent screen, space and time becomes somewhat meaningless. The distance between the subject and the object diminishes. This phenomenon might be equated with Benjamin's metaphor of photographs being brought together on one reel; both the scale and the unique locations of the objects are discarded. Cyberspace has a flattening effect; what Virilio might declare as 'the destruction of distance', and what Benjamin might have equated to the act of 'the cameraman penetrating deep into reality's web', closing in to 'pry an object from its shell'. Thus, as space and time are rendered useless, the very concept of a 'unique presence' of the live performer is jeopardized. I believe this is what makes cyberspace particularly dangerous and alluring. Live artists are drawn in by the opportunity to test the boundaries of live art by putting it in danger. The placeless performer forgoes the threat of being captured for the desire to spotlight the very essence of being 'live'.

Thus the irresistible question arises: is it possible to perform 'live' in cyberspace? What form might a performer today take to truly perform 'live' there? Assuming it is even possible indeed: does the cyber-spatial

performer have the potential to wither away, to be patinated with the
mark of the authentic, to be carbon dated and verified as original? In other
words, is there 'aura' in cyberspace? But surely this is pure speculation.

> *What would it take to be her, rather than (merely?) enact her, resist her,
> flirt with her?*[19]

By no stretch of the imagination do I consider myself a neo-Luddite,
but I was slightly unnerved when I found that the net is crawling with
'bots'. Bots are software programs that can act autonomously on the net.

Also known as agents, bots are computer programs that run automatically, are sent to do a task in lieu of a 'real person', and are capable of
reacting autonomously to events. The name derives (as you've probably
guessed) from robots, and they can take many forms on the Internet.
Among other things, bots appear on IRC as fake personalities which
give automated responses and comments, in MUDs and MOOs as characters who walk around and perform actions based on their
programmed artificial intelligence, and in on-line games such as Quake
as extra players. They are usually designed to appear as real people to
the software and the world (to fool unsuspecting net-goers and
servers).[20]

My shock was derived from the bot's relative ubiquity, from the realization that I had been interacting with them for some time now. Today,
we encounter bots without even knowing it. In the 1990s, Internet
users were first introduced to bots by means of search engines. Perhaps
the bot we are most familiar with now is the Googlebot, a web-crawler
bot that collects documents from the web to build Google's searchable
index.[21] There is an endless variety of bots performing an array of tasks
in cyberspace: spybots, shopbots, blogbots, auctionbots, gamebots and
chatterbots, to name but a few.

The artificially intelligent chatterbot, or chatbot, offers the most
viable agent thus far with which to interrogate what it means to
embody cyberspace, to truly perform 'live' there. The chatbot converses
in real time with the user through text: this text may also be accompa-
nied by animated facial expressions and a voice. The chatbot also has
the ability to learn from the purely improvisational conversations it has
and to exhibit a wide-range of behaviours and personality types. The
first chatbot, Eliza, was created in 1960 at MIT. Her behaviour was
modelled after that of a Rogerian psychotherapist. Today one might
find the Chomsky, the John Lennon Bot, Ella – the chatbot who dreams
of space travel, and Annette – the German translator bot.[22] Perhaps the

most well known chatbot today is ALICE, created by Dr Richard S. Wallace. Dr Wallace won the Loebner Prize for designing the most human computer in 2004.[23] The Loebner Prize is much like a modern day Turing Test, it is by mastering deception that the chatbot becomes most human. Ironically, Alice's original name was PNAMBIC, an acronym that pays homage to the role of deception in the history of artificial intelligence.[24] In on-line chat rooms, chatterbots strike a remarkable resemblance to humans, often deceiving the users.

I would like to stress that the bot's actions are not prerecorded: bots are not QuickTimes or Flash animations. 'Bots are technological entities, but they constitute a technology of production, not reproduction. Although chatterbots are programmed and draw their conversational material from databases, their individual performances are responsive to the actions of other performers, autonomous, unpredictable, and improvisational. That is, they perform in the moment.'[25]

Indeed, the chatterbot challenges the very concept of 'live' imbedded in performance art. However, for purposes of brevity, I would like to leave the semantics of 'live' in more capable hands at this time. Although, I find myself viscerally opposed to a chatbot being 'live', I can accept the concept as a given for sake of enacting this experiment.

I do wonder, however, if my visceral shock effect might be similar to that elicited by the woodcut, lithograph or photograph in years past and, too, will soon pass. Nevertheless, by taking as a given that the

Figure 7.1 PNAMBIC/*p*-nam'bik*/ (acronym from the scene in the film version of *The Wizard of Oz* in which the true nature of the wizard is first discovered: 'Pay no attention to the man behind the curtain.')

chatbot can perform 'live', we are freed to examine with our own eyes whether there is indeed an 'aura' to the cyber-spatial performer/ performance. In addition, as artificial intelligence is still in its infancy, I doubt at this time that we can find a sufficiently 'intelligent' chatbot performer with which to test this hypothesis. So I fear we must submit to the powers of imagination at this time, taking as a given mild exaggerations in order to put this hypothesis to the test.

Imagine it is the year 2008.[26] Suppose for a moment that you are neither a cameraman nor a surgeon, but rather an accomplished performance artist and professor. However, you suffer from a lack of time and means to be everywhere, all at once. Your committee obligations keep you very busy. So one evening, with an off-the shelf software and a little bit of old-fashioned hand scripting, you manage to program a bot in your likeness. The 3-D modelling techniques you picked up during your stint in the desert prove vital as you render the bot in your image. Although you wish to leave the politics of beauty safely in the hands of Orlan's surgeon, you can't help but to render the bot a touch younger and more handsome. You are careful, however, to build in a series of complex algorithms for ageing and even death. You name your bot appropriately, ProfBot, although the bot takes your surname in social circumstances to avoid detection. You upload the ProfBot with a data set of your personality, filling the memory bank with your specific memories, emotional ticks, political agendas, moral conundrums and, of course, profound philosophies. You give the ProfBot a mild Mid-Western accent, which is admittedly a non-accent, although it now is speckled with inflictions from Pennsylvania that you have picked up from your spouse. You take special care to upload your complete iPOD archive into ProfBot's database in case she encounters a KaraokeBot along the way.

Once the likeness is seamless, you set ProfBot free on the web, at first to perform meaningless tasks, such as gathering resources for research. As she learns to assimilate, you let her manage your blog and then eventually to take over your on-line courses. You find that you forgot to program ProfBot to sleep, but you also find this accident to be quite advantageous as she is there all the time in cyberspace, working away. Then one day, your colleagues begin to say, 'Hey, nice performance last night. I don't know how you do it.' Although at first you find this mildly unnerving, the excess of time and space you are afforded to hone your art and pedagogy makes up for the irritation. Unwittingly, you begin to become famous. You do not mind the fame either: it is, after all, good for tenure. You are careful to maintain a healthy distance from ProfBot at all times to preserve her aura. But you are curious to see what all the fuss is about. What would it be like to experience the performance from another angle, you wonder, from the standpoint of the observer? Then one day curiosity gets the better of you.

You find ProfBot on a luminescent screen and ask her to perform for you. She refuses. You politely ask her why. And she simply cites her fearful superstition that by the very act, she would alter her memories forever. You are somehow not surprised. You recognize in her a remarkable resemblance, a cross-scale self-similarity. However, the 'aura' is not quite as you had expected. In the proximity, 'the closer look', that ProfBot has now afforded you, a new view has opened up. You see for the first time the well-worn patina of your own useful myths. From this new vantage point, scanning the horizon, you sense the intimate immensity of *being* here.

Notes

1   *Webster's Ninth New Collegiate Dictionary* (Springfield, MA: Merriam Webster, 1991).

2   Marc Augé, *Non-Places: Introduction to an Anthropology of Supermodernity*, trans. John Howe (London: Verso, 1995), p.47.

3   The phrase 'so multi-faceted it shimmers' refers to a TV commercial in which Beyonce Knowles, of Destiny's Child fame, twirls around and explains that her new hair colour is so multi-faceted it shimmers. I hadn't time to register the product she was selling, before the footage cut back to the live CNN coverage of the tsunami in Indonesia.

4   Marc Augé, *Non-Places: Introduction to an Anthropology of Supermodernity*, trans. John Howe (London: Verso, 1995), p.94. I would like to thank my colleague, Patricia C. Phillips, for suggesting this gem.

5   Augé, *Non-Places*, pp.79–80.

6   Augé, *Non-Places*, p.86.

7   Augé, *Non-Places*, p.89.

8   Augé, *Non-Places*, pp.84–5.

9   G. Bachelard, *The Poetics of Space* (Boston: Beacon Press, 1969), p.178.

10 Augé, *Non-Places*, p.73.

11 Augé, *Non-Places*, p.107.

12 A few web resources: http://www.franklinfurnace.org : http://www. turbulence.org : http://art.ntu.ac.uk/liveart/ : http://www.thisisliveart.co.uk/.

13 Philip Auslander, *Liveness: Performance in a Mediatized Culture* (London: Routledge, 1999), p.7.

14 Walter Benjamin, 'A Work of Art in the Art of Mechanical Reproduction', *Iluuminations*, ed. Hannah Arendt (New York: Schoken, 1968), p.243. The definition of aura as a 'unique phenomenon of distance, however close it may be' represents nothing but the formulation of the cult value of the work of art in categories of space and time perception. Distance is the opposite of closeness. The essentially distant object is the unapproachable one. Unapproachability is indeed a major quality of cult value.

15   Benjamin, 'A Work of Art', p.222.
16   Peggy Phelan, *Unmarked: The Politics of Performance* (London: Routledge, 1993), p.149.
17   Augé, *Non-Places*, p.118.
18   Benjamin, 'A Work of Art', p.223.
19   Phelan, *Unmarked*, p.178.
20   http://www.helpdesk.net.au/courses/info/glossary.htm
21   http://www.google.com/bot.html
22   Further resources on bots: http://www.botspot.com/pages/chatbots.html : http://www.simonlaven.com/
23   http://www.loebner.net/Prizef/loebner-prize.html
24   http://www.alicebot.org/articles/wallace/pnambic.html The machine first used to host PNAMBIC was already named 'Alice', so clients started to refer to her as 'Alice' from the beginning. Later we chose the 'retronym' Artificial Linguistic Internet Computer Entity to fit the new name.
25   Please refer to Philip Auslander, 'Live from cyberspace', *PAJ: A Journal of Performance and Art*, 70 (2002): 16–21, and, of course, Peggy Phelan.
26   Context note: by 2008, you have managed to survive the Bush administration with some semblance of your civil liberties.

8
FutureHouse, Blind City: A Life

Johannes Birringer

I found these small green rocks on some of the graves in the old village of Breedon-on-the-Hill. The cemetery was placed in respectful distance to the village, overlooking the valley, keeping to itself. Many of the tombstones were covered with brown moss, their lettering deteriorated from old age, making it difficult to decipher the names of families that lived here. Generations now lying there, in quiet remove, covered with little green rocks. I took one as a reminder, curious to find out what started such a tradition of placing fake crystals on the earth that protects the decomposing of corpses.

Sites and non-sites

Decomposition. A reverse process that indicates something paradoxical at best, or rather, something that points to the nature of 'process' as we understand it today in the arts. This organic understanding emphasizes the temporary, the transitory, the dynamic yet perishable; it links production and destruction, growth and decay as if art were a metabolizing system, nature now looking at its informational doubles wondering what took artists so long to embrace cybernetics and complex systems science. Artificial, generative life forms evolving and mutating into something as alien or uncanny as the once surreal excesses of body art – this is the cutting edge of today's technological art that locates 'performance' outside of the control of human subjectivity. Authorship is dissolved or disappears in the model of 'emergence', yet the scientific model bears a curious resemblance to late capitalism's globalized flows and exchanges and thus to the business model transforming the cultural form of art today. We rehearse collective process. Artistic practice, especially when it diligently records and reflects everyday life, is valorized by the neo-liberal market as creative social technique. Since the 1990s, art in some sense was asked to function as a social service in the aesthetic production of reality. Such process reflects on how we live and how we want to live, how we comprehend architectures which are not built to last.

I should therefore mention my capitalist venture into building new infrastructures for performance and media research, except that so far it has not turned up any profits but lingers precariously, another 'alternative site' struggling to assert itself and survive briefly, a familiar predicament in the life of an independent choreographer. After early training in theatre, I discovered that the stage holds less interest to me than dysfunctional industrial architectures and other locations we tend to call 'site-specific', for no particular reason other than their apparent inadequacy as functional (useful) places holding commercial or exploitable interest or cultural value. Vacant, abandoned and crumbling buildings caught my fantasy, and inspired performances that could only be devised in such environments that smelled and tasted of a bygone history, showed wounds or proudly held on to the engineering feats of a nineteenth-century era when such buildings provided work and livelihood for many people in the region of my ancestors. My grandfather was a coal miner, and his father before him also tilled underground while the family continued to have livestock and cared for a small area of farmland.

After many years living abroad, far removed from the coal mining region of my province, I returned home one day to discover that the old industry had expired. The mines had been shut down when it was decided they were no longer profitable and deserving of the large subsidies that kept them alive. The mine closest to my home, established long ago in the village of Göttelborn, lay there like an albatross, barely alive but guarded by security personnel looking after the rotting corpse. The guards make sure no one gets lost or hurt in the vast territory of the pit. They've turned water and electricity off, but many dangerous looking cables still lie around exposed. There might be gas leaks and damaged machinery, inverted signs of technological progress.

Progress here has come to a halt, and the regional government, eager to invent solutions to growing economic malaise, structural unemployment, increasing immigration, population density and strained social relations, likes to convert the corpses into monuments to industrial culture ready to be exploited for tourism on the one hand, while seeking investors to create pockets of emerging high-tech industries on the other. The Göttelborn Mine has now been declared a 'heritage', but the redevelopment agency that commissioned my proposal for an interactive media lab dreams already of a different future in the *cité* and the *boulevards* of the pit: it envisions the mine as coming back to life with new energies, new settlers, new innovative inhabitants who start another cycle of creation amongst the proud white towers that overlook the cemetery.

The dream of the future *cité* cherishes its tallest tower as a symbolic landmark, *der weisse Bock*, without necessarily dwelling on the unhappy saga of its construction. The technically advanced Shaft IV Tower, with its colossal pyramidal framework, was a desperate last measure to guarantee production and continued subsidies, yet the engineering feat was paradoxically completed only in the year before the mining company closed everything down. A tower of tragic futility, it offers a splendid view of the surrounding countryside. Research into the sustainability of regional industrial culture needs to be rewritten; surveying the 'urban topography' of the site, the redevelopment agency hopes to attract courageous innovators in such fields as biotechnology, nanotechnology, synthetic material production, computing and artificial intelligence, promoting the integration of nature, landscape design, technological culture and architecture into a new 'information network'.

As we live in this world, we grow more comfortable with the rhetoric of globalization that advertises our survival in the various 'regions' of empire. When I travel between Nottingham (East Midlands of the United Kingdom) and Göttelborn (Saarland, a southwestern state in Germany), I am told that my work in such locations contributes to the development of a 'regional digital culture' which is both regional and global insofar as the region understands itself as a 'portal to the world'. I am not sure whether such understanding is as common among the local population as the development agencies think, but the regional capitals and the business, political and community leaders subscribe to it, and they administer the funding for innovative projects. When I observe the working methodologies amongst fellow practitioners in the creative industries and in my own collaborative productions over the last ten years, the enormous increase in the use of new technologies and networked, distributed communication is readily apparent. Most of such new media work is laboratory-driven, its different parts assembled in different places and brought together temporarily for testing. Some of the work does not have to seek a specific venue to be performed. It is designed to be distributed on-line, conceived as a dynamic system of virtual performance, programmed to be reconstituted in different, changing forms and articulations, and it is thus grounded in a conceptual model of art-making and scientific research which emphasizes process, self-organization and interaction.

In the contemporary context of digital interactive performance, with its specific interdisciplinary techniques of research on the development of pervasive technologies, the programming of interactive design, distributed networks, sensitive environments, artificial life (a-life), complex dynamic systems, and human-machine relationships, the whole question of the 'object' has been muted, and with it the significance of place or origin. Sher Doruff writes:

> Focus on processual interaction over the end-product or art object has implications for definition of aesthetics and classification of media content – a contemporary twist on the conceptualist stance. Dynamic potential within media ecologies (expression through all available mediums, where the mediums themselves are changed by the expression) whose *raison d'être* relies on live processing between medium and between humans, contradicts attempts at classifying symbol or dissecting meaning from layered, evolving sound and image.'[1]

Doruff emphasizes the aesthetic implications of such a collaborative environment, a kind of digital commons with interactive platforms for multi-users, implying that 'the human' is only a medium within such ecologies of diffusion, with an unknown number of input, output and hidden units. The placeless presence of such interactive platforms is a contemporary phenomenon that reaches into countless imagined communities of interest (such as game cultures, hacker and anarchist networks, Attac, eBays, maillists, weblogs, etc.). As we once entered cathedrals to visit their architectures as place-holders for a system of belief, so we now log on to the imagined community of our chat rooms. When I registered with the East Midlands 'Digital Arts Forum' (http://www.digitalartsforum.org.uk), I left a link to a physical resource, in this case my telematic studio in Nottingham, which itself is linked to a network of partner sites in other countries.[2] Once we engage distributed real time interaction strategies and negotiations for data sharing and processing, we tend to operate in a wholly mediated sphere. The phenomenal site or place, where some of the action might be generated, recedes from sight. If performances built on media interaction and databases tend to be disconnected from physical context, and if motion-capture animation and 3-D virtual worlds create projected environments without real performers, then live remediations of the body in digital-choreographic space undermines all our familiar notions of body art and Live Art. The body is no longer in (one) place. It is not obsolete, by no means, but it gradually decomposes.

This is hardly an alarming statement, even as the story of collaborative culture, which has its own romantic and utopian pitfalls, needs some closer inspection. Rather, interactivity today is the new model for our regions, for the knowledge economy, for site-specificity – our spatial and media practices articulate *transactions* between event, site (data) and viewers. Prefiguring the paradox of telematic performances with distributed action, where images and sounds are created not just to be transmitted from one location to another, but to spark a multi-directional feedback loop with participants in remote locations, site-specific performance itself has become transitory. Another way of saying this is to argue that site-specificity is medium-specificity. In regard to genres such as videodance, it has been correctly pointed out that choreography for the camera is site-specific insofar as video creates its own 'site' for the dance to occur.[3] The same is true for net art and on-line interactive performance.

Our organizational process has adopted a new awareness of transactions which are relationship-specific, derived from a combination of palpable practices in engineering, sculpture, film, music, choreography and participatory design. Above all, those who practise such transactions need a room with a view, so to speak, a studio or platform that is connected to the non-physical or virtual environment. The 'local' is understood not as sedimented history but as data mine, a recordable source that can be changed in the post-processing. Place no longer holds a self-evident authority nor provides stable context; it is as fictively constructed as any other mediated reality. This does not mean it is not real, but like any other places where we live or where we travel, it holds potential to become our machine of communication, generate behaviour, or receive our performance envelopes. We model our own habitat as an adoptive process, as we temporarily inhabit and interfere with the ecology of the environment. This is a very material process, I want to emphasize, since performance with interactive design is inevitably focused on sensory processing and heightened perceptual/synaesthetic relationships to audio-visual environments.

There is another way of looking at the site-specific, especially if I relate it to our experience of working in the coal mine. The paradox of site-specific performance here suggests that the 'mine' is replaced by the interactive audio-visual system we build while working together. New properties and networked conditions arise which make the environment a specific media space in which our actions, movements and stories converge. The design of such an environment is aimed at an active 'user' who experiences, not an original place nor a completed work, but an intelligent, responsive system. Such a system requires the participant to engage the various interfaces which control and mediate the aesthetic as well as psychological processes the environment harbours. The 'system' thus becomes a 'place' designed in explicit anticipation of its user: it is always becoming and never completed.

In the summer of 2003 I start working in the abandoned pit, making the 'Interaktionslabor' (http://interaktionslabor.de) a temporal place for experimentation, collaborative brain-storming, designing and creating virtual environments. Twenty choreographers, musicians, composers, architects, media and network artists from four different continents arrive to set up shop in the Schwarz-Weisskaue, one of the largest and most unusual buildings on site, formerly used as dressing-washing room for the 5000 coal miners who worked here for many decades. After a few weeks, we strike the set, dismantle our electronic equipment, and quickly leave, only to return eagerly the next summer, hoping that the mine is still there.

The (repeated) return is not without surprises or complications. Internally, the composition of the group and the focus of the interactive design projects change. Externally, the fictive *cité*, still unpopulated, has begun to look more like a construction site, as one of the old machine halls is being transformed into workshop studios. On top of the dark slack hill, on which we filmed a dance during the first lab, a company is building the largest photovoltaic power plant in Europe. While we set up our equipment, construction workers at the photovoltaic plant are adding solar panel after solar panel. Two other companies have moved in; security is less heavy this year, and the old canteen, where the retired miners still go to have a beer, now features jazz concerts once a month. Children's theatre performances take place in one of the empty buildings; we find remnant signage of a photographic exhibition. Signs of scattered, burgeoning activity, alongside the decompositions.

The Interaktionslabor announced publicly that the team members who come to work here consider the workshop an engine for new ideas in communication technologies and performance with interactive media. The location is treated, with regard to the issue of sustainability, neither as something to be preserved (museum of industrial culture) nor as a theatrical setting for festival entertainment, but rather as an open place of transformation processes. We believe that a laboratory mediates knowledge processes that can be used in other areas of training. This transferability is particularly meaningful in view of communications strategies that involve internet, video and cellular conferencing technologies and wearable computing. They have an impact on new concepts of urbanity, lifestyles and mobility, and they offer a perspective for the younger generations growing up in the region. A study of 'networked environments' takes up questions implicitly raised by the infrastructure development agency (IKS) and its search for investors, although our lab may not initially create jobs, but rather function as a cultural hub for creative practices and a research link in a virtual network with other creative industries in the region and beyond. As a digital laboratory it will also be inevitably non-site specific as it participates in information industries, on the level of research, scientific and artistic production, which cannot be reduced to any single identifiable culture. As models of innovative practice provoking questions, rather than confirming or preserving cultural identities, vanguard laboratories curate projects and complex productions which today are marked by heterogeneity, organizational diversity and mutability, and by collective authorship which we call collaborative culture.

So much for the rhetorical façade. In a basic sense, the lab provides a workshop for skilled labour and artisanship, it converts existing spaces, generates stories, images, sound (including radio broadcasts), hardware and software design, network solutions. Team member move around a lot, dance, make music, debate, film, edit, program, scavenge, tinker and construct. Canadian artist Jeff Mann, for example, constructed a special antenna out of found materials that enabled wireless access from the top of the Shaft IV Tower. From that towering vantage point he was able to send a video stream to Sher Doruff who created a Keyworx configuration that displayed images from Jeff's camera mixed with an audio-visualization of their conversation on walkie-talkies. Queries from the audience, communicated via text messaging from Blackberry PDA's provided by Renn Scott (a user-experience architect working for the RIM Company in Toronto), and chalk drawings made by visitors on the pavement were included in the image mix shown at the Winding Engine Building.

The overall strategy of the 2003 lab was to focus on such hybrid connections, letting the site create the work. The 'site' is the performance interface; it is user-specific to the extent that without interaction, there is nothing to see. Australian media artist Kelli Dipple, for example, showed an interactive improvisation ('Absence') with a triptych of Quicktime movies she had shot of herself in the mine, and then invited the audience to join her and do the same, leaving something of themselves (as trace). In her films, she focused on the mine as a space of disappearing bodies, and her treatment of the interface itself seemed to comment on the disappearing effect of programming that allows for randomness and certain kinds of recognition, not others. Her interface was set up with a video camera as input device for the interactive system (BigEye): it could see space and track motion and colour. Her parameter defined dark colours as a 'present body', and the dynamics of the movement decided which film of her disappearances we would see (and in which direction, forward or backward).

Dipple's 'game', which simultaneously involved spoken passages activated by certain gestures or movements, implicates the visitors and thus potentially motivates and integrates their movement and the interpretation of the collective moment (someone's presence is being decomposed). If interactive design animates the user to make choices, it will inevitably provoke questions about the formal constraints (media properties), control parameters (outcomes predetermined by the programming), and the levels of interaction and reciprocal expertise required in such a space for 'public processing'. Affecting a sense of live processing in the viewer may not be enough if the tools and programming code are not common knowledge, and if the roles of programmer and user are not exchanged. In other words, interactivity is not a common cultural form as long as tacit agreements governing the conditions and variables of a given model of participation have not been defined. The expertise of the user group is a contradictory problem rarely addressed in current discussions of emergent aesthetics which consider artists and audiences as co-producers and assimilate art into the collaborative social practice ('performance') or *improvisation technique* elicited in evolving interactive environments.

How do I want to live?

To examine this question of design and control, we began to work on three parallel processes in 2004:

- an interactive opera about blindness (*Ensaio sobre a cegueïra*)
- a generative/interactive improvisational system in which dance, digital image and sound are algorithmically manipulated creating a hybrid, mutable landscape ('Spiff')
- an architectural project on interactive living ('FutureHouse')

I will end my story by bringing two of these projects into relationship with each other, evoking their connections for you. If you had been with us, you would have received a questionnaire from Marion Tränkle and Jim Ruxton asking you to respond to some queries that are already part of the architectural process the designers have devised for the FutureHouse, which is not a house nor a model of home or place, but an interactive fantasy of how you (dear visitor) would like to live in the future. Do you want to take your house with you? Would you like it to recognize you, respond to your moods, talk to you, make love to you? Think about an idea how you can experience living space completely differently. Spaces as we see them around us all have the potential to change. Architects are skilled to do that. There is a routine when dealing with a restoration project, namely to scan the structure very quickly and decide about qualities to keep and things to change.

During the 2003 lab Tränkle considered the industrial surrounding as so overwhelming that the idea of changing and thinking about different use was nearly a sacrilege. When Tränkle teamed up with engineer Jim Ruxton in 2004, she found a very small, empty building, a former electrical transformer station (*Alte Kompensation*), which was then used to 'perform questions' in an attempt to break down the idea that our surrounding is static. The interactive scenario Tränkle and Ruxton created, with sensors and audio-visual media, was designed to evolve and trigger fantasy. The fantasies of the audience, we figured, would be out of control, while their social behaviour in the interface might be predictable, to some extent. The site-specific medium of collaboration would be improvisation and intuitive recognition of the properties of complex systems: the visitor would feel and imagine possible life forms.

As a framework, Tränkle offered a guided tour through the Future-House. Welcoming a limited number of visitors at a time, she invited them to come inside and successively addressed each of them with the same questions that had been used in the questionnaire to prepare the interactive installation. The central idea of the design concept was to create a sensitive space: numerous sensors (proximity, heat, touch) and kinetic devices reacted to audience behaviour through sound and visual projections, voices started to speak, images appeared on walls, objects in the room came alive, thus conjuring a constantly evolving dynamic that changed the way in which the house was perceived to exist. The house in which you might live lives too.

How do you like the view out of the window? What would you see there? What is essential for you to feel at home? Is it security or connectivity? How secure are you when your house is on-line? What is your image of beauty in a house? The interview form dominated Tränkle's address to the visitors who seemed familiar with so-called show houses (pre-fabricated design), but less so with an empty space that acted upon them. Ironically, in the midst of the specific context of the abandoned pit there was one house already 'ready', stuffed with a little bit of virtual furniture to indicate possible functions within a house that communicates and self-organizes. A house that can also be a bit moody. When it asked a visitor to identify himself by saying something positive about himself, the visitor was so perplexed that he fell silent, whereupon the house declined access to its 'higher levels' of interaction

Tränkle and Ruxton played their roles as hosts with proper dignity and playful humour, also giving visitors time to explore the sensate body of the space, its surprising colours and lights (video images), its stunning views of an imaginary outside (video windows), its mobility (the house becoming an airplane), transformabilty, alertness, cleverness and even erotic dexterity (when one of the walls asked a woman to step closer and touch it). The FutureHouse also contained a database, an archive of imaginary projections that had been collected in the questionnaires and could now be accessed (recreated video animations) by visitors who, as Tränkle implied with mock sincerity, could see themselves as potential buyers. Our laboratory was selling something that is not there yet, but rather than thinking of it as a virtual house, the performance of the interview of interactive living in fact offers people a sensory perception of fantasized space. The mediated 'house' here becomes a sombre version of Hélio Oticica's *Penetrável Tropicalia* – a heterotopic space in midst of the industrial decay.

The processing experience designed by Tränkle and Ruxton offers some fundamental insights into contemporary digital perception. It is perception produced not just by the interactive performance between host and guest, here modestly framed as a theatricalized 'tour' of a 'future house', but actively generated by a sensory environment that invites 'touch' and 'movement', both literally and imaginatively. The sensors which Tränkle and Ruxton placed inside the house do not merely activate digital kinetic objects, and we cannot simply speak here of projected or immersive space which may flood the visitor's sensory perception, as it often happens in contemporary multimedia performances and exhibitions. Rather, the uninhabited FutureHouse acts unpredictably and thus provokes the visitor to move around, hesitate, sit down, change places and postures, and reach towards something which actually takes place in the affected body of the visitor – there is no virtual house emanating from the audio-visual images but the visitor's bodily perception is itself virtualized. When I was in the visitor group, I was asked to close my eyes and imagine where I would fly with the house. I then began to hear the engines start, and my house began to lift off and drift into the clouds and beyond, as the sounds I heard slowly confused my internal sensorimotor logic and made me feel suspended. When I opened my eyes, I looked out of the window of my flying house and saw the sprawling vista of Houston beneath me as we prepared for landing. I had to make an effort to 'place' myself again, feel the reality of where I was since I lost my proprioceptive footing for a while, following a digital process which perhaps begins when I touch an image and it begins to speak, when I perceive a projected object that appears real and familiar, only to become modulated into something fantastic and unexpected.

Decomposing sight

Sensory processing in interactive performance expands our under-standing of affectivity and synaesthetic perspectives. Digital images and sonic frequencies open out, extending the whole body from the inside where virtual (fantasy) movement is affectively and cognitively proc-essed in the cross-modal experience we have when vision does not dominate but is short-circuited by touch and hearing. In my second example, our approach to *Ensaio sobre a cegueïra* (Blind City) focused precisely on the haptic and the auditory, seeking to displace proprio-ception from vision, make us 'see' without seeing. For this workshop, involving numerous lab participants and directed by Brazilian composer Paulo C. Chagas, we chose one of the largest spaces in the mine, the resonating echo-chamber of the Winding Engine Building, gigantic, hollow and dusty, the winds blowing through gaping holes on one side where the cables once hung that pulled the coal from under-ground. *Ensaio sobre a cegueïra*, the Portuguese title of our libretto (adapted from José Saramago's novel), literally means 'essay on blindness'. For the opening scenes of this interactive opera we designed a multi-channel sound environment to combine live voice (soprano), processed voice, chorus, and film projection, emphasizing the live processing and synthesis of the music through performer action with sensors, microphones and feedback. Unlike the FutureHouse and its direct involvement of the visitors, the interfaces for this performance were designed for expert performers to rehearse digital perception.

The rehearsal begins by drawing attention to the moment when a seemingly dominant natural modality of perception (sight) decomposes: people in the city are suddenly struck by a mysterious blindness. This moment is rendered in voice, gesture and action, in performances that access mnemonic techniques harboured by the senses and their self-referencing habits. In this moment the visual, distance from the eye, is not composed. Rather than reciting language (libretto), score and choreography as visual architectures (spatializing memory), the mnemo-techniques for the interfaces climb through the dark. They are soundings that touch the mapping (modelling of sound parameters) for the sensory interaction, which has a graphic or mathematical form in the computer, while the action of the sensitized body relies solely on felt relations, felt quantity and immediate perception of sound, measure, distance, pitch, volume and shape. Carrie Henneman's soprano soars high, reverberating through the entire building. Her voice sweeps and 'guides' the others. Angeles Romero, wearing body sensors on her muscles and joints, moves and modulates digital sound in continuous ineffable waves, seamless loops that keep folding back on themselves as our ears try to focus and 'see' a waveform that is like an incipient direction for such experience of mixed emotions. I am alone in the room, remember colours, objects, shapes that are/were part of my experience; I hear shapes or I might be hallucinating, words forming patterns or movements, remembered rhythms, forming words, decelerating the sensation of forward progression, compressing the multidimensional into intensity without extension. I look inside facing myself, placeless and abstract, my previous life. That intensity, as if we feel we hear our heart beat, is eye-opening, and our poor metaphors crumble when it comes to the non-visual excitement, close to an orgasm, that might drive the self-related movement of the body, my body feeling the twists and turns of Romero's body as she relives the moment with her lover in which she goes blind. This is an analog process for sure, and it thus questions what we do with our computational arrangements, in systems we call MAX or Isadora. On the other hand, the music of this opera is created in the synergy of bodily rhythms, muscles, ears, voices integrating the digital sound, and thus the instruments of an emergent, seismic environment (the technologies), non-localized and abstract, become part of our incipient experience of continuing, moving without sight.

Of course you will say that this is a completely artificial experiment, that the performers were not really blind. Well then, the little green stones on the graves were actually emeralds, and I imagined myself lying there, my body rotting away with these sweet sheets of crystalline tears covering the unimaginable.

Notes

1 Sher Doruff, 'Collaborative Culture', in J. Brouwer, A. Mulder and S. Charlton, eds, *Making Art of Databases* (Rotterdam: V2_Publishing/NAI Publishers, 2003), p.92. For the more esoteric forays into planetary collective consciousness, see Roy Ascott, *Telematic Embrace: Visionary Theories of Art, Technology, and Consciousness*, ed. E. A. Shanken (Berkeley: University of California Press, 2003). See also Katherine N. Hayles, *How We Became Post-human: Virtual Bodies in Cybernetics, Literature, and Informatics* (Chicago: University of Chicago Press 1999); Nicolas Bourriaud, *Postproduction*, trans. Jeanine Herman (New York: Lukas & Sternberg 2000); Amy Scholder and Jordan Crandall, eds, *Interaction: Artistic Practice in the Network* (New York: D.A.P., 2001); and Johannes Birringer, *Performance on the Edge: Transformations of Culture* (London: Continuum, 2000).

2 The Association of Dance and Performance Telematics (ADaPT) was formed in 2001 and includes partner sites in Columbus, Phoenix, Salt Lake City, Irvine, Detroit, Brasilia, São Paulo, Amsterdam and Tokyo. ADaPT on-line performances are documented at http://dance.asu.edu/adapt/ and www.dance.ohio-state.edu/~jbirringer/Dance_and_Technlogy/ips3.html

The Nottingham lab is at http://art.ntu.ac.uk/performance_research/birringer/lat.htm

Doug Rosenberg, 'Video Space: A Site for Choreography'. Available at http://www.dvpg.net/essays.html

I am paraphrasing from the questionnaire and Marion Tränkle's notes for the lab (quoted with permission). Additional commentary and photographs are on our website: http://interaktionslabor.de

3 Following Brian Massumi's suggestion to look at the different logics of affect and emotion, and to consider that 'intensity' is 'embodied in purely autonomic reactions most directly manifested in the skin – at the surface of the body, at its interface with things', we need to examine more carefully the various kinds of connection we make to physical design, content and 'effect'. Especially for performative installations of the kind I describe, with tactile interfaces, images, sound and implied physical action, an aesthetic response which registers affective sensation (and the category of 'intensity' proposed by Massumi) seems promising. See Brian Massumi, *Parables for the Virtual: Movement, Affect, Sensation* (Durham, NC: Duke University Press 2002).

My reflections on digital perception are inspired by Mark B. N. Hansen's (2004) theorization of the 'digital image' and his approach to interactive information environments which *become* a bodily process of filtering and composing images. See his *New Philosophy for New Media* (Cambridge, MA: MIT Press), pp.93–124. Cf. Johannes Birringer, 'La Danse et la perception interactive', *Nouvelles de Danse*, 52 (2004): 99–115.

Part III
On Location

On Location: Introduction

Leslie Hill

The mathematical point through which the imaginary axis of
the Earth's rotation passes.

The North Pole – the point where the wind comes always from
the south, and blows always towards the south, since it is
south in all directions.

The point where the compass itself can only indicate south, since,
being at the absolute north, it can no longer indicate north.

The point where the meridians meet and where, consequently,
it is every hour of the day at once.

The point where the year is encapsulated in an immense day, a
single continual night: dawn, a single continual day, dusk.

The point where the stars neither rise nor set.

The point where the sun neither rises nor falls in the sky, but – in
summer, when you can see it – revolves on the horizon at
the same elevation.

The point where the Earth's centrifugal force comes to an end.
At the absolute north, north no longer exists. Things can
come only from the south. At the heart of the social, the social
no longer exists. Things can come only from elsewhere.
At the heart of the subject, the subject no longer exists.
Things can come only from others.

All magnetic forces reverse.

For every point on the planet, there is no other direction than
the antipode.

(Jean Baudrillard[1])

We either view places from the inside out or from the outside in. These
two views are very different and our composite understanding of places

lingers on the threshold, somewhere in between. It's all about perspective. Our understanding of nineteenth-century Parisian shopping arcades secreted away in the fashionable heart of the city, will be inescapably linked with our experiences of giant American retail-outlet malls that seem to spring from nowhere and stand alone on long stretches of highway. If you have only experienced the arcade or if you have only experienced the strip mall, you can never love or hate either of these two places to the same degree as if you had experienced both. The impact of travel is as much in the way we see things when we return as it is in what we see while we are away. We use places as outposts from which to view and understand other places. We traverse place in order to attain the vistas that shape ideas.

Flannery O'Connor stated that the writer 'operates at a peculiar cross-roads where time, place and eternity somehow meet,' and identified the writer's problem as finding that location.[2] This 'problem' is not limited to fiction. In the theoretical works of writers responding to modernism, such as Walter Benjamin and Siegfried Kracauer through to the post-modern critiques of Jean Baudrillard and the poststructuralist work of Paul Virilio, writers work from and through location – Benjamin's Paris; Baudrillard's Los Angeles; Kracauer's hotel lobbies; Cixous's graveyards and so on. Philosophy shines 'on location'. Writers alight. In Live Art and performance the artist is also faced with O'Connor's problem of location, but in this case on a literal as well as figurative level, as they must orchestrate the siting as well as the setting.

As the practitioner of a transient art form, homeless by nature, the live artist is a cousin of Benjamin's *flâneur*, who wanders through the city, detached and observant, apart from the crowd. Though the family resemblance is apparent if you can get them to stand next to each other, it won't jump out immediately, as the Live Artist is an embarrassing attention seeker, while the *flâneur* is the loner in the family who doesn't like to be photographed with anyone. The live artist comes from a big family, as many migrants do, but is the spitting image of no one. Live artists are mongrels, begotten by unlikely couplings of travellers and architects.

In contemporary urban and architectural discourse, we are increasingly obsessed by figures which traverse space: the *flâneur*, the spy, the detective, the prostitute, the rambler, the Cyprian. These are all spatial metaphors, representing urban explorations, passages of revelation, journeys of discovery – 'spatial stories'. Through the personal and the political, the theoretical and the historical, we all tell spatial stories, we exchange narratives or architecture in, and of, the city.[3]

For all their rambling, eventually the writer must alight, the architect must build and the live artist must break camp. The live artist must settle long enough to make an impression and issue an invitation, for the live artist needs an audience even if only one. Like prostitutes, live artists exist, by and large, outside the official commerce and public space of the city, but must lure people to them, to an alternative place they have temporarily settled, in order for an exchange to take place. So, not only does the live artist face O'Connor's problem of location, they face the problem of finding and drawing an audience to a location. To be honest, it's a lot of work. As O'Connor herself observed: 'you discover your audience at the same time and in the same way that you discover your subject; but it is an added blow.'[4]

In this section Michael Peterson in Chapter 10 takes us on location to Las Vegas, a trip which no book on place and placelessness in performance could be complete without. In Chapter 9 Graeme Miller describes his sound piece *Linked*, which haunts a three-mile stretch, the littoral of the M11 Link Road in East London, with voices of the past, creating a 'memory coral' along a route where houses once stood. Patrick Laviolette looks in Chapter 12 at the performative metaphors of truth, deception and placelessness in the Cornish peninsula through the work of the Kneehigh Theatre Company, an integral part of whose working method is to meld narrative and design into the surrounding landscape. Laurie Beth Clark in Chapter 11 visits and reflects on the placed and displaced nature of trauma memorials at official public sites such as the slave forts of Cape Coast and Elmina and the nuclear holocaust sites of Hiroshima and Nagasaki.

Notes

1 Jean Baudrillard, *Fragments* (London: Verso, 1997, pp.3–4.
2 Flannery O'Conner, 'The Regional Writer', in *Mystery and Manners and Occasional Prose*, ed. Sally and Robert Fitzgerald (New York: Farrar, Straus & Giroux, 1970), p.59.
3 Jane Rendell, 'The Pursuit of Pleasure: London Rambling' in Neil Leach, ed., *The Hieroglyphics of Space: Reading and Experiencing the Modern Metropolis*, (London: Routledge, 2000), p.105.
4 O'Conner, 'The Regional Writer', p.118.

9

Through the Wrong End of the Telescope

Graeme Miller

LINKED is a semi-permanent public work by Graeme Miller consisting of 20 radio transmitters sited along three miles of the M11 Link Road in East London. Using small receivers, listeners on foot are able to hear musicalized and fragmented accounts of the buildings, some 400, which were demolished for the construction of the road. Each transmitter relays material relating to its own vicinity. The work was made in collaboration with the Museum of London and opened in 2003. It will run until the transmitters fail.

A repeating pattern. It begins with the house and cherry tree, then the whole street; 5 minutes away – a parade of shops, 10 minutes – a park. 15 minutes away a small high street, a library. My mental map widened from back step to Woolworth's. Then around the age of 11 or 12 an anxious reality broke: beyond the furthest reach of my domain, in any direction I chose, the pattern repeated itself. My mental map was wallpaper...

The low hills which rise from the basin of London are flocked with semi-detached houses and trees; a fitted fabric with a repeating motif: house – cherry tree – park – high street. Suburban toile. I was marooned in the centre experiencing a pubescent ailment: anxiety-of-place, a dull but constant worry about the arbitrariness of my whereabouts.

The physical edges of this world would be hard to reach for a number of years, but another edge appeared to me by chance. At the bottom of the garden ran a branch line and by it were the stumps of a demolished bridge. A story came up that someone who had lived here before all the houses were built in the 1930s remembered sheep being driven across this bridge. Not only were there sheep, I found out, but fields of lavender and chamomile too. Peel back the present and another pattern, sheep-bridge-sweet-herbs, is revealed. As a world, its claim to existence was as strong, if not slightly stronger, than the houses, including my own home.

From there it wasn't hard to lift off the crust of houses and hedges entirely and reveal the form of the land beneath. Rows of dipping streets, relieved of their houses, would transform into the simple and pleasing shape of a gentle river valley. I built a model, tracing brown contour lines from the map on to layers of grey card which I gummed together. The stepped terraces of the cardboard model of where I lived became a new tool. I had made an object which altered my whereabouts by altering my idea of it. Through it I could make the rivers flow and bombard my own small epoch with Geological Time. The closer I got to inhabiting this distant past space, the further away my native suburbia became. You stand on the street and an image appears behind it of lavender fields. You catch the smell of lavender and the suburban street fades to background. A car passes and the suburb returns to the front, but leaves holes. A gust of wind seems to happen in both places. You are not asleep, but awake. You are not imagining, but reading the land with your own senses.

Seeing these two porous layers at once is to inhabit a new waking space. It is a space with a giddy view through the wrong end of the telescope. You inhabit an observatory, a viewing platform with no noticeable characteristics other than distance from what it is set up to view. It's a rarefied place without the facilities for a full life. You don't necessarily want to be left up the Eiffel Tower for too long after the public have left. You don't want to be there forever – you want to get back down, *prendre un autre café crème* . . .

I finally left the suburbs skilled in distance, craving closeness, making worlds by making things – objects that alter your whereabouts. My made-up worlds were made from bits of the real world. This too – a repeating pattern.

In 1987 I rebuilt a square mile of headland in Kent from fragments of film and audio recorded over five years of random collection. The whole work, *Dungeness: The Desert in the Garden*, ICA 1987, was conceived as a re-creation of the sudden and singular moment of recognition I had experienced there the first time I had visited some years before. A moment overtook me, place-full and timeless, urgent and meaningful with meaning which seems not to refer to anything or anywhere else. In an overpowering second you are revealed exactly where you are. Where you are is a kind of who you are. I compiled the evidence and traces of life found within a square mile of planet surface as if all there was to know could be found there.

In my gathering trips I would often experience the opposite sensa-tion. Wandering over the shingle with a camera, the world around me would suddenly shift as if someone had thrown on the fluorescent lights in the middle of a magic lantern show. Mystery was displaced by flattened banality. The adventurer is suddenly a cow in a field. This sensation is a close cousin of the thrilling rush of place. The anti-epiphanic moment is equally unannounced, is equally about place and threshold, closeness and distance, but has a spoilsport quality. At this point I'd head back home.

A week or so later the processed film hit the mat. Lying on my back with the image projected through a shaving mirror on to the ceiling, I slowed the projector right down to three frames per second. At three frames you can really sense that a projected film is made up of as much darkness as light. You feel a long way off, but the steady clunk of the projector helps you reanimate the scene. The events of a week ago seemed like home movies from ancient Sumeria, only crossed with rusting rail-tracks and strange towers. The vertigo of reaching into the images, of piecing together their still images as movement, creates a sense of space and a sense of being in that space which is not so far from the place-moment I originally felt ten years before. If the sense of place that drained away from me *in situ*, can now be re-created, far away and much later, by its chemical image filtered through rhythmic dark-ness, does this mean we require this dark glass to see what is before our noses? Here I am, looking at the world through the wrong end of the telescope; a street filling with traffic in front of the house a train on the tracks behind. 1986.

Railways at bottoms of gardens feature in my life and for years entered my dreams. A network of single-track lines with secret stations and hidden halts connected scenarios in my unconscious world. This dream-system connects with the houses I have lived in that back on to the tracks. The time line runs through both landscapes.

The trackside world is singular and haunting. It is all place – a know-able pool of locality connected to its own section of track. The track, all time, brings with it distance, animated by the passing train. Here is the certainty that where we are is connected to otherness in a rushing moment. The vanishing tracks in either direction constantly suggest a wider picture that might transform what we are. Parallax draws us to distance and from there we might see ourselves. What we, at the track-side, see pass is also something we may also be viewed from. In June 1968, the mourners of the passing funeral train of Bobby Kennedy stand beside the rails in an act of witness. In the photographs taken from the train the onlookers stand like ambassadors of their own back-yards, themselves witnessed by the momentous and momentary and so made briefly legendary. The camera craves closeness but has to keep riding. Time's tracks run straight through place.

Now I am striding over Salisbury Plain, with artist, Mary Lemley, we have been making a network of walks (*Listening Ground, Lost Acres,* Artangel 1994), in 100 square miles around Salisbury. Suffused with knowledge of the underlying rocks and the time it took warm seas to lay it down as sediment, I am run on geological time and I realize how easy it is to trespass. No fences will stop me while my stride is measured by eons . . . In fact, no fence seems to exist in anything but a flimsy way.

Time line to London. Houses are disappearing. This is for real. It is not a mental trick, yet it tricks the mind and haunts it. It is hard to describe how disturbing I find this random demolition. For two years the familiar landscape has been developing holes. Gaps appear in terraced rows that leave the remaining houses standing like loose teeth. A man leaves Leytonstone Tube and stands bewildered and upset at the corner of Fillebrook Road where the house he has walked by every weekday has now gone. He cannot put it back into the space it occu-pied. The gaps seem to breed a collective anxiety, which expands as the houses are demolished and the rate at which they vanish increases.

Back in Salisbury, I trace a straight line across 20 miles of map and place radio transmitters along it. The map's aerial view, a bird's-eye god's-eye perspective where scale corresponds to the height of the flyer, invites speculation about the places it encodes; a solitary building by a copse, a bend in the river. Our mind's eye can open this surface like a window in an advent calendar and reveal an imagined or remembered scene. We zoom in from above, like a hawk to a rabbit or like a god to a scene of divine intervention. To experience this alignment on the ground is to have walked several miles of land, shuffling passing external events with introspective thought. It is to be present in the flow of real time and to find a place, by the telegraph pole in the middle of a ploughed field. At this point we can align ourselves with landmarks on the horizon. The distant poles mark the edge of our perception. These places are themselves far away, but also seem to see us in between, caught by their long lens, threaded on their telegraph wire. Distance brings us into presence. With boots caked in mud, our earth-bound position is relayed directly upwards to another part of ourselves. An offering laid on the table for a personal bird-god, who is watching over us, seeing the pattern, spotting the connections, yet craving closeness . . .

In a month's time, where the Central Line runs at the bottom of the garden, at 8.00 a.m. in the morning dozens of police and bailiffs in helmets and body armour will storm the house with a battering ram and summarily evict us from the house where I have lived for ten years.

I spent a decade living on this street and another making a work about its disappearance. Over this time I ran back and forth over these 20 years. Commuting the time line you can get off at different stops. Here the five-bedroom, double-fronted, yellow-brick of Number 159 Grove Green Road. Here the 30-foot, four-lane, carriage-way trench where Number 159 used to be. These are only a year apart, but it takes me that year to pluck up the courage to return. When I do I am utterly unable to fit ten years of my life – the double-fronted Victorian holdall of my biography – into the space it once inhabited. My decade of waking, feeding, working, childbirth, heartbreak, sleep, dream, meals, convivial moments and isolated thoughts were suddenly without a hook to hang themselves on. The new surface rejected them. The house – a brick vessel of memory contained at its demise almost exactly 100 years of narrative yet it would not root for a moment into the excavated channel that in five years time would brim with traffic. The view across the road is the same, but there is no place to view it from. The separation of these partnered buildings made each one, in a different way less plausible. One vanished, (from the present), but the other lost its prime witness. The inhabited building becomes a kind of pinhole camera, and in a street laid out this way, the constant witnessing of one building by its partner seems to glue the whole place together. I cannot retro-fit my story into the space it occupied because it has become a *sterile zone*. This was also the name of the high security area condoned off by the police in the final days of the anti-road protest.

Walk 50 yards away from the road into a side street and you can palpably sense where history starts to flow again. We sense this because we are narrative monkeys and city streets are the rainforest of human recounting; they provide a habitat for history. Some places are better habitats than others and some, (recall the no-time, no-place, nothing-to-tell feel of the hard-shoulder of a motorway should you spend any time there), are utterly hostile. In narrative ecology an exhausted and depleted space will no longer sustain a viable system of history. This is history's natural history. I was told that birds, though they hunt and feed on the motorways' edges, will tend not to nest within 50 metres of it. Could this be true of the nesting habits of stories? Were the gaps in the rows of houses that appeared in the early nineties more than evidence of single extinctions? I see now they were small holes in the narrative fabric which would not only resist any future occupancy, but also bleed the area around them of meaning. These pockets would join to form a continuous strip in which placelessness would reign because it is starved of time and where timelessness would reign for lack of a sense of place. The soft verges would become hard shoulders.

In Bratislava, they told me, the new bridge built in the early seventies demolished a medieval synagogue. Under the elevated carriageway the ground-plan of the building was chalked out where it stood. The drawn footprint was cleaned away then re-chalked, cleaned and drawn again. This was not done by an individual, but realized in a collective act of defiance. They told me that when you spoke to people they spoke as if the synagogue was still there and the road not. Defiance lay in collective belief and the traced ground-plan was its trigger. The narrative integrity of this place was not only restored, but the absent effectively replaced the present.

LINKED follows the littoral of the road. Its broadcasts fill the space and entice the listener, on foot, into the margins where narrative time starts and stops. It broadcasts fragments of accounts of the very space they refer to. It is not a history of the area, although its fragments do contain the upper parts of events, ordinary and extraordinary, tales, short and tall, that took place in it. Rather it is an object within history – a stick in the stream. It participates directly in the narrative life of the area and alters its flow. The purposely broken half-stories are half-stories because they are really bait. They are there to draw the witness into the neighbourhood and force them to finish the tale or overwrite it with their own conflicting account. In doing this, the houses are rebuilt, re-chalked and the absent replaces the present. The half-stories are also half-stories because they are heard from a long way off. They are the aural equivalent of the view from a high building, (the wrong end of the stethoscope?). They reveal themselves as pattern and offer the listener the hark-I-can-hear-my-house sense of how you yourself might fit into this pattern. Like my grey-card model of the suburbs, LINKED is an object that alters your whereabouts by altering your idea of it.

LINKED is $100\,m \times 5\,km \times 200\,yrs$ in dimension. It opened at the mid-point of its purpose, marking space back 100 years and built with transmitters that should still be broadcasting in 100 years' time. Century forwards, century back; it's an interesting time scale because just about anything happening in between is phrased and framed by two distant satellites of perspective. It's time-based work and, because it can only be accessed on foot it always places the listener in their own present moment. All present moments are haunted by their absence. I'm not sure what the official duration of the moment is, but it is certainly something which can be halved 100 times and still exist. The moment is shadowed by the past and future but is of neither. It seems to be made up of pure place: a Place sandwich in Time bread. Place seems to share the inherent poignancy of a musical moment – its instant death at the second of its birth. It exists in its fading trail, in memory. Perhaps place too requires memory and engaged faith to hold its music. The fleeting nature of a sense of place and its ability to suddenly fill and empty of meaning leaves us with the job of holding its musical shapes in the afterglow of our mental map, or in the rhythm of our body.

Place is not purely mental, I know this. I do believe that places continue to exist after I have left. I believe that the fridge light goes off when the door is shut. I believe that history happened. Yet I also see it is an act of faith, that in our human narratives we are constantly having to invent and compose the present lest it fall away. We do this each alone and we do this collectively. Place is the surface in which we write our narrative, but our neighbour's is also written. The overlapping, confused and evolving texture of shifting and made-up presents is a work of inter-authorship – a co-composition which can be read as well as written. It is a view of place that might seem it would consume you with its countless versions and endless mis- and reinterpretations, yet somehow is capable of reassurance as long as you remain active within it. In this landscape of hellishly bewildering possibility we seem to trade our story lines with amazing ease. We are making it all up as we go along and yet are capable of a felt consensus in a shared landscape; a kind of quantum neighbourliness.

By bringing listeners into its field, the chain of 20 transmitters is there to act as an artificial reef. Like the 1300 Redbird subway cars sunk off the Delaware coast, it is their shape and form that attract a complex range of species to a relatively barren patch of sea floor. LINKED, I hope, functions the same way in the narrative ecology of East London.

This photograph is the trace of a time when the houses of Grove Green Road were still not built. The view remains, but the anonymous photographer and their camera have gone. The girl in the picture sees and knows the photographer. Because she is patiently there and looking, she invites us to stand behind the tripod, fill the shoes and the moment of her photographer with our belief. She is a performer who invites us, asks us, makes us re-cloak the grey trees with green, the lengthening shadows with warmth, the distance with sound. In making

Figure 9.1 Grove Green Road before houses

LINKED, this photograph became important to me, not just because it miraculously conjures belief from its grainy silver gelatin marks, but because it was taken just before the century of inhabited space between the 1890s and the 1990s which LINKED deals with. It is a place far down the track beyond the start of my map and a connecting station for all stops via the Dark Ages to the Pleistocene. In dream it is close to the lavender fields of South London. Another suburb of the same city – another wallpapered sprawl and beneath it, another remote layer that seems to govern it. My own years in a house are made absent by the present motorway, but both the motorway and the houses are rendered thin and porous by this moment before either came into being.

The Central Line still runs beside the motorway. Run time's arrow backwards from the present moment and the Link Road will fill itself in, the houses will reappear and steadily renew themselves until, in the 1890s, they pour back into their foundations and grow over with rye-grass, hawthorn and elm. Strangely, the blighted neighbourhood began to revert to something more like the fields near Bent's Farm. In streets built for a middle-distance, contained a view of time, untended gardens merged and roses tangled with the born-again descendents of Victorian trees and grasses creating swathes of dense vegetation inhabited by birds and animals which literally migrated in along the railway tracks, but seemed to have arrived down the track from the past.

Run time's arrow forward 100 years and another image emerges, more grainy and doubly obscure, impossible to focus, this time unwritten. I screw my mind's eye up tight and briefly as this volatile pool of future fills with weather, sound, atmosphere and daily ordinariness, it offers me the view backwards. Here I am, a century ago, wrong end of the telescope, titchy on the bridge over the Link Road, in the early days of transmission. What I can see clearly is the penumbra of obscurity that surrounds this circular image of myself. It is the shadow of a time-tunnel in which I will die and the transmitters will fail. This work and it will outlive me and then erase itself. Time-based. The dizzy view back to my own residency on Earth from a point when both my life and death are almost entirely unremembered is a little chilly. It is the ultimate step back to get some perspective – an aerial view high enough to have escaped gravity. Earth from Apollo13. A one way ticket. Is this what underlies every distance? If we pull back, the helicopter shot at the end of the movie were to keep going, is this where we end up? Oblivion.

Still, the view from this great distance reveals things to the hopeful mind. It shows me the weather within the self-image of this area over decades and discloses the living corporeal history growing around the transmitters. Memory coral. I imagine clusters radiating from the trans-missions and strands strung between them: a narrative necklace specific to this site. This long view shows that against the flux of meaning, over time the place remains relatively constant. Future moments will break on the consciousness with the same sharp sense of overwhelming atmosphere. A passer-by in 2090 may be struck by the same resonance in the same spot as a photographer in 1890. Places assert their signature on the psyche repeatedly and human history sticks to its old haunts. At night, mist still gathers in the same hollows it did 1000 years before.

10
Walking in Sin City
Michael Peterson

She did not decide to stay in Vegas: she only failed to leave. She spoke to no one. She did not gamble. She neither swam nor lay in the sun. She was there on some business but she could not seem to put her finger on what that business was. All day, most of every night, she walked and she drove. Two or three times a day she walked in and out of all the hotels on the Strip and several downtown. She began to crave the physical flash of walking in and out of places, the temperature shock, the hot wind blowing outside, the heavy frigid air inside.... By the end of the week she was thinking constantly about where her body stopped and the air began ... [1]

Corporate place-making

While anecdotally persistent, they must be a bit of a rarity, those dedicated gamblers who supposedly travel to Las Vegas, proceed directly to a hotel, park themselves in front of their favoured table or machine, and hardly move for the duration of their stay. Instead, visitors to Vegas seem to wander, on routes bigger or smaller according to taste and economics – or the kind of compulsion driving Didion's character. The tourist town seems built for a constant oscillation between rest and motion.

Performance can offer Vegas tourists both at the same time. One of the original advantages of casino showrooms is that performances gave gamblers the experience of 'going out' while keeping them in. A specific strength of the variety format that so long dominated Vegas stages is that it offers seemingly distinct performance experiences in a single package. *Jubilee!* at Bally's is the strongest vestige of this tradition, with lines of feathered showgirls offering the visual thread on which are strung scenes ranging from a Samson and Delilah number to the sinking of the Titanic. Yet there is also a variety impulse at work in other Vegas performance forms. Magic, which can appear as a variety element in reviews such as *Splash!*, also often includes other variety elements in productions marketed primarily as magic acts. Erotic reviews, such as the otherwise quite formalist *La Femme* ('the art of the nude'), also frequently include comedians, comic jugglers and impressionists. All of these performances serve multiple business purposes: they generate revenue, they create value which casino managers can give to valued patrons as 'comps', they attract visitors staying at other casinos and, for hotel guests, they add a strongly visible element to the experience of the large casino as a self-sufficient place.

Commentators make much of the casinos' attempts to keep gamblers in place once they've got them, and it is true that some casinos can seem literally hard to leave. But tourists who go somewhere often seem to insist on going on. Just as seaside resort areas can become clogged with the 'internal' traffic of visitors protecting their sunburns by going on shopping expeditions or admiring historical sites of often dubious authenticity, so Vegas streets and sidewalks can seem jammed by crowds of people who project the sense either of 'taking a break' from gambling, or of waiting for their more serious gambling companions to finally finish. The resorts, then, know you're going to move around, and they recognize that the risk of losing one customer is the potential to attract another. Casinos don't try to imprison customers; they do try to construct semi-permeable membranes that absorb wandering tourists and then tend to keep them in.

You can feel this working in the littlest itineraries suggested by their obviousness: walk out to the pool or down to the restaurant. Almost all the big casinos now have shopping malls attached or bundled inside. The New York New York not only mimics the famous skyline on the outside; that exterior contains another exterior, city streets contained within city buildings. Paris is across the street, where, inside, the Eiffel Tower disappears into a ceiling of sky. While the absence of clocks in casinos is often cited as evidence of an institutional denial of 'the outside world', casinos have no interest in an absolute separation of inside and outside. The spatial grammars on the exterior are contiguous with related strategies of casino indoor space, and in fact one of these strategies is to conflate inside and out. Besides the streets inside New York New York and the Paris, there are new cars, waiting to be won, parked on banks of slot machines in every casino. These *inside outsides* aren't just for walking, either, since you can get a pedicab in the Aladdin shops, a gondola ride at the Venetian.

The architectural traditions of the theatre entrance have in Vegas a conflicted relation to the construction of these *inside outsides*. Many casino showrooms are barely marked, by signs too modest to do justice to their flashy logos. Lobby spaces are no more interesting; typically, the need to mediate between performance space and the place around it is met in the blandest, least marked way. These reticent thresholds suggest an anxiety on the part of the comprehensively themed casinos ('fake' places) about containing the potentially competing meaning-making within their theatres (places of faking, or what Foucault referred to as heterotopias). An interesting exception to the inconsequential entrances and non-lobbies in most casinos is New York New York, where theatre exteriors are a logical part of the architectural theming (contradictory though it may seem to have theatre façades on both the outside and inside of the building).

Restless still? Go a bit further, then, to the *outside inside*.

Downtown, the Fremont Street Experience has made the whole sector an inside, a sort of civic atrium ringed by hotels. It's like the courtyards of inns in Spain in the so-called Golden Age, a space created by the commerce that surrounds it, a space which calls out for its own performance form. Where the Spanish courtyards were filled with drama, the space between the Golden Nugget, Fitzgerald's, Binion's, the Golden Gate and so on is filled nightly with spectacle. But the light show that plays over the digital ceiling, while it does provide an event to draw gamblers up from the Strip, is less interesting than the arcade itself. The 'Fremont Street Experience', as it's called, is a performance designed for a non-place, a generic piece of technology usually showing animations of limited imagination. But its installation did achieve a kind of corporate-civic place-making in spite of this. Architecturally, it's like a hi-tech barrel-vault stretching the blocks from Main to Fourth. In daylight, the street is a literal breath of fresh air, like a sunporch offering relief from dark smoky casino interiors, which in turn take on a mysterious allure. As Walter Benjamin scribbled about the Parisian arcades: 'Since the light comes only from above through glass roofs and all stairways to the left or right, at entranceways between the shops, lead into darkness, our conception of life within the rooms to which these stairways ascend remains somewhat shadowy.'[2]

The canopy also turns those casino's *exteriors* into indoor artefacts, like museum pieces, or like 'found' instances of the theatre exteriors built into the artificial New York. Along with the resurrected neon signs that literally *are* part of a museum, the physical structure overhead, so unimaginative in its own visual impact (and certainly unimaginative in its programming), is wildly innovative of this urban tourist space, creating across this relatively modest street a place-making physical space that the Strip can only aspire to. But aspire it does. The problem for lower Las Vegas Boulevard is the clash between its enormous scale – its literal volume as well as its traffic flows – and the need for each specific location to call out to customers. It's a literal conflict between space and place.

Following in the tire tracks of Venturi, Brown and Izenour (who visited the city when driving on the Strip was still a good idea), one might see this conflict played out in the new massive elaborations of the principles of symbolic architecture that have arisen in the past two decades' competition between themed casino resorts. These include new videographic display technologies on architectural signage and the elaboration of symbolic façades beyond thematic association and toward skyline simulation (as in New York New York) and even the literal theatricalization of the resort space itself: a carnival parade is enacted on a regular schedule in the Rio, while a revised version of the pirate show (now with women!) draws large crowds to the lagoon outside the TI (formerly the Treasure Island). This very large scale visual logic certainly carries the legacy of the automotive spectatorship so important to their analysis in *Learning from Las Vegas*, but in many cases its current orientation is toward the pedestrian, so that the very large signifies toward the very small. This architectural shift is arguably a move from what *Learning* calls 'building as sign' to what is, in a very literal sense, 'building as setting'.

Thus it is perhaps equally productive to reverse perspective and, this time following Susan Stewart's lead in *On Longing*, consider how the miniature is mutually constitutive of the gigantic; the tourist experience of Vegas is not only one of being dwarfed by immense sign systems, but also of being offered temporary mastery over the minuscule symbolic in the form of souvenirs, financial/symbolic exchange, and the framing of views and vistas and *scenes*. Instead of being only a masochistic submission to complex systems of control, Vegas tourism, seen in this light, might be an experience of empowerment. Of course this immense space is obviously homogenously corporate in some ways.[3] Yet within so much vastness is a continuous appeal to difference, so that the themes of the resorts leak out into the sidewalks – spectators of the pirate show at Treasure Island 'walk the plank' of the boarded sidewalk, and the incongruous moving sidewalks outside the Venetian are encased in décor consistent with the hotel, leaning down to the street as if to ingest passers-by. This tension produces a lot of the excitement of being on the Strip – the sensation of being shouted at by buildings, signs, hawkers, leaflets and the illuminated butts of the *Crazy Girls* revue on top of every second taxi.

Spatial criticism

As in my analysis of these spatial practices on the part of casino culture, descriptions of Las Vegas frequently take spatial form: list-making walks through the city. For example, James Howard Kunstler's rather crabby description of the Strip is rich in spatial language, even if his geography is not literal and some of his place names are inaccurate:

> The volcano at the Mirage has been joined next door by a pirate ship extravaganza, in front of the Buccaneer Bay Resort [sic], complete with cannon fire and live swashbuckling actors, enacted every two hours.... New York, New York, has, on the outside, an enormous roller coaster weaving up and around the cartoon skyscrapers of its fanciful façade. Inside it offers a food court done up in a pastiche of Greenwich Village and Times Square (yeah, both in the same place, why not?). Across Tropicana Avenue stands the Excalibur... Across the street – that is, across the ten-lane strip – from Excalibur looms the baleful glass box of the MGM Grand, the casino of which is larger than Grand Central Terminal.[4]

His tone, I think, invites serial guffawing or tongue-clucking in response to each new item. This is a common tactic, but people who *enjoy* Vegas write this way too, only they ask for a repeated 'wow' or 'cool!'. Either way, these lists seek a bond with the reader; they cement a common sensibility without too explicitly invoking it.

Such peripatetic devices are particularly common in writing about Las Vegas. Vegas is experienced as a set of passages, interconnections of Strip, street, driveway, lobby, hallway. Unlike *les passages* of Paris, the organizing conceit of Benjamin's influential, unfinished *Passagen-Werk* (*The Arcades Project*), the gambling spaces of Vegas casinos are flattened rather than soaring; we speak of casino 'floors' and gambling 'pits'. Yet casino space is constructed along a logic of flow and distraction that is recognizably 'arcadian', so to speak. As Benjamin took the arcades of Paris – with their gambling, prostitution, and new arrangements of commerce and social interaction – to be exemplary of nineteenth-century industrialization, colonialism, urban development and mass commodification, so many see in the passages of Vegas – with their gambling, commercial sexualities, and new arrangements of commerce and tourism – a hot spot of post-industrial globalization, 'new' urban development and the commodification of experience. Considered from this point of view, Ralph Rugoff's eloquent description of the impact of desert space on Las Vegas culture is only half right:

> For such a work of art, there can be no better frame than the hundreds of miles of Mojave desert that surround the city. This frame is the secret advantage Las Vegas has over other places with legalized gambling.... It supplies a prophylactic against reality: the instant you arrive here, you feel marooned from the world you left behind. Dry desert winds convey a delirious frontier freedom, and experience takes on a mirage-like quality. The sky is the limit in Vegas, and the sky here is limitless.[5]

Rugoff's strong aesthetic sense of the implicit optimism of the physical context of Vegas rings true, though the growth of suburban sprawl around the city threatens to erode the feeling of being in a desert oasis. More importantly, the sense of separation from 'reality' is no doubt a key part of the phenomenology of Vegas; however, a 'Benjaminian' perspective requires that we ask how 'reality', in the form of material social relations, in fact underlies the seeming unreality of the place.[6]

Gerbils or *Flâneurs*?

While navigating the exterior space of Vegas is relatively easy, given its organization along the major axis of the strip and the minor one of Fremont Street, negotiating interior space can be more challenging. Elsewhere in the same essay Kunstler mocks the condition of the casino workers, who he says became inured to the purposeful disorientation of the casino floor and in fact 'lived in the disorienting housing complexes east and west of the Strip ... They were accustomed to spatial confusion. Most had learned to navigate their way around the workplace by means of gerbil-like dead reckoning – *take a right at the "batter up" slot machine, hang a left at the "winners' circle bar"*.'[7] I think Kunstler misunderstands both gerbils and casino employees; those directions say more about the workers' understanding of tourists than about their own spatial practices.[8] While some of his other writing about cities is more complex, here Kunstler sounds as if he would raze the city. By the end he imagines the future of Vegas as a looted, deserted ghost town.

It is surely more productive to look specifically at human movement *within and among* these radical shifts in scale and vectors of public and corporate influence, and how, as Certeau, Benjamin and many others might observe, to walk (or to drive and park) can be to remake the city. In my view, the caged gerbil is a poor figure for the Las Vegas tourist in motion. It's the very immensity, complexity and counter-intuitivity of Vegas spaces that allow the visitor not just a 'making do', but a *mastery* of time and space that is immensely and, I think, democratically pleasurable. The gerbil is a worker (or a guest) frustrated in search of a destination, who pitiably – to Kunstler – stumbles through arbitrary landmarks to a meaningless destination. That's not usually what I see when I watch people walk here, even the drunk and bankrupt, or the parents with children Kunstler mocks. Yes, there is spatial frustration fostered by the visual density, the repeated motifs and the winding paths laid out for maximum exposure of gambler to game. This experience is comparable to the ordeal arranged by supermarkets which deliberately spread products in a manner that defies convenience. Still, more often, I see purposely purposeless movement, perhaps a kind of *flânerie*.

Glossing Benjamin's notes on the *flâneur*, Rob Shields explains:

> *flânerie* is more specific than strolling. It is a spatial practice of specific sites: the interior and exterior public spaces of the city. ... *flânerie* consists of strolling at an overtly leisurely pace, allowing oneself to be drawn by intriguing sights or to dawdle in interesting places. ... As an ethic it retrieves the individual from the mass by elevating idiosyncrasies and mannerisms as well as individuality and singular perspective...[9]

The *flâneur* is a privileged, elite figure, almost always rendered as male. And just because he is able to flaunt his non-productivity, he is not necessarily a subversive force. In Benjamin's words, 'The *flâneur* is the observer of the marketplace. ... He is a spy for the capitalists, on assignment in the realm of consumers.'[10] Central to many descriptions of the *flâneur* is an individualism defined against a mass; the elite *flâneur* is 'in the crowd, but not of it'. If we were to settle for that as a representative of the Vegas tourist, we'd simply celebrate the hipster lover of kitsch, and reinstate condescension as the optic for viewing the city.[11] So perhaps it's best not to dwell too long on the historically authentic *flâneur*, if he exists, and instead consider Benjamin's interest in *flânerie* as a methodology of looking. Because Vegas tourism is so concentrated in a now pedestrianized space and so structured around a sightseeing based on a queer equivalence among multiplicitous 'inauthentic' spectacles, the aimless but critical wandering of *flânerie* is a promising model of tourist behaviour along the Strip. The 'real' *flâneur* is slippery as a historical figure, and might be thought of most productively as an urban legend[12] but the *interest* in *flânerie* by writers such as Benjamin, who devotes considerable energy to it in *The Arcades Project*, points to an intense desire within radical modernism for spatial practices that could engage with commodity capitalism and colonial globalization while maintaining a kind of agency.

A striking quality of Vegas tourism is the degree to which so many visitors, regulars and first-timers alike, explicitly construct their own expertise in dealing with travel, casinos, specific machines and table games, and the city's culture. This is most obviously apparent in the twin pursuit of luxury and bargain that are stereotypical of the Vegas visitor. The emblematic space where these pursuits are joined is the famed all-you-can-eat buffet offered by almost all casinos. Here is a meal that *is* a bargain, but is so because the consumer can choose individuated luxury. It is a meal one *walks* through, and while often eaters make straight for 'destination foods' such as snow crab legs, equally common is the ambling diner, the *grazer*. It's probably absurd to try to make a *flâneur* out of the units of this ritualized gluttony, but if the discernment or discretion of the 'average' Vegas tourist is to be seen as anything other than 'false consciousness' – and I think it has to be – then we must at least start with the kind of creativity or authorial agency that Certeau sees in the urban walker.[13]

A kind of will toward *flânerie* is part of the *savoir-faire* cultivated by most Vegas tourists. The Vegas tourist is a connoisseur of unnoticed details, seeking them out, sharing them, making a minor literature of pedestrian, amateur travel writing.[14] And more, the Vegas tourist is forearmed with the basic tools of cultural criticism, savouring rather than regretting (to quote Dean MacCannell out of context) 'the distance that separates him from what he is seeing'.[15] Seeking to understand the spatial practices of Vegas tourists as forms of *flânerie* at least theoretically constructs visitors as 'democratically' empowered potential critics of globalization.

The limits of walking in 'Sin City'

> As a consumer of sights and goods, the *flâneur* is a vicarious conqueror, self-confirmed in his mastery of the empire of the gaze while losing his own self in the commodified network of popular imperialism.[16]

Across all these places and spatial practices are layered the ornament and detritus of globalization, a set of forces acting on and through the city. Globalization's most brazen appearance in the Las Vegas cityscape is as *theme*, most notably in the form of symbolic architecture referencing cultures across time and space from the elite Bellagio to the Kiplingesque Mandalay Bay. To this extent, globalization, or at least global themes, are part of industrial 'place-making' in Vegas. John Hannigan argues that the contemporary commercial developments he calls Urban Entertainment Districts are 'the end-product of a long-standing cultural contradiction in American society between the middle-class desire for experience and their parallel reluctance to take risks, especially those which involve contact with the "lower orders" in cities'.[17] With regard to Las Vegas, which Hannigan cites as an extreme example of the kind of urban development he discusses in his book *Fantasy City*, I suggest that beyond this conflict between desire for experience and the racism and class-ism which characterizes bourgeois US attitudes toward cities, lies a conflict between a desire for *international* sophistication (global domination in the eyes of some) in conflict with xenophobia and classic American provincialism.

Classic Vegas performance has long relied on ethnic *schtick* and exotic settings, and more recent developments continue that tradition. For example, at the Excalibur casino, the dinner-theatre banquet features a *Tournament of Kings*, in which various European stereotypes joust from horseback. Following the geopoetics of professional wrestling, the Russian is the bad guy. But 'classier' Vegas performance also processes global identities. As part of this, the 'nationality' of international performers, like other identity factors, is at times exploited and at times repressed by Vegas entertainment interests, with Cirque du Soleil's various productions notable for emphasizing international talent while tending to anonymize individual performers. It is instructive to contrast these 'arty' and sophisticated performances with the identity strategies of some relatively new performances which share more aesthetic affinity with 'old Vegas' entertainment styles. For example, *EFX!* was a review show combining old-style extravaganza style with what are meant to seem amazingly up-to-date stage effects. Until recently its star was musical theatre legend Tommy Tune. Of note here is that this show was remarkably rooted in Vegas as its immediate context. The show was full of tacky universalisms (like the 'Welcome to Your World' number) and casual racism directed at a presumptively multi-national audience (like the opening bit where a 'stagehand' gives a pre-show announcement in fake Japanese and Spanish). But these gestures occur within an open, campy, reflexive structure which arguably disarms the Vegas mix of universality and homogenization. For one thing, the review format allows for a frank acknowledgment of the performance context, and Tune would acknowledge this, for example, by noting how many shows he'd done (I saw the 875th) and interviewing members of the audience. Most obviously, almost every number in the show refers to another Las Vegas show, as in the Merlin and the Dragon number or the space circus act.

Another way to frame this distinction between performance structures is to ask whether a given performance moves spectators toward *place* or toward what Marc Augé calls *non-place*. Augé discusses the emerging global network of generic, anonymous transitory spaces (malls, airports) as an emerging paradigm of non-places 'where the habitué of supermarkets, slot machines and credit cards communicates wordlessly, through gestures, with an abstract, unmediated commerce'.[18] While many aspects of Vegas contribute to its uniqueness, its 'only in Vegas' place-ness, other facets, such as the ultimate similarity of many locations, and the ubiquity of diverse themes which tends to make theming itself a homogenizing effect, tend toward the effect of the non-place. In Augé's words:

> [T]here are spaces in which the individual feels himself to be a spectator without paying much attention to the spectacle. As if the position of spectator were the essence of the spectacle, as if basically the spectator in the position of a spectator were his own spectacle. A lot of tourism leaflets suggest this deflection, this reversal of the gaze, by offering the would-be traveller advance images of curious or contemplative faces... gazing across infinite oceans, scanning ranges of snow-capped mountains or wondrous urban skylines: his own image in a word, his anticipated image... The traveller's space may be the archetype of *non-place*.[19]

Augé implies a kind of neo-colonialism-in-advance, where the structure of tourist desire ensures his own importance as transcendent of place, and best realized in non-place. I suggest that performance is the aspect of the constructed tourist environment that can best alter this abstracting, erasing tendency of tourism, and that it is highly 'placeful' moments of performance that can do this to best effect. The simple locatedness of moments such as those constructed by Tommy Tune in his interaction with the spectator suggests that the best cultural places to consider the material reality of difference is not the theatre of avant-garde imports and meticulously universalized themes and unified production values, but in the explicit texts of exotic/erotic performances, or in marketing spaces like asianlasvegas.com or in the open patter of neo-traditional stage personalities. For all the acclaim that high-culture influences such as Cirque have received in recent decades, they have arguably had a weakening rather than strengthening impact on Vegas' ability to see *itself* on stage.

But globalization also structures the city's commerce; many have noted that Vegas is a type of special economic zone; rather than 'exporting jobs' from the First world and importing cheap products, Las Vegas exists as an international zone of cheap production (for a set of nearly virtual commodities) which *imports consumers*. In the words of one popular economic observer: 'Call Las Vegas a Far West Tiger, and you wouldn't be too far off the mark. Branded, service-driven, globalized, and unhindered by the state, the Las Vegas casinos do sound uncannily like models for the economy into which we appear to be moving.'[20] Globalization also shapes the demographics of those visitors and of the service laborers who tend them. While detectable at ground level as a theme, globalization is thus an aspect of the city that is only *in part* visible.[21]

'Looking down on Las Vegas' has become a key concept for me; in part I'm inspired by the opening of Certeau's essay 'Walking in the City', in which he contrasts the view from the top of the World Trade Center with the lived writerly activity of pedestrians on New York streets. Now, there's no World Trade Center in the New York, New York (though following September 2001 there was erected a pedestrian shrine like those at ground zero, now formalized in lighted glass cases). But an oscillation between looking at the city from above, as if it were a plan, and immersion in the very different experience of motion through space is central to the Vegas experience, if only because the very airport immerses you in the city. But the looking down of the tourist, even of the slumming hipster, is different, it seems to me, from the downward look of the cultural critic who reserves for himself the overview and assigns to the consumer only the desire to be lost within immensity. Here's Zygmunt Bauman on postmodern *flânerie*:

> One may say the shopping-mall world, the world of theme parks, holiday packages – those many small-size and medium-size insides struggling to match the big-size ideal of the Disneyland, that ultimate inside that puts paid, for a pre-paid time, to all outsides – are designed with the sole purpose of rendering the aimlessness obsolete.

Their tremendous attractive power they owe to the catering to the needs of *flâneurs* with the lavish profusion of which the old *flâneur* could hardly dream. They are, one may say, the world made to the *flâneur's* measure: the world of the *flâneur* expanded into the entire world, a complete world, a world without residue or alternative....This they have achieved...through expropriating the *flâneur's* own right and capacity to invent the rules of the game he would play and to supervise their execution.[22]

While this is a clever linking of subversive motion and totalizing market, it also evacuates all agency, leaving the *flâneur*/tourist/shopper *not knowing any better*. Dean MacCannell's classic work *The Tourist* makes a similar error: 'If distance exists for the tourist, it is not between him and what he sees. As a tourist, he can only be alienated from the *meaning* of what he sees since this meaning is secreted in unnoticed details.'[23] But it is the unnoticed detail which is the proper concern of the *flâneur* in the first place. And more, the Vegas tourist (and most tourists, for whatever other sins they may rightly be damned) savours 'the distance that separates him from what he is seeing'.

All this is not to say that the 'democratic' *flânerie* of Vegas tourism is not in its own way elitist, privileged and neo-colonial. For what is served up in Vegas is in many ways a miniature, though gargantuan, buffet of cultural capital, generated through unequal exchange; and walking in this city conserves this set of global social relations even as it challenges the apparent subjectification of the tourist by the spectacle. As Shields puts it:

What better way to map the diversity and distance of empire than to encounter its characters in cosmopolitan public places? The gaze of the *flâneur* is thus part of a tactic to appropriate not only the local, physical spaces of the city as one's own 'turf'...but also to participate in the popular sense of empire, to master and even revel in the 'emporium'.[24]

Indeed, if Vegas seems to make globalization 'safe' for the tourist consumer, it is in part through exploiting the very ambivalence that is evoked in the confrontation between spectator and 'excessive' spectacle – it cannot be *too safe*. As an infamously unique cosmopolis, Vegas enjoys a form of cultural 'monopoly rent', but, as David Harvey points out, 'the bland homogeneity that goes with pure commodification erases monopoly advantages...some way must be found to keep...places unique and particular *enough . . .*'.[25] Vegas is not simply a site for cultural criticism, it is a site of little else, and the 'critical' glance of the tourist is in some sense merely another of globalization's tactics. And all this is also not to say that there is no horror for the individual 'emporiumist' in Vegas. But rather than imagine the horror of a walk in the city as a gerbil's futility or a robotic shopping spree, why not a relation to official meaning and spatial organization that is, if not heroic, at least active? Why not a 'long poem of walking'?[26]

Walking as performance tactic

Restlessness turns inward again – no visitor wants to stay outside here for very long. Roaming inside Vegas leads again to options for rest. But aside from actual hotel rooms – which, after all, are really the heart of the apparatus for the reproduction of gambling – resting spaces by and large point back to the business of the city. There are precious few places to sit down that don't involve gambling, eating or performance.

To pay for performance in Vegas (or to be 'comped' to it) is often to hire others to be restless on your behalf; there is no element of Vegas choreography more important than walking. Having exhausted yourself, whether at the games or on your feet, you can watch others risk, and watch others walk. From the aestheticized militarism of marching chorus lines to the strut which is the basic move of erotic reviews such as *Crazy Girls*, it's no wonder so many Vegas stages have both broad prosceniums and runways reaching out into the audience.

If walking is a 'tactic' for the Vegas tourist, it is a 'strategy' for the Vegas performer.[27] Moving through space is a central part of the oscillation between distanced spectacle and intimate exchange which characterizes so much Vegas performance. And no performer in Las Vegas walks with as much purpose as 'Mr Las Vegas', Wayne Newton. In the theatre at the Stardust that bears his name, Newton promenades around a runway that brings him as close as possible to as much of the audience as possible. He shakes hands and kisses cheeks and poses for photos, all while his band vamps incessantly at the chorus of 'Suspicious Minds'. This one song can go on for what seems like hours, as everyone in the house tries to touch the star. While his act is full of stiffness, classically bad humour, and frequent near-failure of his ageing vocal chords, Newton is master of one essential Vegas skill. This circulation among the people – repeated night after night with brutal efficiency to the same brutal accompaniment – seems charmingly authentic. He appears to eagerly search through the crowd, responding to spectators as if they surprised him, absorbing our restlessness into his own robotic performance. With his dazzling teeth, his grasping hands, and especially his purposeful, striding legs, Mr Las Vegas transforms a modest theatrical space into an archetypal Vegas passage.

Notes

1 Joan Didion, *Play It As It Lays*, 1970 (New York: Pocket Books, 1978), pp.168–9.
2 Walter Benjamin, *The Arcades Project*, trans. Howard Eiland and Kevin McLaughlin (Cambridge, MA: Harvard University Press, 1999), p.923. Contrast this effect with that earlier identified by Venturi, Brown and Izenour: 'Time is limitless, because the light of noon and midnight are exactly the same. Space is limitless, because the artificial light obscures rather than defines its boundaries' (R. Venturi, Denise Scott Brown and Steven Izenour, *Learning from Las Vegas*, rev. edn (Cambridge, MA: MIT Press, 1972), p.49).
3 Dean MacCannell sums up the sense of Vegas as exemplary of corporate place-making, which he sees as largely a failed enterprise: 'Large companies own the airlines and major hotels and attempt to market entire countries as "destinations". But with the exception of theme parks and Las Vegas, they have encountered difficulty in their efforts to manufacture and purchase important attractions and entire destinations. . . . One of the few remaining freedoms under advanced capitalism, if we choose to exercise it, is to abjure commercialized entertainments, to continue to set our own touristic itineraries' (Dean MacCannell, *The Tourist* (Berkeley: University of California Press, 1999), p.197). See also Susan Stewart, *On Longing: Narratives of the Miniature, the Gigantic, the Souvenir, the Collection* (Baltimore: John Hopkins University Press, 1984); and Robert Venturi, Denise Scott Brown and Steven Izenour, *Learning from Las Vegas*, rev. edn (Cambridge, MA: MIT Press, 1972).
4 James Howard Kunstler, *The City in Mind: Notes on the Urban Condition* (Free Press, 2002), pp.149–50.
5 Ralph Rugoff, *Circus Americanus* (New York: Verso, 1995), p.6.
6 For example, just as Benjamin identified 'the boom in the textile trade' as the commercial precondition for the fantastic spaces of the Paris arcades, and the development of iron construction methods as their physical precondition (Benjamin, *The Arcades Project*, p.15), so historians of Vegas note its dependence on legalized gambling to create its industrial possibility and such things as the invention of the air conditioner and the building of the Hoover dam as its infrastructural necessities. Yet Benjamin did not want to 'explain' the arcades by simple economic and technical determinants; his project rather sought to question the entire way of life we know as modernity. For the most thorough treatment of *The Arcades Project*, see Susan Buck-Morss, *The Dialectics of Seeing* (Cambridge, MA: MIT Press, 1989).
7 Kunstler, *The City in Mind*, pp.152–3.

8 Even more tellingly, he takes what some might call 'cognitive mapping' and what Michel de Certeau and others might label 'spatial stories' as *abject* forms of spatial knowledge.

9 Rob Shields, 'Fancy Footwork: Walter Benjamin's Notes on *flânerie*', in Keith Tester, ed., *The Flâneur*, (New York: Routledge, 1994), p.65.

10 Benjamin, *The Arcades Project*, p.427.

11 In the popular conception of Las Vegas, the city is either not a 'real' place, or it is a place only in a very specific, sordid way. Vegas is usually seen condescendingly. Either it is the ultimate fake, a capital of simulation and thus a non-place, or it is a place characterized by petty, vulgar reality, defined by the disappointments of commercial sexuality and the implacable microeconomics of the gambling table. Often these two representations are merged, as in the title of Hal Rothman and Mike Davis's recent anthology *The Grit Beneath the Glitter: Tales from the Real Las Vegas* (Berkeley: University of California Press, 2002). This approach is not without merit (as Davis and Rothman's important work shows) but as the performance scene in Las Vegas illustrates, binary distinctions such as 'real' and 'fake' miss the crucial dimension of the social production of the tourist experience.

12 Shields, 'Fancy Footwork, pp.64–5.

13 The usual starting point for this insight is 'Walking in the City' (Michel de Certeau *The Practice of Everyday Life*, trans. Steven Rendau (Berkeley: University of California Press, 1984), pp.91–110).

14 This is the subject of a different study, but in the meanwhile, I suggest the reader might be convinced of the breadth (if not depth) of 'vernacular' cultural studies of Las Vegas through a simple Google search of the phrase 'our trip to Vegas.' A Google image search for the same phrase reveals the strength of vernacular photography as an analysis of the city.

15 MacCannell, *The Tourist*, p.68.

16 Shields, 'Fancy Footwork, p.78.

17 John Hannigan, *Fantasy City* (London: Routledge, 1998), p.7.

18 Marc Augé, *Non-Places: Introduction to an Anthropology of Supermodernity*, trans. John Howe (New York: Verso, 1995), p.78.

19 Augé, *Non-Places*, p.86.

20 J. Surowiecki, 'Lessons From Las Vegas: Are Casinos a Model for the New American Economy?', *Slate*, 21 November 1997: The Motley Fool, 'The Motley Fool', 29 December 2003; http://slate.msn.com/id/2629/#sb43122

21 It is a part of what Rob Shields describes as 'visualicity', in 'Visualicity: On urban visibility and invisibility', *Visual Culture in Britain*, 3:1 (Summer 2004): 23–36: www.carleton.ca/~rshields/index.htm

22 Zygmunt Bauman, 'Desert Spectacular', in Keith Tester, ed., *The Flâneur*, (London: Routledge, 1994), pp.149–50.

23 MacCannell, *The Tourist*, p.68.

24 Shields, 'Fancy Footwork, p.74.

25 David Harvey, *Spaces of Hope* (California Studies in Critical Human Geography 7. University of California Press, 2001), vol. 7, p.396 (emphasis added).

26 Certeau, *The Practice of Everyday Life*, p.101.

27 For a discussion of these terms, see Certeau, *The Practice of Everyday Life*, pp.35–39.

Bibliography

Augé, Marc. *Non-Places: Introduction to an Anthropology of Supermodernity*, trans. John Howe, New York: Verso, 1995.

Bauman, Zygmunt. 'Desert Spectacular', in Keith Tester, ed., *The Flâneur*, London: Routledge, 1994, pp.138–57.

Benjamin, Walter. *The Arcades Project*, trans. Howard Eiland and Kevin McLaughlin, Cambridge, MA: Harvard University Press, 1999.

Buck-Morss, Susan. *The Dialectics of Seeing*, Cambridge, MA: MIT Press, 1989.

de Certeau, Michel. *The Practice of Everyday Life*, trans. Steven Rendall, Berkeley, CA: University of California Press, 1984.

Didion, Joan. *Play It As It Lays*, 1970, New York: Pocket Books, 1978.

Hannigan, John. *Fantasy City*, London: Routledge, 1998.

Harvey, David. *Spaces of Hope*, California Studies in Critical Human Geography 7: University of California Press, 2001.

Kunstler, James Howard. *The City in Mind: Notes on the Urban Condition*, New York: Free Press, 2002, pp.149–50.

MacCannell, Dean. *The Tourist*, Berkeley, CA: University of California Press, 1999.

Rothman Hal. and Mike Davis, eds, *The Grit Beneath the Glitter: Tales from the Real Las Vegas*, Berkeley, CA: University of California Press, 2002.

Rugoff, Ralph. *Circus Americanus*, New York: Verso, 1995.

Shields, Rob. 'Fancy Footwork: Walter Benjamin's Notes on *flânerie*', in Keith Tester, ed., *The Flâneur*, New York: Routledge, 1994, pp.61–80.

Shields, Rob. 'Visualicity: On Urban Visibility and Invisibility', *Visual Culture In Britain*, 3.1 (Summer 2004): 23–36. http://www.carleton.ca/~rshields/index.htm.

Stewart, Susan. *On Longing: Narratives of the Miniature, the Gigantic, the Souvenir, the Collection*, Johns Hopkins University Press, 1984.

Surowiecki, James. 'Lessons From Las Vegas: Are casinos a model for the new American economy?', *Slate*, 21 November 1997: The Motley Fool. 'The Motley Fool', 29 December 2003, http://slate.msn.com/id/2629/#sb43122.

Venturi, Robert. Denise Scott Brown and Steven Izenour, *Learning from Las Vegas*, rev. edn, Cambridge, MA: MIT Press, 1972.

11
Placed and Displaced: Trauma Memorials

Laurie Beth Clark

I started thinking about trauma memorials in the days immediately following 9/11 2001, when the streets of New York were full of impromptu shrines. Like many Americans, I was deeply moved by the proliferation in and around Manhattan of homemade flyers for missing friends and relatives. Like many artists, I felt most compelled to respond to the crisis through my work, yet knew it was unlikely that I would ever have a meaningful opportunity to participate in the memorial design process.

When I visited the place of World Trade Center for the first time on 20 September 2001, I was part of a steady stream of thousands of people who poured out of the Fulton Street subway station and circled the still-smoking ruin counter-clockwise. I did not take any pictures that day but a few people did. By my next visit in May 2002, the place could genuinely be described as a tourist destination. Within eight months, the city had constructed a viewing platform and a mechanism for diverting pedestrian traffic by sending visitors to South Street seaport to pick up tickets for a specific entry time for the platform. There was a tour bus there from Oklahoma, and we heard the students on it sing God Bless America in Cherokee. One of the strongest feelings I remember having when I visited the World Trade Center in May 2002 was that, after waiting several hours for access to the viewing platform, there was, in fact, nothing to see. People had to point out to one another where the buildings had been.

Already by May, the place demonstrated its contested nature, the conflict between the state's impulse to define the location and individuals' impulse to engage. The platform was covered with what on the subways would have been called graffiti, and the place was a repository for mementoes and 'offerings'. This parallel negotiation of

popular participation with state construction is what led me to begin
to consider trauma memorials beyond the United States. Since May
2002, I have visited the 'hallowed ground' (or perhaps more accurately, the desecrated ground) of traumatic places on four continents.
For this project, I have spent time at the slave forts at Cape Coast and
Elmina in Ghana, at the peace parks at Hiroshima and Nagasaki in
Japan, at Dachau concentration camp in Germany, and at My Lai (Son
My) and other war memorials in Vietnam. I also hope to have the
opportunity to include locations in South Africa, Rwanda, Cambodia,
Chile and Argentina in the larger project. In addition to these 'placed'
or 'site-specific' memorials, I am also considering 'displaced' or 'off-site'
memorials, like the Anne Frank House in the Netherlands, the holocaust
museums in Europe and the United States, or the Vietnam Veterans
Memorial in Washington DC, as well as those that are 'placeless' or
'siteless' such as cybermemorials and the peripatetic AIDS Quilt. As a
visual artist sometimes engaged with trauma memorial content, I have
used these opportunities to reflect on the strategies used by existing
cultural institutions.

Some of the key elements that have emerged in my research are the
ways in which architecture and guide services are deployed to create
and reinforce identification (as well as dis-identification), the parallel
between the tropes and devices of pilgrimage in use at 'placed' and
'displaced' memorials, the role that preparation plays in the probability
of a transformative outcome, the dilemma of intrusive quotidian experiences, the use of 'educational alibis' to counteract the suspect nature
of 'trauma tourism', the kinds of rituals enacted and other staged forms
of interactivity, the place of nationalist pride at the place of grieving,
and the ambivalence regarding suitable souvenirs.

I do not mean, by analysing together the memorials we make at the
locations of trauma, to suggest any equivalence between very different
instances of genocide. What these places have in common is not the
nature of the events they recall but rather the memorial impulse, the
challenge of 'curating' intractable places, and the sometimes contradictory performances that visitors enact at these places.

'Placed,' 'displaced', and 'placeless' memorials create social spaces in
which spectators embody and enact memory. The body in space comes
to know its relation to the past very differently in works that must be
navigated interactively with the spectator choosing both the sequence
in which content is engaged and the length of each engagement, than
in works constructed for static theatrical seating and linear dramatic
reception. Both the temporal and the corporeal engagement of spectators

at memorial installations are integral components of the staging of cultural memory. There is a pilgrimage component to visiting the location of trauma, whether the concentration camps at Dachau or the former prison at Robben Island, but when the place of trauma is unavailable as was the case initially with the World Trade Center, the pilgrimage impulse can be accommodated by 'displaced' memorials as readily as those location at the place of violence.

As a holocaust memorial, Anne Frank House must be considered 'displaced', more like the memorial shrines and altars at Union Square than those at 'Ground Zero'. While Anne Frank's secret annex provides an opportunity to reflect on the Shoah, what actually happened here was survival, not extermination. The house is a monument to Anne's humanity rather than a testament to Nazi inhumanity, and the invitation to readers of the diary is to identify with her life, her heroism, her creativity, her discomfort. The tragedy of her death, both individually and metonymically, is located in a physical and a historical elsewhere. Yet the tropes and devices of pilgrimage work in remarkably parallel ways for 'placed' and 'displaced' memorials. The sense of passage begins with waiting in line, the prototypical pilgrim structure. On busy days, the line for the Anne Frank House may stretch around the block to the next canal, and often, given that it is the Netherlands, involves inclement weather. Victor Turner points out that the physically difficult nature of the trip to the pilgrimage place is integral to the transformation experienced by the pilgrim.[1] In fact, the language of transformation permeates trauma memorial places. The helpful staff at the information desk at Anne Frank House told us, 'However they come in, they come out differently.' While there are no lines at Cape Coast or Elmina, the journey is more arduous: there is a 24-hour plane flight from the Americas, the discomfort of the equatorial heat, and an emotional encounter with the extremes of West African poverty that threatens to exceed the emotional impact of the place itself.

For pilgrims as for tourists (and Turner is quick to point out that these are often one and the same), preparation is one of the most important elements in the successful transformative experience and the greater the preparatory investment, the more substantial the transformation. Theatre, movies, television, books, and museums, all play a role in this preparation process. As a Jewish child or a North American child or a Dutch child, I am likely to have read the diaries, seen a film or a play, and to have imagined myself visiting these places. Similarly, African-Americans and others visiting the slave forts will have repeatedly and vividly imagined the genocide enacted there. Other than the African heat, there's not much in the sanitized slave fort that would account for the frequency with which spectators faint and/or hear the voices of ancestors. Rather, this is a place at which a lifetime of imagining these atrocities surfaces.

However, preparatory content is no guarantor of emotional engagement. For example, the 'placeless' touring exhibition of missing-person flyers failed utterly to produce either the sense of destination or the opportunity of engagement necessary to trauma memorials, in spite of the receptivity of the public to multiple mourning places for the World Trade Center events.

One of the most effective spatial structures for participatory performances is the passageway and it is the predominant vehicle for embodied knowledge in all my case studies. Passageways reproduce, internal to the memorial place, the journey that has taken place, to arrive at the trauma place, in the same way that pilgrimages are structured to offer intensified and microcosmic trails that mirror the larger and more diffuse voyage the pilgrim has made from home city to sacred ground. At the slave forts and the concentration camps, the place's architecture offers a natural chronology. Tours at Cape Coast and Elmina fort follow a path that invites identification with the shackled slaves. Nowhere is the use of passage more determined than in the path to the 'door of no return', the route by which captured slaves who survived the slave forts were marched to board the slave ships to cross the Atlantic. This door is most often enlisted in performance rituals of return: the return of slave remains from the new world, the return of the descendants of slaves through these doors, and an annual symbolic embrace by Africans of African-Americans.

In contrast to the slave forts, where our passage, at least through the dungeons, is meant to mirror the path taken by captives, the path we follow through Anne Frank House has no particular referent, but stairways and passages figure importantly to engage us narratively in the story of the place, a drama with its own climactic structure, the revelation of the actual diary. While many memorial places are interior, architecturally analogous to the mental states they hope to induce, Anne Frank House is thrice so, reflecting in addition the inner life of the secret annex and the inner life of Anne's mind, with few tourists paying much attention to the exterior of the house, nor is the museum structured to draw our attention there. But even at Hiroshima and Nagasaki, where there is no useful residual architecture, a number of passage structures have been constructed. The spiral descent into memorial hall at Hiroshima is highly effective, but the overdetermined use of the lighting and sound effects of the museum at Nagasaki invokes haunted house more than it does pilgrimage.

In Ghana, the magnificent architectural exteriors and the extensive portion of the place taken up by the living and working quarters of the European governors, merchants, clergy and soldiers present a problem for the identificatory, architectural narrative. When our tour guides walked us through the governor's quarters, the visit was rushed, perfunctory. Even the irony expressed about the placement of the church directly over the slave quarters was discussed physically within and from the point of view of the slave dungeon. The problem of identification permeates the slave fort tours. It is there in the careful choice of language by our Cape Coast guide, who explained that slaves were captured in wars and raids by '*some* Africans' while emphasizing the role the introduction of European firearms played in trapping Africans in a kill or be killed cycle. It is clear that he has negotiated this sensitive terrain numerous times with multiply identified spectators.

There is evidence at all of these places of a struggle to find the proper 'voice' for providing information. Are the institutional presenters represented as, or identified with, perpetrators, victims or members of the resistance, and to which of these groups is the information addressed? The position of the administration of holocaust memorials is complicated by the re-emergence of anti-Semitism in Europe *and* by the untenable political position that Israel has – often in the name of the holocaust – come to occupy. Even as they unflinchingly insist on the reprehensible nature of the development and deployment of the A-bomb, the Japanese places also carefully report their own militaristic culpability, something I am sceptical that the United States will ever do at the World Trade Center memorial.

At Cape Coast, we were invited to stand first in the courtyard where female slaves were brought for selection and then on the balcony where the slavers could choose one for sexual violation. Moreover, our guide told us that the administration has found it necessary to segregate the three major groups of spectators – blacks from the Americas, whites from Europe and North America, and Ghanian school groups – to avoid altercations over perceived appropriate behaviour. Spectators may disapprove of others' attitudes, may find inappropriate acts of shopping, smiling, taking or leaving mementoes, photography, and even the state in which the monument ought to be preserved. At the World Trade Center, points of contention include degrees of jingoism and religiosity.

There is little risk of anyone identifying with the perpetrators at Anne Frank House. The only narratives available are that of the attic residents (victims or survivors) or of helpers consistent with Dutch emphasis on honouring resistance. As though what Susan Bernstein calls 'promiscuous identification',[2] were not already thoroughly insured by the diary (and its movie and stage play versions), Anne Frank House goes beyond the stairways and passages to stage sight lines: doors, shutters and shades are not only left cracked open, but historical photographs of what Anne might have seen are carefully positioned over, outside or through.

Because trauma tourism is intrinsically suspect, seen as the moral equivalent of gawking at a traffic accident, all the memorial sites make some effort to 'alibi' their existence. The two most common strategies for this are 'never again' and 'making common cause' with social justice efforts. The former is exemplified by a Cape Coast plaque that says: 'May humanity never again perpetuate such injustice against humanity.' A typical example of the latter is a panel from the Anne Frank House quoting Nelson Mandela about reading, and being inspired by, the diaries while he was in prison. This strategy is most pronounced at Hiroshima and Nagasaki where the declared mission of both peace parks is to put an end to nuclear weapons. The museums are in large part devoted to a critique of nuclear weaponry and both the city government and the museum administration participate in an ongoing nuclear disarmament effort. A letter written by the delegation sent from Hiroshima to New York to pay respect after the World Trade Center attacks begins with an expression of empathy for the pain of the people of New York but transitions quickly into a harsh indictment of the United States for perpetuating the arms race.

At Cape Coast and Elmina, visitors bring their ritual materials to the site, such as wreaths and mementoes. United States-based tour leaders and African Americans who have resettled in Ghana also run businesses that help in the staging of rituals for mourning and reconciliation that may include the lighting of candles, the recitation of prayers, and other opportunities for what our guide called 'making physical what is in your mind'. Visitors at Cape Coast are offered also the opportunity to have the resident 'priest' pour a traditional African libation with palm wine for a token fee. Such rituals, whether spontaneous or orchestrated, have no analogue at Anne Frank House. According to the staff, visitors seldom leave mementoes, although this is sometime done at her statue around the corner. In fact, we were told at the information desk, they have more often had to deal with the opposite impulse, the desire to take something away, and I was led to believe that this accounted for the ways in which the star photos in Ann's room had been partially torn from the wall although these are now protectively covered. Even though the concentration camps provide little opportunity for individual participation, which is discouraged explicitly by signs and also tacitly by showcasing artefacts of state participation, small gestures are made, particularly the transcultural gesture of placing stones.

By far the most extensive infrastructure for participation can be found at Hiroshima and Nagasaki, where not only are protected repositories and even archives provided for the ubiquitous paper crane wreaths throughout both cities, but also receptacles for flowers, incense- and candle-holders, and room for offerings. Perhaps the widespread practice of leaving water, food and memorabilia at shrines creates the ready context for memorial participation. Interestingly, the impulse towards participatory gestures following 9/11 was not limited to the relatively inaccessible lower Manhattan site, but was enacted immediately after 9/11 at sites that could be identified with New York all over the world, including US embassies and even American hotel chains abroad and even at the New York, New York casino in Las Vegas.

Memorials in economically privileged countries often use interactive technologies to channel the participatory impulse. Hiroshima and Nagasaki have extensive interactive databases that include victim and survivor registries, The Anne Frank House tour concludes in a room of computer terminals that offer a 3-D walk-through simulation of the house, perhaps targeting a generation for whom the virtual is more engaging than the tangible.

Whatever else it is, trauma tourism is still tourism. At Nagasaki, there is a large statue of a man pointing at the sky – where the bomb came from. Tourists like to stand in front of this sign and take pictures of themselves posing in the same position as the statue, so much so that at the tram stop the signage for the memorial park actually uses this gesture of posing for a photo as the marker of the park location. This anticipation of the souvenir brings to mind Benjamin's discussion of the relationship between 'authentic' places and their reproductions.[3] Just a week after 9/11 there were entrepreneurial vendors in lower Manhattan selling homemade photos of the burning towers and the news-stands were sold out of postcards of the New York City skyline that still included The Twin Towers.

Every memorial site I have visited has a gift shop, though the offerings differ widely based on economy, propriety and clientele. At Dachau, everything in the gift shop is in black and white – as though colour were deemed too festive – and there is a sign explaining the rationale for the sales – visitor demand – as well as the use of the proceeds – site maintenance. But at Hiroshima and Nagasaki, 'Hello Kitty' souvenirs are sold unabashedly alongside origami paper for making cranes, t-shirts that make the dome look like a rock concert mix with social justice t-shirts, and Hiroshima and Nagasaki phone-card sales compete with large and very serious book sections. One should not discount the importance of the museum shop as an opportunity for spectators to engage with traumatic history. The Cape Coast and Elmina shops sell 'pride' in the form of kente cloth and local crafts. The museum store at Anne Frank House offers copies of the diary in many languages, returning us physically to the text that we carried mentally to the site, but also reiterating its universal impact.

The role that art plays in mediating these sites is part of a larger discursive effort that includes the press and also community groups, in short, all those who seek to influence both the production and the reception of historical events. Sometimes this mediation is highly personal and arguably therapeutic, as in the pictures made by survivors. It can also be quite intentionally propagandistic. Often art serves multiple and even conflicting functions, depending on who is speaking/ presenting and who is listening/looking. There is almost no accounting for the ubiquity of bad sculpture, both representational and abstract, that abounds at and near trauma memorials.

When individual artists have the opportunity to construct trauma memorials, we may borrow strategies from these living history museums, but we also have some unique challenges. While we can use techniques like physical immersion and interactive spectatorship to invite embodied reception, we cannot rely on the preparation of spectators to trigger emotional transformation. Whether we are working with displaced or latent content, spectators are more likely to have travelled to the site based on the reputation of a particular artist or institution than with the intention of engaging with particular content. The job of the artist, then, is to devise aesthetic strategies that integrate content delivery with sensory impact.

The three holocaust memory projects I've worked on have been 'displaced' in the sense that they are not located at the place of the events they commemorate, yet all three have been produced in the context of 'pilgrimages' I was invited to make to Germany. Like this research, the projects try to think about the relationship between very different instances of cultural violence. Although my 1990 project *Approach/ Avoidance*, which looked at denial as a social force by staging an apocalypse that has not yet occurred, can be productively discussed as a 'future trauma memorial', more recent site-specific projects in Germany take the holocaust as their point of departure. *Klanglos Verschwunden* (disappeared without a sound) in 2001, because of its domestic setting, was more subtle, posing the question, 'Was vergessen sie?' (What do you forget?), that could be taken up to consider a broad range of social and personal denials. *Versteckte Kinder* (hidden children) in 2002, consisting of small houses in honour of the children who survived the war by hiding in the forest, was more blatant yet remarkably hidden from the many in southern Germany who can no longer recognize a *mezuzah* as a marker of a Jewish home. *Halteschtellen* in 2003 was a series of posters for bus shelters that look at genocide from the perspective of children who have lived alongside it, but were not directly threatened.

Epilogue

In some ways, the World Trade Center site is a more effective memorial right now (December 2004) than it will ever be again. A fully functioning train station, evidence of the resilient city, is literally immersed in the excavation. It's harder than it should be to see through the mesh fence, though it's clear that is what everyone wants to do. There is a more substantial, enclosed viewing platform that spans the site and can accommodate a sufficiently large crowd so that viewing times no longer need to be assigned and ticketed. The formulaic tropes of memorial display have started to appear. There are text panels with historical photos that celebrate the vibrant cultures of lower Manhattan and there are banners with quaint things famous people have said about the city. At street level, the site is already less satisfying. The signs on the metal barriers, and the style of the barriers themselves make clear that the World Trade Center administration wants to limit memorial gestures. Still, the determined structure is contested, by protesters with banners and leaflets critiquing the 9/11 investigative commission and by individual mourners who leave flowers and mementoes. No doubt a monumental building and some form of more or less effective memorial architecture will come to occupy the lower Manhattan site in the next few years. But what people feel compelled to do there will somehow be different, in subtle yet meaningful ways, from what the structure officially allows.

Notes

1   Victor Turner and Edith Turner, 'Introduction: Pilgrimage as a Liminoid Phenomenon', in *Image and Pilgrimage in Christian Culture: Anthropological Perspectives* (New York: Columbia University Press, 1978).
2   Susan David Bernstein, 'Promiscuous Reading: The Problem of Identification and Anne Frank's Diary', in Michael Bernard-Donals and Richard Glejzer, eds, *Witnessing the Disaster: Essays on Representation and the Holocaust.* (Madison: University of Wisconsin Press, 2003).
3   Walter, Benjamin, 'The Work of Art in the Age of Mechanical Reproduction', in *Illuminations* ed. Hannah Arendt (New York: Schocken Books, 1969).

12

Where Difference Lies: Performative Metaphors of Truth, Deception and Placelessness in the Cornish Peninsula

Patrick Laviolette

> We no longer believe that truth remains truth when it is
> unveiled, – we have lived enough to understand this...To-day
> it seems to us good form not to strip everything naked, not to
> be present at all things, not to desire to 'know' all. Tout
> comprendre c'est tout mépriser.[1]

These are some of the closing lines to Friedrich Nietzsche's *Nietzsche Contra Wagner*. He ends a preceding work, *The Case of Wagner*, with the requisition that music, in its 'pure' form (whatever that might be), should not become an art of lying. By claiming not to be partisan to the stage, to actors, to drama – Nietzsche seems to have problems stomaching showmanship, of which he accused Wagner of being a particularly gifted master. Rather, as a good sophist he sought to preface logic, reason or reality. But in this regard I am inclined to follow Jean-Paul Sartre when his protagonist in *La Nausée* writes in his diary: 'I admire how we can lie by putting reason on our side.'[2] In this sense, it is far from inconceivable that Nietzsche himself was performing a certain deception upon his reader, one of which he was fully aware and deliberately intended. Indeed, he repeatedly and rather overtly indicated that if he despised much of Wagner's *oeuvre*, it was only because he understood both the work and the man all too well.

In 1865 Wagner's Arthurian opera *Tristan und Isolde* had its debut in Munich. Based on a legendary tale of love, honour, deceit and death this epic is set in the Celtic triangle of Cornwall, Ireland and Brittany, whereby the Duchy of Cornwall is centre stage. This story has since been retold and rewritten countless times. Nearly 140 years after Wagner's rendition, *Tristan & Yseult* has come back to its land of inspiration. The nationally acclaimed Cornish group the Kneehigh Theatre Company have transformed the opera into an elaborate multimedia production, featuring live and recorded music, acrobatics and dance. For the past two summers they have performed this tragi-comedy at dozens of outdoor venues across Cornwall, such as the Eden Project, Restormel Castle (near Lostwithiel) and the Minack Theatre (near Porthcurno on the south-western extremity of West Penwith). They have also performed the piece at selected sites 'up-country', for example, Nottingham's Rufford Abbey. An integral part of Kneehigh's theatrical orchestration is to fit the story and the set design into the surrounding landscape. Places like St Michael's Mount and Pendennis Castle have thus served as interactive backdrops, whereby their historical and mythical legacies are used and re-invented. In this sense, the theatrical appropriation of each site transgresses both time and space.

This chapter explores the relationship between this process of redramatization and the concepts of place and placelessness from an anthropological perspective. That is, it ethnographially considers the age-old cycles of changing and modernizing historical narratives. It provides a brief cultural examination of the reuse of myth, legends and deception as expressed through theatre and the performative arts in Cornwall. By looking at the recycling of truth and lies as well as the reformulation of local identities and historical ideas, I shall draw together various metaphors of socio-cultural distinction. Given that theories about the performance of identity often collide, the chapter ultimately hopes to push understandings of literary metaphor towards considerations for material, visual and embodied metaphor, whereby identities open up to a more postmodern and phenomenological framework concerned with the fragmentation of experience. The idea is thus to explore the realms of drama, place and placelessness in a way reminiscent of ethnographic work on the performance of locality in a rapidly globalising world.[3]

Afloat on stage

The story-telling group *Scavel An Gow* provides an ideal example of theatrical adaptations of local myths, legends and stories. Indeed, they deliberately mix and manipulate local metaphors of identity. The group began as part of Kneehigh and has since become an independent Cornish collective. It is made up of seven regionally known writers and storytellers, who perform and publish their own Cornish stories. They also recount some local poems and tales from various authors that have been influential in the South-West. Their shows generally take place in church or village halls while they are on one of their tours of Cornwall. They also perform outdoors at places like the Eden Project or summer events like Penzance's Golowan Mazey Day festival. When I met them for the first time in the grounds of Pendennis Castle in Falmouth at the Dewhelans (Cornish Homecomings) festival, they were going through some of their own material from *Dream Atlas*, a collection of stories commissioned by Radio 4. They also read from the book *Chasing Tales: The Lost Stories of Charles Lee.*[4]

A typical performance by *Scavel An Gow* begins with one of the group's members giving a brief profile of the troupe. He or she then sits on a bench built into the upright 'boat-stage', with doors that close in over the top. This 2-metre high stage was made by the Botallack artist David Kemp, the partner of one of the groups' founding members Mercedes. It is designed out of a recycled vessel and is meant to encourage the audience to think about Cornwall's traditions and future. Before reading their stories or poems, each performer tells us something about the author's connection to Cornwall and gives an overview on the geographical area in which the story occurs. The principal justification for choosing the material is that they are examples of written work based on periods of residency in a particular area of Cornwall. These are thus performed within the community that has inspired them.

By entangling distinctly recognizable markers of tradition with issues of alternative realities, deception and fabrication, these storytellers are in effect performing the open-endedness of culture. For instance, the very name of their troupe – *Scavel An Gow* – inscribed on the portable boat-stage, is Cornish for both 'a bench of lies' and 'gossip in dialect'. In calling into question what is often taken for granted in Cornwall's history and traditions, this little boat-stage and the stories that are voiced from it challenge the stereotypes regarding Cornish identity. Consequently, the 'deception' inherent in the local myths and legends that are told becomes part and parcel of a process to sustain claims of historical and cultural distinction.

David Kemp addresses these idiosyncrasies in his art. Animals, masks and the myths of past societies feature prominently in his work, as does music or sound and plant 'life'. The anthropomophization of artefacts as well as their animistic relationship with cultural narrative are things that David deliberately plays with and reconstructs. He enjoys working with junk, which he once salvaged regularly from the beach. Now, however, he finds most of the materials for his smaller pieces in car boot sales. He admits to being equally inspired by both Cornwall's natural as well as post-industrial landscapes. This versatility means that David is keen on 'piecing together curious connections between past and emergent mythologies and technologies'.[5]

In this vein, consider the Eden Project to which David has significantly contributed. Interestingly, it has been officially promoted as 'The Living Theatre of People and Plants'. Sue Hill, the Art Director at Eden, emphasizes these timeless and placeless relationships between horticulture and mythology in her work. Sue has also worked for what has famously become known as the Lost Gardens of Heligan and makes most of her sculpture with her brother Peter Hill, who incidentally is the set designer for Kneehigh: 'Pete and I made some living sculptures for Heligan Gardens – a huge sleeping Mudmaid and a Giant's Head. Just mud and sticks and Cornish plants.' Sue has herself been a member of Kneehigh Theatre for 12 years and now mostly works with artists on the designs and interpretations of the exhibits at Eden. She matches artists to particular projects and develops ideas with them and the scientists. An interesting parallel exists here with the work of Paul Richards[6] on the performance of indigenous agricultural knowledge in West Africa. Richards argues, for instance, that local cultivation skills are often developed through performance knowledge rather than through any type of technical knowledge of an indigenous or traditional sort. Consequently, good gardening, like good art, depends on adaptation and improvisation instead of the rehearsal of strict protocols.

Inward bound

One such artist is Heather Jansch who makes driftwood pieces. One of her sculptures is a life-size driftwood horse that stands at the gates of Eden. The horse stands on beach pebbles, some of which are lodged within the bone structure itself. This skeletal wooden steed is far from dead, however. It is open to the elements and thus alive with a micro-world of insects, mould and stains from seagull droppings. The only physical isolation that the piece has to the public is a shipping-towrope outline on the floor that encloses some beach pebbles. This link to the elements of nature is further displayed in an outdoor installation at the Eden Project. This demonstrates how twine- and cord-making materials for such ropes were traditionally (and occasionally still are) obtained from plant fibres such as cotton, hemp, manila and sisal.

Rope is, of course, a hugely significant material icon of Cornish distinction which goes hand in hand with boats, knots and nets. Its association with ambiguously fluid seascapes is highly evocative and symbolic. Such binding artefacts, to use a term that Alfred Gell[7] and Susanne Küchler[8] have worked on extensively, are crucial to dock works and survival at sea. As Robert Flaherty illustrates so well in his film *Man of Aran*[9], these elements of material culture are essential in maintaining enduring social relationships. They are physical manifestations of the connectivity between land and sea – between place and placelessness.[10] Furthermore, they embody the transgressions that materiality can make between life and death as well as between nature and culture.

The relationship that these artefacts have with a legacy of maritime lifestyles and seafaring tragedy has equally been brought to life by the use of a 72 mm-wide mooring towrope as part of the 'Located Exhibition'. This show was organized by the MA students of the Falmouth College of Art and took place in the summer of 2003. It was itself a meeting point between performance art and a more formal visual art exhibition. The show drew together 18 MA artists who each contributed objects that they collected locally and which were the equivalent weight of their own bodies. Each day three different artists would get together and transform the objects into a new interactive piece that took up the entire Gallery. This process was chronicled in numerous forms such as photography, video, guestbook commentary, text and the presence of an anthropologist. Over the course of the week, the artists and the public were constantly situated within a creative space that was significantly related to performing the local in a global world of discarded things.

Of particular relevance is the cargo ship towrope that one student obtained from the Falmouth Dock Master. In outliving its functional life and becoming part of an artistic installation, the rope's post-sealife transgresses the seaport, its working identity and effectively its local biography. It has become an enigmatic art/artefact with a significant, if cursory, liminal life. That is, this rope has transgressed normal processes and networks of reuse. Instead it has become an object that exists out of time and out of place. It possesses characteristics of both life and death, nature and culture. Indeed its very life force is tangled up between land and sea. Conceptually one can extend these levels of meaning further. In pointing out the ties that exist between trap-hunting, death and art, Gell's[11] reflections on artefacts as artworks in and of themselves is an attempt to lure the reader into a tight rhetorical mesh. Indeed, his paper deliberately mimics in prose and visual language what hunting or fishing traps achieve in the material relations between hunter and hunted. Here we can talk of 'the death of the reader' in a vein quite different to that suggested by analysts in the post-Roland Barthes era.

During the summer of 2004, the whole of Cornwall could have been described as bound to the stage. The Seen Outdoors initiative promoted and sponsored dozens of plays, musicals and dramatizations of one kind or another. One implication behind these outdoor theatre performances and their associated set designs is that they have begun to stand for a collective form of social remorse.[12] The transformation of lighthouses, derelict boats and mining landscapes serve to socially bemoan the decline of the region's pillar industries. Mary Douglas's[13] work on risk can illuminate for us here. Indeed the loss of tradition is often lamented in the context whereby modernity and tourism are impure polluting factors. But this message is not just a dark one. A cultural salvation is also taking place through the immutability of displaying a reviving material culture associated with the sea and post-industrial landscape. One side of the story is that the roles of such performance art projects is to mourn the past and maybe the ambiguity for the future. But it is far from inconceivable to suggest that we are also dealing with regenerative efforts. Such projects serve Cornish society as focal points in docking social relations associated with the decay of traditional industries to different moorings of identity to do with pan-regional heritage.[14]

Hence the 'deception' intrinsic in reciting or acting out local myths and legends as well as the region's cultural capital becomes integral to processes of sustaining assertions of socio-historical distinction. The stance that difference does indeed 'lie' in this region therefore begins to make sense in that it at once rests there waiting to be woken and does so because of the ambiguous or deceitful nature of all that one could ascribe as a unique trait or authentic place. In ways that are obviously not contemptible, a culturally created scenario exists in which placelessness is overcome by claims to difference that are staged and acted out. Senses of identification that are lulled, deceptive or ambivalent are therefore, in this case, part of an elaborate metaphorical construction of distinction. Scrutinizing the creation and contention of identity through theatre and the performance arts provides one avenue for understanding how such metaphors of belonging and placelessness are actually materialized. In challenging the clichés regarding Cornishness many performative expositions have been tangibly readapting traditional artefacts and local landscapes.

The Cornish peninsula is a disparate region that is filled with plural spatial identities whose pasts are contested, if not paradoxical. That is, even though Cornwall demonstrates aspects of being insular and exclusionary, it is also associated with a plethora of more generic disjunctures dealing with the Celtic, the diasporic, the impoverished, the (post-) industrial, the mythical, the rural, the touristic, the traditional and the inherently creative.[15] To an extent then, Cornwall has been transformed into a marginal territory where identities play off against each other. Hence, while it is many things to many people, certain coherences and half-truths are nonetheless created through dramatizations of cultural distinction and social relationships.

Conclusion

This chapter has sought to highlight how many performative exposi-tions challenge the stereotypes regarding Cornishness; how they call into question what is often taken for granted in Cornwall's history and heritage. The findings presented here thus outline some of the ways in which performance art contributes to a creative, metaphorical and spatio-temporal framework for understanding cultural difference. Or more specifically, for examining differing perceptions of Cornwall's relationship with transformation, whereby social identities are (re-)invented and abandoned, created and contested. The groups and people that I have referred to are therefore acting as performative intermediaries. They bring a diversity of creative people into contact with members of environmental campaigns as well as those people in the business, political and research realms. Together they are seeking to put heritage and investment tourism at the forefront of national, European and international attention.

And yet many expressions of Cornishness are a kind of statement about existing on a somewhat topographical edge. In a sense then, the prevalence of the sea and coastal lifestyles contribute to the distancing from, as well as the criticism of, contemporary views of modernity. Such a form of Cornishness subverts modernity insofar as it contests an overall rat-race worldview. Such an alternative consists of harbouring a place where different values and a different pace of life are desirable; a place where, according to one informant, 'a day up-country is a week down 'ere'. Hence, as a different way, the Cornish way is one that challenges what is taken for normality. By striving to modify the pace of the Western way of life, Cornishness has a rather tenuous relationship with modernity. Here the discourses of modernity meander into postmodern or hyper-real realms. Jean Baudriliard[16] and Umberto Eco's[17] allegorical stances are possible routes of analysis. Eco's recent book *Baudolino*, for instance, scripts out some familiar lessons of history: that in the absence of absolute truth we are directed into labyrinthine inventions and half-truths, dead-ends and white lies.

Equally, we can always return in our footsteps to Nietzsche's attacks on the modern world. In his conclusions to *The Case of Wagner*, the human condition under modernity is a 'contradiction of values'. 'No wonder that it is in our age that falseness itself became flesh and blood'.[18] I therefore suggest that to understand Cornwall one has to come to terms with these types of paradoxes because the people and even the landscape articulate paradox as something of a regional or cultural character. This is itself a roundabout way of stating the Duchy's centrality on the social and geographical margins.[19] Given that its borders of identity are not static, Cornwall does not only exist on the periphery. Instead, people associated with this place are continuously redirecting their identities – crossing, disturbing and renewing boundaries. This challenges Western notions of modernity and marginality, truth and deception.

From such a perspective, it is difficult to trace a comprehensive boundary around the local – the essence of what it is to belong to Cornwall. Yet definitive indicators in 'identifying' this identity come across, if not clearly, then through their nuances. If anything the eclectic, oblique and disparate nature of what we could define as the Duchyesque might be the homogenizing force. As Simone de Beauvoir reminds us: 'existence – others have said it and I have often repeated it – does not reduce itself to ideas, it does not lend itself to enunciation: we can but evoke it through imaginary objects; we must therefore seize from it the flashes, the whirls and the contradictions.'[20] As a simple point of clarification to this statement, I would suggest that we can, of course, evoke existence through the tangible materiality of visual, embodied and landscape metaphors as well. Indeed, we need to think beyond non-material formulations of the imagination. That is, we need to overcome what is arguably a Nietzschian conception of pure sensual experience.[21] Rather we should strive for more syneasthetic blurrings in our understanding of the relationships between the senses, the imagination and the landscape – between, spatial perception, deception and performance.

Acknowledgements

An earlier version of this chapter was presented at the Cambridge Social Anthropology Conference, Truth: Truth in Anthropology and the Anthropology of Truth, Pembroke College, 23–24 September 2004. Thanks to the organizers and participants.

Notes

1 Friedrich Nietzsche, *The Complete Works of Friedrich Nietzsche: Vol. 8, The Case of Wagner*, ed. Oscar Levy (London: T. N. Foulis, 1911), p.82.

2 Jean-Paul Sartre, *La nausée* (Paris: Gallimard, 1938), p.24.

3 Patrick Laviolette, 'The materiality of metaphor: tensions between landscape and landscapelessness', paper presented at the ASA Conference, Locating the Field: Metaphors of Space, Place and Context in Anthropology, Durham, March 2004; C. Tilley, 'Performing culture in the global village', *Critique of Anthropology* 17: 1(1997): 67–89; Marc Augé, *Non-Places: Introduction to an Anthropology of Supermodernity*, trans. John Howe (London: Verso 1995); V. W. Turner, *The Anthropology of Performance* (Baltimore: PAJ Publications, 1988).

4 'S. Parker, *Chasing Tales: The Lost Stories of Charles Lee* (Callington: Giss'On Books, 2002).

5 David Kemp, *Things Reconstructed* (Penzance: Alison Hodge, 2002), p.5.

6 Paul Richards, 'Cultivation: Knowledge or Performance?', in M. Hobart, ed., *An Anthropological Critique of Development: The Growth of Ignorance* (London: Routledge, 1993).

7 Alfred Gell, 'Vogel's net: Traps as artworks and artworks as traps', *Journal of Material Culture* 1: 1(1996): 15–38.

8 Susanne Küchler, 'Why knot? Towards a Theory of Art and Mathematics', in C. Pinney and N. Thomas, eds, *Beyond Aesthetics: Essays in Memory of Alfred Gell* (Oxford: Berg, 2000).

9 Robert Flaherty, *Man of Aran* (United Kingdom: Gainsborough Pictures, 1934).

10 E. Relph, *Place and Placelessness* (London: Pion, 1976).

11 Gell, 'Vogel's Net'.

12 Patrick Laviolette, 'Landscaping death: resting places for Cornish identity', *Journal of Material Culture* 8: 2(2003a): 215–40.

13 Mary Douglas, *Purity and Danger: An Analysis of Concepts of Pollution and Taboo* (London: Routledge & Keegan Paul, 1966).

14 E. Laurier, 'Replication and restoration: Ways of making maritime heritage', *Journal of Material Culture* 3: 1(1998): 21–50.

15 Patrick Laviolette, 'Cornwall's visual cultures in perspective', *Cornish Studies* 11: (2003b): 142–67.

16 Jean Baudrillard, 'The Precession of Simulacra', in J. Natoli and L. Hutcheon, eds, *A Postmodern Reader* (Albany: State University of New York Press, 1993).

17 Umberto Eco, *Baudolino* (Orlando: Harcourt, 2002.

18 Nietzsche, *The Complete Works*, p.51.

19 V. W. Turner, *Dramas, Fields and Metaphors* (Ithica, NY: Cornell University Press, 1974).

20 Simone de Beauvoir, *La force des choses* (Paris: Gallimard, 1963), p.342.

21 E. Blondel, *Nietzsche: The Body and Culture: Philosophy as a Philological Genealogy (London: the Athlone Press, 1991).*

Part IV
Border Panic

Border Panic: Introduction

Leslie Hill

> At the atomic level, then, the solid material objects of classical physics dissolve into patterns of probabilities, and these patterns do not represent probabilities of things, but rather probabilities of interconnections. Quantum theory forces us to see the universe not as a collection of physical objects, but rather as a complicated web of relations between the various parts of a unified whole. This, however, is the way in which Eastern mystics have experienced the world, and some of them have expressed their experience in words which are almost identical with those used by atomic physicists.
>
> (Fritjof Capra[1])

Finding and articulating the boundary between the perceiver and the perceived has been one of the most elusive quests of philosophy and science in human history, especially since the 'new philosophy' of Newton's day. A good border is definitely hard to find. Complex theories and explanations have developed around these subtle border check-points right across art, science, religion and philosophy. Through the diverse approaches of their various disciplines, people have engaged for hundreds of years in the impossible task of trying to mark the borders. Physicists conducted sub-atomic experiments with light photons to determine if, on the atomic level, they would act as particles or as waves, and made the uncomfortable discovery that if you zoom in closely enough there are no real borders at all between one thing and the next. Anthropologists made global surveys of human cranial measurements to prove the existence of distinct races, distinctions contemporary DNA analysis dissolves at the same time it seeks out the infinitely small distinctions of chromosome mutations. Semioticians have interrogated the relationship of the signifier and the signified, only to conclude that a one-to-one relationship between them is impossible. Political leaders have engaged, throughout human history, in outright warfare over territory, aiming definitively to settle the questions of borders by force. Yet the borders still ebb and flow. Borders and boundaries are by nature placeless.

The fiercest distinctions break down under close examination. Even socio-political situations that appear to offer more clear-cut divisions than the quantum conundrums of waves and particles begin to blur when we zoom in.

> Many of the harshest conflicts in the world today are between people who are physically indistinguishable. If someone took a room full of Palestinians and Israelis from the Middle East, or Serbs and Albanians from the Balkans, or of Catholics and Protestants from Ireland, or of Muslims and Hindus from Northern India, or of Dayaks and Madurese from Indonesia, gave them all identical outfits and haircuts and forbade them to speak or gesture, no one could distinguish the members of the other group – at least not to the point of being willing to shoot them.[2]

Still, people seem hardwired to think in terms of borders and will seek divisions and boundaries in any given situation, then pour enormous resources into maintaining them. Every human civilization has had a boundary concept of 'us' and 'them', manifested in a myriad of different discriminatory behaviours. Right-wing politicians in particular have historically played on ethnic and economic anxieties over immigration, inciting border panic among nation-states from generation to generation. In sharp contrast to our early ancestors, who migrated from Africa across the globe with a scarce awareness that they were moving, today we move swiftly and with a high degree of political self-consciousness.

For all the philosophical and sub-atomic hair-splitting, boundaries are certainly experienced as real for those who find themselves on the wrong side of them. Examining social boundaries on an urban scale, Lieven de Cauter sees the contemporary city as a cluster of self-contained capsules, capsules that separate the 'haves' from the 'have nots' both in real space and cyberspace.

> The *gated communities* and the detention camps for illegal refugees mirror one another. The counterpart of the fortress is the camp. The former is a machine of exclusion, the latter a machine of inclusion. Similar is the relation between the tourist zone and the ghetto, the City

Walk and the containment zone. Or in other words: no man without a wall. The hype concerning the abolition of frontiers is but a sham. The World Wide Web, mobility and the boom in communication are in direct proportion to capsularization. The one is not conceivable without the other. The famous globalization is at the same time a re-delimitation of territories. Transcendental capitalism cannot function without camps and capsules because it is still based on the accumulation of capital through unequal trade between centre and periphery, and because this contrast is presently clearer than ever. To put it more directly: our society cannot exist without barbed wire.[3]

For de Cauter, the evolution of the capsularized city results in a flattened, placeless urban experience that mirrors the evolution of the flat, placeless interface of cyberspace. This is not unlike the modernist nightmare Siegfried Kracauer envisaged in his description of the transmogrification of the city into a giant, placeless hotel lobby, a space purpose built for human non-interaction.

Live Art is a homeless art form in the capsularized city, for it doesn't occupy the high-brow cultural-economic bubble of a national opera or a national theatre with listed architectural space and season-ticket holders, nor does it occupy the more pedestrian but far more vast and lucrative spaces of the shopping mall multiplex cinemas. There are few cities in the world where you will find a Live Art 'capsule' – a cultural space dedicated to producing Live Art. If you do find a space that produces Live Art, it will be part of a hybrid programme of other boundary-blurring art forms such as installation. Live Art is a lurker, now a dweller. Borders are familiar to live art, both as campsites for temporary occupations and as subject matter, but borders are among the most angst-ridden places on earth, so it isn't an easy gig. The following section looks at four different types of 'border panic' through the lens of a performance work or works. Paul Heritage describes in Chapter 16 his recent project, 'Love in Time of War', which was literally staged on the heavily guarded border wasteland between two favelas in Rio controlled by rival drug gangs. In Chapter 13 Jennifer Parker Starbuck analyses the presentation of transcendent capitalism in *Alladeen*, a collaboration between **moti**roti and the Builder's Society, which focuses on the lives of call-centre workers in Bangalore who are trained to try and 'pass' as Americans. L. E. Bogad looks at the placing of performance in Chapter 14 in the context of art activism in the 'Billionaires for Bush' movement that evolved around the 2004 election, a movement in which the performers placed themselves in the 'enemy' camp. And finally, in Chapter 15 Helen Paris examines the delicate membrane between performer and audience member in several works which feature one-to-one encounters between the two, asking how close is too close for comfort.

Notes

1   Fritjof Capra, *The Tao of Physics* (London: Flamingo, 1982), p.150.
2   Lieven de Cauter, 'The Capsular City', in Neil Leach, ed., *The Hieroglyphics of Space: Reading and Experiencing the Modern Metropolis* (London: Routledge) p.278.
3   Steve Olson, *Mapping Human History: Genes, Race and our Common Origins* (Boston, MA, and New York: Houghton Mifflin, 2002), p.226.

13
Lost in Space?: Global Placelessness and the Non-Places of *Alladeen*

Jennifer Parker-Starbuck

> Place and non-place are rather like opposite polarities: the first is never completely erased, the second never totally completed: they are like palimpsests on which the scrambled game of identity and relations is ceaselessly rewritten.
>
> (Marc Augé[1])

In the 2003 production of *Alladeen*, a collaboration between New York's Builders Association and London's **moti**roti, there is a moment when a young Indian woman, calling the United States from a phone centre in Bangalore, reaches a fellow Indian transplanted to Silicon Valley. She momentarily forgets the reason for the call and begins to ask him imploringly about life in America, a life she would clearly love to be a part of. However, in accordance with her on-the-job training, she has taken on an American name and persona and must feign 'Americanness'. Remembering this she reverts back to the purpose of her call, preventing her from an honest human exchange.[2] *Alladeen* is an exploration of identity, isolation and hopeful wish-fulfilment, weaving the romantic orientalist tale of Aladdin and his magic lamp into and through a story about the rise of International Call Centres in places like India, in which young people aim to 'pass' as American (or British) in order to fulfil an increasingly corporate need for cheap labour. A growing phenomena, these call centres field and place a wide range of calls to the United States and Britain, from people calling in to make travel and hotel reservations to call centre operators' marketing a host of products to 'unsuspecting' Americans. Although it is hard to penetrate the slick surface of *Alladeen*'s dazzling technological presentation, beneath it a tension exists between (1) the displacement of certain forms of cultural and economic globalization as exposed within the show's content and echoed through its website counterpart/extension; and (2) the paradoxical re-place-ing of the individual's placelessness within the embodied space of the theatre. I contend that this type of international call centre poses another form of what anthropologist Marc Augé would call a 'non-place', and that presenting it within the space of the theatre has the potential to replace the placeless global workers within a 'First-World' local imaginary.

In *Non-Places, Introduction to an Anthropology of Supermodernity*, the source of the above epigraph, Marc Augé adds to wide-ranging contemporary discourses of space and place his concept of the 'non-place' of the condition of supermodernity.[3] As he defines it, supermodernity is marked by its excesses – of time, space and ego – and most importantly, by its production of 'non-places'. These non-places, for Augé, are different from anthropological place, in that they 'cannot be defined as relational, or historical, or concerned with identity'.[4] For Augé, 'place' is inhabited – those well-travelled, but not simply passed-through spaces defined precisely by their relationalities, identities and histories.[5] Writing in 1995, Augé describes how an excess of general space through rail transport, space travel, satellites and broadcast images have forced 'considerable physical modifications: urban concentrations, movements of population and the multiplication of what we call "non-places".'[6] In this excess, access to space has expanded and thereby altered our relationships to place. Augé describes an increased retreat from the place of the city (Paris) and how it has shifted human–spatial relationships:

> It is at the city limits, in the cold, gloomy space of big housing schemes, industrial zones and supermarkets, that the signs are placed inviting us to visit the ancient monuments; and alongside the motorways that we see more and more references to the local curiosities we ought to stop and examine, instead of just rushing past; as if alluding to former times and places were today just a manner of talking about present space.[7]

In the 'rushing past', which is also indicative of a growing ease in traversing broad spaces, the non-place has emerged. The non-places Augé describes tend to be physically grounded – airports, highways, supermarkets – and are always passed through; they are not formed with internal identity or relations in mind, but instead 'in relation to certain ends (transport, transit, commerce, leisure), and the relations that individuals have with these spaces'.[8] This provocative notion that the 'passed-through', transient space is as crucial to a cultural understanding as the anthropological or social spaces of, for example, Bachelard's focus on homes, leads me to attempt an expansion of Augé's notion to address a recent form of non-place exhibited in *Alladeen*, the call centre, a transient place for workers to pass through in order to facilitate an inexpensive transnational need to sell products, provide services and collect data. This non-place is formed in relation to a certain end (commerce) while also subjecting individuals to 'ordeals of solitude, directly linked with the appearance and proliferation of non-places'.[9] Within the non-place the individual is thus rendered placeless; within the non-place of the call centre the individual is also rendered faceless.

What interests me in reading the call centres as 'non-places' is examining how this 'passing through' space, which, in Augé's description is not concerned with any specific identity, can act as a site for a cultural 'passing' of identity that, when filtered through the place of the theatre, re-emerges as visible. Additionally, Augé's notion of the non-place attempts to interrogate the fluid and often unacknowledged experience of moving through spaces that are rendered invisible, spaces in which people are placeless, spaces worthy of analysis, especially as globalization has made transnational travel, trade and tourism more and more ubiquitous.

At a time when popular conceptions of globalization range from an all-consuming evil force to a utopic promise of international sharing, I would like to take up cultural historian Peter Hitchcock's argument for a transnational cultural studies and his assertion that 'the crisis of globalization is a crisis of imagination, something that exists in the material limits of a global imaginary as currently constructed.'[10] His project is to re-imagine transnationalism as a positive and hopeful resource by urging an interrogation of the transcultural in such exchanges as Nike's appropriation of Indonesian workers for its shoe production, or literary displacements in the Caribbean (to gloss over his complex and intricate analysis). By focusing on representation and non-representation rather than solely economic aspects of these exchanges, Hitchcock attempts to 'underline the importance of imagination to both the aesthetic and the economic in cultural transnationalism'.[11] Using Hitchcock's cultural transnational imagination and Augé's idea of non-place, I hope to re-evaluate the themes of identity presented in *Alladeen* within the context of the theatrical space, to imagine it as a hopeful (if not completely successful) site to replace the face effaced in the non-place.

Alladeen is framed by a paean to globalization. It begins and ends with nearly identical segments that take place in New York and London, a structure which emphasizes the international global team-work that makes up the piece as well as the interchangeability of the global city. It opens with a young woman of Indian descent 'multi-tasking' on her cell phone, switching between languages while discussing karaoke bars. She appears successful and business-like, the very epitome of having 'made it' in a global world. As her 'call waiting' clicks in, a large screen behind her begins to simultaneously transform; effortlessly, blocks of images slide into place like a puzzle, creating the image of a Virgin Records megastore in New York.[12] Immediately the audience is seduced by the polish of the technology on stage and the mesmerizing sound composition.[13] The show is full of seductions, tech-nological certainly, but also in its humour – the audience laughs at the clever erasure of cultural differences as phone lines, megastores and money blur the geographic distance and distinctions between three distinct global city locations, all within an Anglophone sphere – New York City, Bangalore and London. Yet, as alluring as the production may be, it is also crucial to confront this cultural blurring which erases the very real world of corporate greed and capitalism. As Peter Hitchcock so beautifully states in his investigation of cultural transnationalism, 'the true face of globalization is precisely its facelessness', an idea that is exposed, if not critically presented, beneath the seductive elements of globalization presented in *Alladeen*.[14] *Alladeen*, by blending the techno-logical and the live in what I would call a 'cyborgean' theatrical framing, has the potential to challenge this facelessness, exposing the defacing act of globalization to the theatrical relation, while also repeating the polish which hides the realities of the labour that produces it.[15]

Directed by Marianne Weems and conceived by Weems, Keith Khan and Ali Zaidi of **moti**roti, *Alladeen* was created on several distinct levels: the theatrical production, a website (www.Alladeen.com) and a music video. I am interested here in how the stage production and the website work almost in opposition in their critical portrayals of the call centres and the operators. Both contain examples of the non-place: the produc-tion seeks to depict it through actors within the embodied space of the theatre, while the website is itself a non-place where the real-life opera-tors have a chance to directly express themselves. Although both rely heavily on the viewer's seduction, and parts of each are exchangeable within the other – clips from the website are projected on stage and clips from the production can be sampled on the website – the website, by nature of its persistence, assists in the reproduction of global capital but offers a depth and complexity that is muted on stage. It is ultimately the stage, by virtue of its evanescence, which has the potential to subvert the seduction of global capital.[16] Performance, as Peggy Phelan has written, 'cannot be saved, recorded, documented, or otherwise participate in the circulation of representations of representations'.[17] While this production may not have been, or, for that matter, even tried to be, successful in its subversion (particularly when the website component is taken into account), I assert that the cyborg theatre form this production takes ultimately begins to engage potentialities for exploring identity in a global supermodernity.

The main story-line of the stage production takes place in the Bangalore call centre where we, as audience, are witness to both the training (for they are not unskilled workers) and the employment of four hopeful operators. The operators are trained to 'speak American' and learn common pronunciation differences. The enactment on stage is juxtaposed with clips from an extended video (which can be viewed on the website) called, 'How to Neuter the Mother Tongue', in which supervisor Sharu Jose describes the system of teaching SAE, or Standard American English, the preferred accent for the call operators. Jose explains the common mistakes in pronunciation and intonation and then describes the need for cultural knowledge, such as the politically correct terms 'physically challenged' so that the operators can 'get a feel of America without going to America'. This linguistic reorientation serves to empty out the real grounded place that is America; the place here rendered placeless by discursive effect. A knowledge of American culture is expected – the ubiquity of US cultural productions within the Anglophone world – and the operators are encouraged to use this knowledge to make personal connections with those they call. However, the lack of a 'real' grounding in the non-place of the call centre – pretending to be America while instead being Bangalore – produces humorous incongruities within the theatrical space. For example, (this excerpt can be seen on the website) a panicky young woman from the United States calls the travel number 'On the Road' looking for directions to Las Vegas and says, 'I'm utterly confused as to where I'm going I'm feeling a little lost in space out here', at which point she is interrupted a bit too hastily by the call operator, '*Lost In Space*? That was a great show, remember Angela Cartwright?' This moment refracts the possible meanings of lost in space; as the call centre's non-place itself becomes lost in the space of this exchange, the theatrical imaginary contextualizes actual transnational flows that attempt to transmute cultural identification into a 'global' (read: American) identification.

In the production, a great deal of humour results from the cultural misappropriations of 'Americanness' by the workers. We watch as they are drilled about US geography as well as the rules of American football. On stage, this classroom sequence is quite funny as statistics fill in for lived knowledge and the operators attempt to project a feeling of local understanding from across the globe. In one instance, one of the call operators is thoroughly stumped by a caller's use of the word, 'smacka-roonies', to mean money. The operator puts the caller on hold and frantically attempts a search for the word, yielding only perplexed comments from her colleagues on the floor. Although the callers have been schooled in typical American idiomatic expressions, there are always phrases and words that make impossible a total cross-cultural exchange. Non-places themselves, as Augé defines them, 'are defined partly by the words and texts they offer us: their "instructions for use",'[18] Here it is the words themselves which are both the commodity and the objectives of this non-place; while for Augé, it is words that tell us how to act in the non-place, here the callers must act to fill in for the lack of words provided by the non-place's attempt to hide its placelessness. The Indian callers attempt to learn the codes and instructions for use, but often maintain the stilted formality of loudspeaker announcements; however, these texts, meant to guide the workers and navigate their journey into an imagined America, seem to only serve to displace them.

In the non-place of the actual call centre, the operator role-plays willingly. Unlike the unskilled, 'absent' workers Hitchcock attempts to replace within his discussions of the transnational production of the Nike shoe or Starbucks coffee production, the Indian call operators, according to what is presented in the media, are often college students looking for a little extra cash.[19] Another important distinction to be made here between the call centre operators represented on the *Alladeen* website and in the media and Hitchcock's workers is that many of the call centre operators are often not dependant upon this work for long periods of time. One article reports that the work 'involves gruelling hours and can be mind-numbing. The average call-centre worker stays in the job for only four months.'[20] However, in all of these examples the identity of the worker is intentionally erased in order to market goods within a global economy.

What is never fully examined in *Alladeen* is the underlying need for the operators' pseudo Americanness, their attempts to 'pass' vocally and culturally. Their exchanges are based largely on a fundamental lie, to serve a corporate need to make money. The occasional honest glimpse at the long night-shift hours the operators endure and the effect on their social lives hints at the downside to their financial boon. The stage production gets lost in the clever representation of the passing, instead giving way to a 'let's all be *Friends*' glossing over of the questions of political economic structures.

The stage production of *Alladeen* visually points to the erasure of identity within global capitalism. The *mise-en-scène* is such that on a split stage (a large screen the width of the stage is raised above the playing space) the actors below become only part of a composite image, much like a computer screen with many open windows. On the screen, footage from actual call centre operators is blended with projections of contemporary cultural images, such as the characters from the (now retired) popular TV series *Friends*. This becomes an amusing structural gimmick in the production – each of the call centre operators selects the name of one of the *Friends* characters as their alter ego. Augé suggests that 'the link between individuals and their surroundings in the space of non-place is established through the mediation of words, or even texts'.[21] By selecting such cultural texts and commercial figures, the production team plays on the audience's cultural awareness of the fame and success of the real actors playing these roles, but the cultural realities of these as definitions of 'American identity' and the funny moment of receiving a phone call from 'Rachel Green' and realizing 'that's the same name as the character on *Friends*' are foregrounded in this exploration. As well, this also gives the production team a chance to work with technologies of image processing in which the faces of the live actors are at times merged on screen with the faces of the *Friends* characters. In one particularly cyborgean moment, while operator 'Phoebe' takes a call her face is projected on the screen above. There, her image begins to morph into the face of *Friends* character Phoebe. Their features become blurred and it becomes difficult to distinguish who is who. The non-place is not concerned with particular identity and this blurring of real individuality with invented character becomes the only way for the operator to navigate the space. If, as Hitchcock suggests, 'the true face of globalization is precisely its facelessness', then perhaps it is successfully achieved only through this complicated blurring of identity, which, in this case merges actors performing characters based on real call centre operators with fictitious televised characters played by other actors! The layers create a visually interesting and thought provoking, but eerily disconcerting, erasure of all the identities involved.[22]

Hitchcock points out that 'the number of people who either are forced or choose to move beyond and between national borders is reason enough to examine whether the Nation State remains an adequate identitarian formula. The alternatives, however, are marked by fluid but no less contradictory forms of subjecthood.'[23] The capitalist project of selling parts of the production chain out to the lowest bidder who can ably do the work links Hitchcock's unskilled workers with the more highly skilled Indian callers, although with the call centres there is no tangible commodity, such as the Nike shoe, involved. However, what is perhaps most provocative within the example of *Alladeen* and the call centre is that the commodity in this case can be read as the false identity, the 'Americanness' by which the caller identifies him or herself in order to market the variety of services and products the call centres provide. The production falls a bit short here, for the humour and gorgeous visual production mask an underlying critique of what it means to live as the workers, or how it feels to be culturally erased in order to serve American interests. The gloss of the production, in effect, reperforms the central act of capitalism, the forced erasure of visible labour in the production of the commodity. While the playbill lists all those involved in the production, in the live moment, the technological wizardry stands out not for the human production of it, but for its own slickness as commodifiable/commodified theatre. However, as I will discuss, the fact that this slickness remains grounded on the theatrical stage, and that the production engages live, placed bodies, recoups it somewhat in light of Phelan's notion that 'performance clogs the smooth machinery of... representation necessary to the circulation of capital'. The commodifiable aspect of the production is best seen through its website counterpart. While, as I discuss below, the production itself can create a place for the replacing of the erased identity, the website, although it attempts to do exactly this, remains as a persistent loop back into a globally capitalist trajectory.

Itself acting as a non-place, www.Alladeen.com, attempts to provide instructions for the viewers of the more anthropologically placed stage production. As slick as the stage production, the website is also worth scratching the surface to find the hidden links and embedded articles – navigating the site is worth the trouble. The reported facts and figures reveal some of the economic structures of the call centres (as of their posting in 2003), for example, at the Wipro Call Centre in New Delhi, president of financial services Girish Paranjpe reports that, 'out of our client list, about 350 clients, about 70 per cent are in the Fortune 1000'.[24] This same article reports that call centre agents earn between

$2300–$3200 annually, versus ten times that amount in the United States. Research also expected 'more than 3.3 million US jobs to move offshore by 2015 – the bulk of those to India'.[25] It is also possible to locate the impulses behind some of the theatrical choices on the site, and there seems to be a real desire to address the larger issues of globalization and cross-cultural 'exchanges'. In an interview with Katherine Wessling of the magazine (*ai*) (also found on the website), director Marianne Weems explains that:

> The piece is grounded in questions about materialism and colonialism in literature, global technology, and real life. So our exploration of the Indian operators is emblematic of all these questions about unilateral positions and, really, unilateral arrogance on America's part. One of our original impulses was to look at the ways that America looks at India and India looks at America – how [America is] perceived by the rest of the world.[26]

The New York production seemed weighted more heavily toward America looking at India in that any real exchange was shrouded in humour or splashy effects. However, on the website is a link to 'Cyber Immigrants' within which another link, called 'Perception of America and American Culture', provides short movies from actual Indian call operators revealing their impressions about America. It seems that overall, their perceptions derived from media representations are augmented or reversed after speaking with many Americans. For instance, one operator, Ateef, found that music videos are not a good indication of what Americans are really like, and another, Mathew, felt that Americans are not as great as they are made out to be, in fact, he found them 'really dumb'. Aarti recognized that there were similarities between Indians and Americans and noted with interest that 'spouses never make decisions without the other'. Natasha decided that the American family structure was not very close knit and that many Americans are lonely. The movies are a refreshing counterpoint to the humorous fun the audience has at the actors' malapropisms, and here honest critiques can flow back. There is, however, also a danger in these brief generalizations, but they ask to be juxtaposed in the ways in which they mirror back to an American audience its own generalizations and stereotypes.

The non-place of the website offers a more complex navigation of the issue so that in addition to economics offering a potential critique of the capitalist machinery in place in the real call centres, it also adds to a statement such as, 'per agent cost in the USA is approximately $40,000 while in India it is only $5,000', the assertion that 'just to put this figure in perspective: despite the comparatively low wages, in India a call centre operator still makes more than the average doctor'.[27] This to me was the first hint of the website's non-place being a passing back through for the viewer into the economy of capital. This is a non-place which circulates outside of the theatrical space; the web address is projected on to the screens during the performance, literally intending to loop the viewers back into this circulation. The website's instructions are contradictory, or perhaps neutralizing – a segment promoting IT and outsourcing acts as a counterpoint to Weems's previous comments when it states the components of locating 'lower cost of factory inputs' as:

Agricultural Age – British used the colonies to grow indigo
Industrial age – Nike shoes being made in Indonesia and toys being made in China
Virtual age – From looking for lower cost of manufacturing to reducing transaction cost.[28]

The reference to Nike shoes made in Indonesia, for example, could link to Hitchcock's argument that 'the athletic shoe industry has inscribed itself in a particular form of nation building that is nevertheless uninterested in the Subject that such a process confers. To imagine the links in the aura of the shoe is what must be risked if criticism is to be responsibly positioned in global analysis.'[29] If Hitchcock's analysis was yet another link from the website, this would generate a more nuanced critique toward replacing the placeless. However, like the non-place of the call centre in *Alladeen*, the non-space of the website endlessly loops back into global capitalism. The production, too, relegates the non-place of the call centre to a literal 'passing' through space toward a wealthier future; the character 'Joey', for example, is able to successfully pass well enough to earn a promotion as representative. However, through 'Joey' emerges the production's critique of this endless cycle. Even if 'Joey's' humorous bid for personal economic capital serves the theatrical without ever explicitly engaging capital's slippery complexity, it also renders him incapable of moving beyond this point into a human exchange, as I discuss below. This story-line within *Alladeen*, coupled with Phelan's notion of the disappearance of performance, stops this loop in its tracks.

The final scene of the production repeats the structure of the first, beginning with the same woman, now in London and still talking about karaoke. An almost identical Virgin megastore slips into place and then pulls apart as the screen lifts up to reveal a flashy karaoke bar complete with light boxes and a dance floor. This jet-setting woman here meets up with the character 'Joey', once he has risen up through the ranks in Bangalore. It is a happenstance meeting, but one which fleshes out a critique, albeit a nuanced one. 'Joey' has successfully navigated the non-place of the call centre and travelled to the place of the city, where identity and relations are key elements. 'Joey', perhaps the modern day Aladdin, has been granted his wish – he has successfully passed into global capitalism. However, when he approaches the woman in the karaoke bar he is met disdainfully. She clearly finds his line of work beneath her and is dismissive of him. The desperate hope for wish-fulfilment that global capitalism has perpetuated renders 'Joey' faceless and alone. Augé's evocative statement, 'the space of non-place creates neither singular identity nor relations; only solitude, and simili-tude' resonates here.[30] Although Augé was most likely referring to the displacement within the non-place, his provocative notion has led me to ponder the condition we are left in after passing through so many non-places. If the excesses of supermodernity lead to the formation of the non-place then these non-places are inherently linked to late capitalism. In the final moments of *Alladeen* a projection on the screen reads *Bitter Magic*, and underneath it rapidly scrolls the cryptic, 'be careful what you wish for', a warning almost too brief to comprehend its potentially ironic message: in searching for visibility through non-places leading to capital you may render yourself placeless and faceless. Phelan argues that 'visibility politics are compatible with capitalism's relentless appetite for new markets and with the most self-satisfying ideologies of the United States: you are welcome here as long as you are productive. The production and reproduction of visibility are part of the labour of the reproduction of capitalism.'[31] As visibility increasingly takes on an American face, it is difficult to understand how to negotiate the non-spaces that represent only First World products and faces. The very materiality of the theatrical place, however, does allow bodies to be represented but perhaps not, following Phelan, reproduced. The buck stops there. In this place we come face-to-face with the material bodies that are placed; here we can recognize the faceless and placelessness of the workers. I will never again take a call without questioning the iden-tity of the caller.[32] The website, which is a part of this production, does reproduce and recirculate this performance as a non-place endlessly looping around and around as a global extension of the place of performance. However, it at least represents some of the actual faces and workers, speaking their own ideas even if masking the realities of the labour.

Perhaps this argument is too great a stretch. Like Phil Auslander, I am wary of making too much out of the liveness of these bodies in a mediatized age. In this case, I agree whole-heartedly with Auslander that 'the general response of live performance to the oppression and economic superiority of mediatized forms has been to become as much like them as possible'.[33] Likewise, I agree that in *Alladeen* the live production does in fact 'derive its authority from its reference to the mediatized',[34] however, while Auslander argues that the 'live itself incorporates the mediatized',[35] I remain convinced that while the live production does this, the live bodies do not. The face-to-face encounter remains ontologically and ethically a different space from that of the non-place. However, this reading of *Alladeen* is not immediately apparent. I admit to initially being completely caught up in the polish of the technological wizardry. Despite the rush, I was, that night, left with an empty feeling of uneasiness that there should have been more critique within the production. However, despite my fear that the underlying issues or content are 'white-washed' in the production of *Alladeen*, it is ironically the very blurring of form that makes this a provocative collaboration. One of the potentials for this type of cyborg theatre is that it integrates multiple forms – live performance, music video, film – in a shared place while simultaneously creating a space for the interrogation of the very issues of identity and subjectivity the live body faces in a technologically mediatized, First World society. The use of technology here need not be merely spectacle but can pose questions about its influence in our lives. To read the simple 'be careful what you wish for' under the gigantic block letters BITTER MAGIC hovering above a scene of highly saturated orange and yellows within a simulated karaoke bar on stage seemed to be the production team's way of making a joke, of acknowledging that their own movement through the non-spaces of a global society could force them out of the theatre altogether – but as of yet, it has not.

Notes

1   Marc Augé, *Non-Places: Introduction to an Anthropology of Supermodernity* (London: Verso, 1995), p.79.
2   Sections of this chapter are reprinted from Jennifer Parker-Starbuck, 'Global *Friends*: The Builders Association at BAM', *PAJ: A Journal of Performance and Art*, 77 (May 2004), XXVI: 2: 96–102.

3   On place and space, see, for example: Gaston Bachelard, *The Poetics of Space: The Classic Look at How We Experience Intimate Places*, trans. Maria Jolas (Boston, MA: Beacon Press, 1964); Michel de Certeau, *The Practice of Everyday Life*, trans. Steven Randall (Berkeley: University of California Press, 1984); Michel Foucault, *Power/Knowledge* (New York: Pantheon, 1980); David Harvey, *Spaces of Capital: Towards a Critical Geography* (London: Routledge, 2001); Henri Lefebvre, *The Production of Space* (Oxford: Blackwell, 1991); Doreen Massey, *Space, Place and Gender* (Minneapolis: University of Minnesota Press, 1994); Edward Soja, *Thirdspace* (Oxford: Blackwell, 1996).

4   Augé, *Non-Places*, pp.77–8.

5   Augé, *Non-Places*, pp.77–8, Augé seems to incorporate Michel de Certeau's 'frequented space' into his notion of anthropological place, relegating the term space to a more general use, or in non-symbolic surfaces of space. See pages 79–85 for his differentiation of terms.

6   Augé, *Non-Places*, p.34.

7   Augé, *Non-Places*, pp.73–4.

8   Augé, *Non-Places*, p.94.

9   Augé, *Non-Places*, p.93.

10 Peter Hitchcock, *Imaginary States: Studies in Cultural Transnationalism* (Chicago: University of Illinois Press, 2003), p.5.

11 Hitchcock, *Imaginary States*, p.5.

12 The night I saw the production, this moment of technological 'magic' caused the audience at the Brooklyn Academy of Music (BAM) to break into applause, apparently over the technological innovation of the creation.

13 The sound for the production was by Dan Dobson with original music samples by Shrikanth Sriram.

14 Hitchcock, *Imaginary States*, p.188.

15 I have coined the term 'Cyborg Theatre' to differentiate between random uses of multimedia in production and that which interrogates the ideas of human subjectivity through its integration with technology on stage.

16 I want to thank Josh Abrams for his invaluable advice in the shaping of this piece and for offering up the terms persistence and evanescence at a time I needed them most.

17 Peggy Phelan, *Unmarked: The Politics of Performance* (London: Routledge, 1993), p.146.

18 Augé, *Non-Places*, p.96.

19 For a specific example of this, see David Rohde, 'Sleepy city has high hopes, dreaming of high tech', *New York Times* International Section, 20 November 2003 (article included in press kit).

20 Rohd, 'Sleepy City'.

21 Augé, *Non-Places*, p.94.

22 Production credits list several 3-D animators as well as Rick Kjeldsen, DinoVision Inventor (image processing software provided by IBM). See www.Alladeen.com for a list of individuals who worked on this project. Additionally, in preparation for *Alladeen* the artistic team travelled to Bangalore to observe the actual centres and in the photo credits section of the website, one real operator, Natasha Sabharwal, has, in fact, taken on the name of Rachel Green (the Jennifer Aniston character on the TV show).

23 Hitchcock, *Imaginary States*, p.6.

24 See article *India at Outsourcing Revolution's Core* (2003 [cited 2003–4]) at http://www.msnbc.com/news/983161.asp?vts=102220030513 for access to this article by Sue Herera, CNBC.
25 See website in note 24.
26 Katherine Wessling, 'Dreaming of Genies', *(ai)*, Fall 2002, p.30.
27 Found on www.alladeen.com, 'The Economics of Outsourcing', in which another website is embedded: www.outsourcetoindia.com
28 See website in note 27.
29 Hitchcock, *Imaginary States*, p.151.
30 Augé, *Non-Places*, p.103.
31 Phelan, *Unmarked*, p.11.
32 During much of the piece I thought back to many of the recent calls I had received and wondered if I had perceived an Indian accent, or whether the caller had tried to relate to the weather in New York, or say something about the sightseeing possibilities? Later, I learned that many other audience members were processing similar thoughts.
33 Philip Auslander, *Liveness: Performance in a Mediatized Culture* (London: Routledge, 1999), p.7.
34 Auslander, *Liveness*, p.39.
35 Auslander, *Liveness*, p.39.

Bibliography

Augé, Marc. *Non-Places: Introduction to an Anthropology of Supermodernity*, London and New York: Verso, 1995.

Auslander, Philip. *Liveness: Performance in a Mediatized Culture*, London; New York: Routledge, 1999.

Bachelard Gaston, and M. Jolas. *The Poetics of Space*, Boston, MA: Beacon Press, 1994.

Carlson, M. A. *Places of Performance: The Semiotics of Theatre Architecture*, Ithaca, NY: Cornell University Press, 1989.

Certeau, Michel de. *The Practice of Everyday Life*, Berkeley: University of California Press, 1984.

Chaudhuri, U. *Staging Place: The Geography of Modern Drama, Theater – Theory/Text/Performance*, Ann Arbor: University of Michigan Press, 1995.

Cresswell, T. *Place: A Short Introduction, Short Introductions to Geography*, Malden, MA: Blackwell, 2004.

Lauretis, T. de. *Technologies of Gender: Essays on Theory, Film, and Fiction, Theories of Representation and Difference*, Bloomington: Indiana University Press, 1987.

Foucault, Michel, and C. Gordon. *Power/Knowledge: Selected Interviews and Other Writings, 1972–1977*, 1st American edn, New York: Pantheon Books, 1980.

Garner, S. B. *Bodied Spaces: Phenomenology and Performance in Contemporary Drama*, Ithaca, NY: Cornell University Press, 1994.

Harvey, David. *Justice, Nature, and the Geography of Difference*, Cambridge, MA: Blackwell Publishers, 1996.

Harvey, David. *Spaces of Capital: Towards a Critical Geography*, New York: Routledge, 2001.

Hayles, N. K. *How We Became Post-Human*, Chicago: University of Chicago, 1999.

Herera, Sue. *India at Outsourcing Revolution's Core* (2003 [cited 2003–4]. Available from http://www.msnbc.com/news/983161.asp?vts = 102220030513)

Hitchcock, Peter. *Imaginary States: Studies in Cultural Transnationalism, Transnational Cultural Studies*, Urbana: University of Illinois, 2003.

Jameson, F. *Postmodernism, or, the Cultural Logic of Late Capitalism, Post-Contemporary Interventions*, Durham, NC: Duke University Press, 1991.

Lefebvre, Henri. *The Production of Space*, Cambridge, MA, and Oxford: Blackwell, 1991.

Massey, Doreen. *Space, Place, and Gender*, Minneapolis: University of Minnesota Press, 1994.

McAuley, G. *Space in Performance: Making Meaning in the Theatre, Theater – Theory/Text/Performance*, Ann Arbor: University of Michigan Press, 1999.

motiroti, The Builders Association and *Alladeen*, by Marianne Weems, Brooklyn, 2003.

McAuley, G. 2003 www.alladeen.com

Nightengale, B. 'Aladdin as customer service genie', The *New York Times*, 30 November 2003.

Parker-Starbuck, Jennifer. 'Global *Friends*: The Builders Association at BAM', *PAJ: A Journal of Performance and Art* XXVI, 2: 77 (2004): 96–102.

Parker-Starbuck, Jennifer. 'Shifting Strengths: The Cyborg Theatre of Cathy Weis', in Carrie Sandahl and Philip Auslander, eds, *Bodies in Commotion: Disability and Performance, Corporealities*, Ann Arbor: University of Michigan Press, 2005.

Performance Research, 'On Place' vol. 3:2 (1998).

Phelan, Peggy. *Unmarked: The Politics of Performance*, London and New York: Routledge, 1993.

Rogoff, I. *Terra Infirma: Geography's Visual Culture*, London; New York: Routledge, 2000.

Rohde, David. 'Sleepy city has high hopes, dreaming of high tech', The *New York Times*, 20 November 2003.

Sassen, S. *Cities in a World Economy*, 2nd edn, *Sociology for a New Century*, Thousand Oaks: Pine Forge Press, 2000.

Sassen, S. *The Global City: New York, London, Tokyo*, 2nd edn, Princeton: Princeton University Press, 2001.

Soja, Edward. *Thirdspace: Journeys to Los Angeles and Other Real-and-Imagined Places*, Cambridge, MA: Blackwell, 1996.

Wessling, Katherine. 'Dreaming of genies', (*ai*); Interview, (*ai*): *Performance for the Planet* (2002): 30–5.

14

A Place for Protest: The Billionaires for Bush Interrupt the Hegemonologue

L. M. Bogad

Prologue

Public protest is out of place in the United States. It has no place. It's on the run, running in place, running out of space.

Or at least this appears to be the goal of those who sanction protest only in Orwellian 'Free Speech Zones': out-of-the-way lots and streets ringed by fences, with police-controlled access and egress. Creative dissenters have resisted being 'put in their place' by defying permit bans or using art, direct action and diverse tactics to project their objections over the fences and out of the margins, hoping to disrupt the dramaturgy of state, corporate and political events.

This struggle over protest-place was particularly intense in New York City – where real estate is always a hot item – during the Republican National Convention (RNC). The RNC, backed up by massive state power, demarcated, occupied and fortified a heavily mediated space from which they could project to the nation a hegemonic monologue that would elevate their candidate to saviour status while overwriting any inconvenient details, facts and ongoing wars of choice. The anti-Bush Counter-Convention contradicted the RNC in both content and form; this was a multi-vocal, dialogical, placeless and many-faced mass entity, which flowed throughout the city, enacting the global justice movement's slogan 'We Are Everywhere'. The Counter-Convention infiltrated and engulfed RNC events and contested space in the streets and in the local media.[1] Lacking the RNC's strategic power to lay claim to a secure space, the Counter-Convention nevertheless attempted to disrupt Republican symbolism and dramaturgy with oppositional imagery while building and deepening intra-movement coalitions and connections for future action.

The Billionaires for Bush, a street theatre/media intervention group, made a unique (and no doubt tax-deductible) contribution to the Counter-Convention: using irony to focus on issues of class. Like public protest in general, the very concept of socio-economic class, or the identity of a ruling class, is denied a place in mainstream American discourse; indeed the term 'class warfare' has become a term with which pundits and politicians denounce not the elites, but anyone who critiques the elites or even acknowledges that they exist as a class. Commentators on all sides do flips in order not to say the phrase 'working class', resulting in such terms as 'the working poor' and 'working families'. The Billionaires for Bush use cartoonish irony to bring issues of class back to the forefront of discussion, and to mock the exploitive policies of the Administration wherever they perform; they also add an element of tactical ambiguity and playfulness to street confrontations where tensions can run high.

Place, protest and permission

Frisbees and grass. In the lead-in to the Republican National Convention in New York City in the summer of 2004, the Republicans made it clear that both of these things were more important than the First Amendment to the Constitution. The United for Peace and Justice (UFPJ) coalition wanted to stage a massive rally on the Great Lawn in Central Park, a space big enough to accommodate the hundreds of thousands of demonstrators expected to gather to protest the Bush agenda. However, the Republican Mayor, Michael Bloomberg, backed up and pressured by the Bush Administration, insisted that so many people in the park would kill the grass. Bloomberg further claimed that such an enormous mass of protestors would violate the rights of people who wanted to play frisbee in the park.[2]

These were the excuses for the marginalization of a mass demonstration that threatened to disrupt the painstaking dramaturgy of the RNC. The RNC, like all such conventions, is a tightly co-ordinated ritual designed to overwrite the differences between the factions of the host megaloparty (that is, between fiscal and social conservatives), and to present compellingly emotional and strategically vague symbols and personas to the national public through the television. To make all of this cohere, the convention needed a powerful event-narrative, and perhaps this was why the RNC was scheduled later than any other RNC ever: so that it would be closer to 9/11. By occupying this hallowed time and space, the Republicans hoped to stage a pageant with a story-line in which a grateful New York would embrace their President-protector-avenger as he co-opted the memory of that tragedy for his re-election campaign.

The battle for the right of peaceable assembly was key. A massive, peaceful, festive, creative public rejection of Bush at a historic, picturesque site in the city would certainly speak against the event-narrative. Beyond the Great Lawn, protestors wished to stage a Counter-Convention all over the city that would express a wide range of voices in dissent against the monolithic monologue that was the RNC. Thus the pressure on Bloomberg to marginalize the protestors as much as possible, claiming it was for their safety in the post-9/11 era, or for the grass' sake. Without a legal permit, many people, fearing arrest, would be intimidated and stay home. If the protestors were denied a viable permit, some frustrated protestors might engage in civil disorder, confirming the 'culture war' for the viewers at home and mobilizing the law-and-order Bush base.

The protestors were told they could exercise their constitutional right to peaceable assembly . . . in the borough of Queens, several miles and a river from Madison Square Garden where the RNC was to be held. When they refused, they were told they could gather on an inhospitable strip of the West Side Highway, also far from Madison Square Garden, where many would pass out from standing on the shadeless blacktop, superheated by the NYC summer sun. The UFPJ gave in to the city's hardball negotiating tactics and accepted this place for protest. However, UFPJ's outraged grassroots members threatened to drop out of the coalition and march *en masse* on Central Park, permit or no, rather than stand on the Highway. Finally, the city and UFPJ agreed to a march, without a rally, that would mass west of Union Square, pass Madison Square Garden, and double back to disperse at Union Square. This was hardly ideal, but UFPJ decided to make it work, all the while resenting the fact that the people were not allowed to meet in their own park.

The movement staged many responses to the government's restrictions on peaceable assembly, and to the privatization and overregulation of dissent in public space in general. Massive anti-Bush banners were illegally hung from hotel roofs; some groups rented billboard space, while others creatively altered commercial postings, to make them anti-RNC. ACT-UP got naked outside of Madison Square Garden; their stencilled skin screamed, 'STOP AIDS DROP THE DEBT'. Times Up!, the bicycle-riders' group, staged the largest Critical Mass bike ride in the history of New York, which clogged the avenues of Manhattan for hours. For 40 weeks, Reverend Billy staged a recurring action in the recently reopened World Trade Centre subway/PATH station. Every Tuesday evening rush hour, anonymous performers would join the swarms of commuters, scuttling around and talking in their cell phones; however, as they did so, instead of chatting to their spouses or giving orders to subordinates back at the office, they recited over and over the First Amendment to the United States Constitution:

> Congress shall make no law respecting an establishment of religion, or prohibiting the free exercise thereof; or abridging the freedom of speech, or of the press; or the right of the people peaceably to assemble, and to petition the government for a redress of grievances.

This mass recitation would gradually escalate from invisible theatre to a crescendo of screaming glorious First Amendment worshippers, and police found it hard to arrest them as they chanted those sacred words.

The Clandestine Insurgent Rebel Clown Army (CIRCA) ran pell-mell through the streets without a permit, alternating between clownarchic swarming, strict military formation marching ('Left-Spit! Right-Sneer!'), cowardly fleeing, 'sneaking' in plain sight, and hiding behind very small objects. CIRCA was determined to remind spectators of Bush's now-infamous jetfighter landing on an aircraft carrier, costumed in a flight suit, putting his thumbs up, and announcing the end of major combat operations in Iraq under a 'MISSION ACCOMPLISHED' banner. This intrepid appearance was stunning in its crafted, mediated placelessness; in fact the carrier group was just outside of San Diego. Normal conveyance for such an executive visit would have been a quick shuttle on a helicopter. However, the jetfighter was much more daring and exciting looking. The supersonic warplane and the aircraft carrier were commandeered as the set and backdrop for the heroic figure of Bush. The entire carrier battle group did circles as it stayed out of port for Bush's dramatic visit; the cameras were arranged to aim out to sea so the nearby shore and city would not be in the frame. The crew, who by the rules of military discipline had to cheer their Commander-in-Chief, served as adoring extras in this high-seas adventure. CIRCA Harpo-Marxed on this Bush moment by wearing flight suits that said 'MISSION ACCOMPLICATED' while searching for weapons of mass destruction in restaurants, mailboxes and the body cavities of passersby, and using giant straws to snort the white lines in the streets and crosswalks, thus evoking both Bush's delightfully contrived moment on the aircraft carrier and his narcotic pastimes.

While the Republicans had the Federal, city and state governments and their massive strategic power to occupy and hold space, the opposing social movement had a tactical advantage in working on familiar home territory amongst a mostly supportive population and enjoying a wide diversity of skill sets, identities and modes of performance and protest. The Counter-Convention staged meetings, councils, conferences, cultural events and many kinds of street actions all over Manhattan and Brooklyn; the Republicans found that they had a more limited range of motion outside of the cordon of police protection at scheduled events. Some RNC delegates may even have experienced a sense of out-of-placeness that the invisibly white, unmarkedly privileged and entitled had perhaps never felt before. Republican delegates were taunted as they went to their Broadway shows and finely dined at Tavern on the Green. Delegates attending an auction of Johnny Cash memorabilia were confronted by over a hundred Johnny Cash look-alikes, who denounced this co-optation of that people's musician by strumming and singing Cash songs that advocated for the poor and the imprisoned. The pseudo-right-wing Missile Dick Chicks infiltrated a Republican private party as the 'entertainment'; it took a while for the partiers to realize they were being laceratingly lampooned by their hired 'showgirls', and it took them longer to throw the Chicks out.

Bush had scheduled a ceremonial visit to the site of the World Trade Center. This offended many New Yorkers who felt that Bush had never delivered the promised economic or security aid that he had promised to the city after 9/11. The movement planned a mass bell-ringing all over the neighborhood to non-verbally signal a protest to Bush's presence even if police kept protestors far away. P. Diddy, whose office looks down on the site, had put up anti-war posters on all of his many windows, a visual that would have disrupted the event's solemn obeisance/obedience to Bush. The RNC chose to cancel the event, keeping their dramaturgy within the more manageable, nigh-hermetically sealed Madison Square Garden. This was no small victory for the Counter-Convention movement; disrupting a planned ritual at the site of those horrific terror attacks made the Republican co-optation of 9/11 less explicit and thus less powerful.

However, there is one voice that the author has shamelessly neglected in this tract: that of the elites. Their response to all of these provocations was crucial to an understanding of the civic dialogue that was happening in the streets of New York. Accordingly, and in the interests of objectivity, I will report the following: on Sunday, 29 August, the day of the big march, about a dozen people showed up on the Great Lawn, in lovely opera gowns and tuxedos, and festooned with blinding jewellery. These were the Billionaires for Bush, and they archly informed the massed media that, in fact, the real reason one million 'hoi polloi' were denied the Great Lawn on that day was because they, the upper 0.00001 per cent, had already reserved the space to play lawn sports. They went on to point out that this was part of their agenda to 'Privatize Everything', from the Park to the City Library, to the electoral process itself – 'one dollar, one vote!'

The dazzling gaggle of haute-reactionaries then spread out all over the massive lawn, playing croquet and badminton. The sight of a few well-to-do cartoon characters scattered about, having their elitist way with that massive green space, sharply evoked the absence of the million protestors. This was a typical Billionaire action: riffing on reality; using satire to surprise, amuse, and engage; and satirically straight-arming the 'red-state/blue-state' culture-war binary by trying to get Americans to once again think about *class*. Through ironic adoration they attempt to disrupt Bush's constructed persona as a straight-talking, dirt-under-his-nails Everyman, reconstructing him as the upper-class wastrel-turned-warmonger that the Billionaires love so much. Of course class is a key component of the base-line irony of the project: the sight of 'plutocrats' marching in the streets with signs underscores the reality that of course, this sort of 'grassroots' performance in public space is something elites need never resort to. The Billionaires manifest as a funhouse-mirror image of the very elites whose disembodied, globalized 'liquidity' is one of the very foundations of their power. Since the real oligarchs won't come out and play in the street, the Billionaires provide the punch lines, playing both sides of the debate with joyously heavy-handed mockery. They were out in force with signs such as 'Corporations Are People Too', 'Small Government, Big Wars', and the mischievous 'Cheney Is Innocent'.

Figure 14.1   Billionaires for Bush, photo: Fred Askew

Billionaires flash-mobbed the city in actions planned and spread by internet and cell phone, such as waltzing *en masse* in Grand Central Station. In an intra-social-movement bit of theatre, they played a smack-down game of basketball with the organizers of the Poor People's Coalition.[3]

Billionaires spread their ironic message on radio, TV and the web (www.billionairesforbush.com); this multimedia approach added layers to the campaign, while the Billionaires' performative irony allowed them to play both sides of the debate. As my Billionaire character, 'Ollie Gark', I found that doing a radio interview on a left-wing gay radio station show enabled me to draw connections between class and gender oppression with a smarmy, condescending smile. The affable, self-satisfied demeanours and a repertoire of one-line jokes led to a great deal of media and press attention for the Billionaires.

The website, designed to present both the satirical group-persona and an earnest political critique, also served as a modular tool to help spread the concept: people looking to start a chapter in their home town could download many excellent graphics, slogans, performance ideas and even original songs in karaoke version so they could sing them with the back-up of a blinged-out boombox. This helped the consistency of costume, graphics and 'branding' of the group across the country, while allowing for flexibility, creativity and idea-sharing amongst and between the local groups. Thanks to the website, media coverage and relentless proselytizing, there are now 100 Billionaires for Bush chapters in the United States and abroad. The website provided a virtual place to co-ordinate performances in far-flung actual spaces.

The Billionaires had already bird-dogged Bush on the swing-state campaign trail, setting up their red-white-and-blue piggybank banner and cheering him on with 'Two Million Jobs Lost: A Good Start!' as he drove by.[4] The Billionaires also swung through the swing states during their Get On the Limo tours, spreading the gospel of greed and seeding new chapters as they went. Their 'Block the Vote' tour in Florida, snarkily celebrating (and publicizing) the tradition of Bush-family Republican disenfranchisement of African-Americans, was enhanced by the soundtrack of rapper 50 Billion:

> The Billionaires are in the house
> The Billionaires are in the WHITE House . . .
> Buying access
> Seeing progress
> And making a mess
> Of the political process
> Oh yes!

Irony can always be misinterpreted, especially when a group uses the same shtick on multiple simultaneous audiences. We found that police tended to treat us more politely, perhaps because of our generally genteel, entitled demeanour, or perhaps we were activating some ingrained instinct to protect the propertied? There were incidents when the police would put us in with pro-Bush demonstrators...and at least one time when those Bushites took us seriously, joining in on our chants such as 'Four More Wars!' in earnest, a chilling example of the complexities of irony as a tactic. Still, Billionaires such as founding plutocrat Andrew Boyd (aka 'Phil T. Rich') have found that irony has been an effective tool for engaging people who would otherwise tune out the message, creating momentary confusion and a pleasing 'Ah-ha moment' for passersby.

Now that the election is over, sadly, the group will not be changing its name anytime soon. Thanks to targeted voter suppression/intimidation, an insufficiency of voting machines in minority districts, and a well co-ordinated character assassination of Kerry, the day ended in victory for Our Benefactor. When confronted with the devastating consequences of this 'victory', the cadres may have faltered, and the joke may have worn thin. The class warriors of the radical Right will drive to further Privatize Everything, from our genes to our prisons to our national forests, while striving to overwhelm discussion of class with culture war at home and wars of choice abroad. They will strive to further dominate all branches of the government, all sectors of civil society, and farther flung corners of the world. Nevertheless, the Billionaire website immediately hailed the results and noted that the group had, after all, 'paid for eight years', and celebrated 'the disappearance of over 1 million votes'. It remains to be seen how, or if, this extended multimedia subvertisement will regain momentum after the election, or/and how it will fit into a greater long-term strategy. Clearly, this kind of performance is only one tool in the repertoire of the movement of movements, only one approach of many, and not to be relied upon exclusively or inflexibly. Groups like the Billionaires will continue to experiment with techniques that are not purely reactive but that help to create a culture of shared meanings that can in turn sustain an oppositional movement even in the darkest of times. The satirical struggle continues.

Creating a place for protest necessitates building a joyous, dialogical space that can attract and include the voices of many diverse counterpublics. The movement of movements contains differences not only in beliefs but about how to act on those beliefs. Some feel that an oppositional movement should not even ask for a permit from the state, or that only direct action is effective and not mass demonstrations. Places for protest should look and feel different from those created and occupied by States or Parties, who, in the words of one Republican advisor, 'create their own reality' in fortified, hegemonological, placeless spaces where the waters off San Diego stand in dramatically for the Persian Gulf, where Madison Square Garden is the HQ Central of the culture war, where war is peace and ignorance is strength. The movements do not have the power to create such places. All the better. They are rooted in localities while reaching out to each other, co-ordinating virtually and gathering on the street and in (surveilled and scrutinized) meeting places. This is not only about pandering to the 'swing states' in the parlance of the day. Movements perform not only against what they oppose but to embody and enact visions of the world we want to see, to invest our place with our own cultures. These places, created and sustained through performance, are not merely reactive encampments outside the castle but the beginnings of a new place to live. Oppositional places need to be constructed not only in response to events such as the RNC, but, as with the Counter-Convention, they must deepen intramovement connections and coalitions across boundaries of geography, identity and privilege, through co-operation, performance and praxis under pressure.

Acknowledgements

The author would like to thank the Arts and Humanities Research Council and the British Academy for their support.

Notes

1   Here geographical place really mattered, in the literal sense of physical sites and sight lines: local papers were forced to acknowledge the reality of the massive actions, as citizens could see them for themselves; the Counter-Convention received much less coverage outside of New York in the mainstream media.
2   Organizers considered showing up *en masse* with Frisbees decorated with anti-Bush slogans.
3   As the highly corrupt referee, I can report that the Billionaires were losing to the Poor People's Coalition by somewhere around 96 to 2. Fortunately, in the course of the game the Billionaires were able to privatize the city basketball court, purchase it and evict the Coalition from the grounds. It still took them several days to score enough baskets to officially win the game.
4   In fact, in York, PA, Bush gave us the double thumbs-up as his motorcade whooshed by.

15
Too Close for Comfort: One-to-One Performance

Helen Paris

Performer: I'm glad you came. I didn't know if I would recognize you. I had a picture of you in my head. Did you miss me? I mean did you ever think of me? Did you want to see me again? I mean did I make any difference? Did you want to say something just to me? Did you want to catch hold of something that you thought you might have seen or at least thought you'd caught a glimpse of and, at least for a little while, not want to let go? Am I too late? Did I say the right thing but at the wrong time? And what I'm really asking is do I get another chance?

I will miss you, I miss you already. Goodbye.

Come on baby, I'm here. I'm here right now in this time, in this space just for you. It's just you and me. Come on, come in, come over here. I have something to tell you. Something I want to show you; only you. What is it? You are scared? Don't be scared. Just come over here. Just cross the line. Just one little line that lies between us, that separates us. Just one line that keeps you in your place and me in mine. You are the reason I am here. Didn't you know? You are the reason I come here every night. Without you – why without you I am nothing! No one. Without you, I am not here. Without you I am speechless. Without you I don't know what to do with my hands. You make me what I am. I need you. Come on. You know you want to. Yes you do. Why else did you come?

How close can you get? How close is too close? In this chapter I will describe three performances explicitly created to push, pull, provoke and tease at the borders between audience member and performer. I will explore how intimacy, proximity, language and the placing and displacing

179

of performer and audience facilitate this border manipulation. *Vena Amoris*[1] was a performance in which a one-to-one interaction between performer and audience member was designed – not through face-to-face communication, but rather relayed via a mobile phone. The performer was 'placeless' through most of the performance, a disembodied voice down a phone guiding the audience member on a journey through a building. The second performance, *On the Scent*[2] was a performance about the relationship between smell and memory, set in domestic spaces for discreet audiences of no more than four at a time. The exclusive audience number meant that the audience entered the house as if they were specially invited guests. The final piece, *Deserter*[3] was formally inspired by some of the outcomes and border crossings experienced in *Vena Amoris*. *Deserter* took on a more conventional shape, taking place in a black box venue for an audience of 40, but within the performance each audience member experienced a moment of one-to-one contact with the performers as they entered and exited the space. Each work experiments with audience/performer border crossings in one-to-one performances and fuels an ongoing journey to find out how close you can get, and just how close is too close.

Vena Amoris

Audience members for *Vena Amoris* arrived one at a time at 30-minute intervals. Throughout each performance the performer remained *in situ* in a studio on the first floor of a large four-storey building containing studios, offices, a theatre space and café, while the audience member waited in the café bar downstairs. From the very beginning of the performance the spectator/performer borders are blurred; the audience member is seated in the bar and suddenly her mobile phone rings.

Performer: Hello. The performance is about to begin so if you'd just like to make your way to the theatre.

Answering the phone and following the performer's instructions to walk to the auditorium, the audience member now collaborates in the performance. The reality is that the audience member becomes *both* performer and audience.[4] The duality of the audience member's role is further signified as she enters the theatre space and is directed, not to the rows of empty, red-plush theatre chairs but to the stage itself where, already positioned, set and waiting for her, is *her* light, an empty spot on the stage which the performer instructs her to enter:

Performer: Could you possibly step into your light? (*Audience member steps into the spot. In the centre of the spot-lit area there is a box of matches and a cigarette.*) Please feel free to smoke.

Taking their place spot-lit and silhouetted centre-stage, the coil of cigarette smoke curling in the shaft of light, the audience member presents an image which is instantly recognizable as Theatre. The audience member is literally in the place of the performer whilst the performer is placeless – disembodied.

Despite the fact the audience member and performer cannot see each other, there is a distinct closeness, an intimacy between them. The intimacy in this flow of connectivity is augmented by the nature of the phone contact. Paul Levinson states that the telephone is 'revolutionary not only in what it may promise, but in the most intimate way it makes that offering. The intimate acoustic distance of the speaker's mouth and voice form the listener's ear on the telephone.'[5] This notion of intimacy – of sound as caress, as touch, the performer reaching out and touching the audience member with her voice reveals the possibility of the depth and closeness of the communication between performer and audience member. At the same time there is a distinct discomfort caused by this shifting of the audience – performer borders. The encounter between performer and audience is an assignation almost explicit in its flagrant disregard of convention. The established codifications have been over-turned; there are no set ways to respond. It could be time to panic...

The performer's voice guides the audience member on a journey through the building, which, trustingly, the audience member follows, and which leads inextricably closer to the real presence of the performer. In the final part of the journey the audience member walks down a narrow corridor, at the end of which is a door with a code lock. A tall blonde woman, elegantly dressed in a black-velvet evening gown is standing outside the door. Upon the audience member's approach, the blonde woman enters the code, opens the door a crack and gently pushes the audience member through. Simultaneously she whispers to an identical tall blonde, her twin elegantly dressed in black velvet, who appears on the other side of the door. She is her exact double; the roles have become so submerged that even the physical borders have dissolved, who is who? What is what?

At the far end of the room the audience member has entered, a door-sized mirror stands surrounded by dressing room lights. A chair is positioned in front of the mirror, which the audience member is invited to sit in by the twin who then recedes to the code-lock door, once again opposite but divided from her 'exterior' twin, mirroring the experience of the audience member and performer, close, yet distant. The audience member sees only her own reflection in the brightly lit mirror, unaware that the performer in the dark on the other side is looking directly through the two-way mirror.

The performer speaks to the audience member, and the words, quoted at the beginning of this article, are at once recognizable and unfamiliar; deliberately abstract and at the same time intensely personal, as if spoken to a lover, and open to individual interpretation. The personal, intense and intimate nature of the dialogue raises the question of whether the text is in fact the *same* for each audience member. Is the journey she has just taken unique? Will the performer be 'true' to them? All the while that the audience member has been making her journey, guided by the words of the performer, the performer has been gazing at her own reflection unable to leave, to take her place on the stage. In some ways the audience member is at last in a place *familiar* to her in which to witness a performance. The room is darkened; heavy curtains block out the light, she is seated and before her is the performer. Yet, still the conventions of her role are confounded, as they have been throughout the journey. The way the mirror is framed with bare light bulbs, seems to signify the traditional theatre dressing-room mirror, the place where the performer sits before and after the show, before and after confronting the audience, where she faces her own reflection before presenting that image to another, seeing herself before she is seen. Throughout the performance the audience member has been watched on her journey, at times feeling a victim of an imagined voyeuristic gaze of the somewhere-present performer. Ironically, the only time that the performer can in fact see her, the audience member feels unseen, unwatched. The moment of visual revelation happens when the performer lights a cigarette from behind the mirror. The flame from the Zippo lighter brilliantly illuminates her face and she is visible to the audience member for the first time. 'The moment comes and goes in a whisper, in a heartbeat. A presence. An absence. Fort! Da!'

How does the audience member respond? The moment the audience member sees the performer, the vision through the looking glass presents her with an equally strong image of herself, still partially reflected in the glass. At this moment the mirror transposes the two illuminated faces on to one another, patina like, creating an almost otherworldly effect, as the performer's eyes are imprinted on the audience member's eyes, mouth on mouth, forehead on forehead. The audience member has entered a double world, through the looking glass – but whose image does she look to find? Truly, performer and audience member are meeting each other, reflected flesh on flesh, shape on shape, feature on feature.

What engenders the intimacy, the immeasurable proximity between performer and audience member is the same as what separates them. They may have shared roles, a journey, an image, but they are separate, in a moment the flame will be extinguished. Each will be left only with their own reflection. The performer created a map for the audience member to follow and yet, in taking the journey, becoming the performer, the audience member is also the pathfinder, the mapmaker. The performer directs the audience member on her journey from start to finish, but within that journey there are moments when such omnipotent control hovers in a fragile balance; when it is no longer so clear-cut who's in charge. This shifting equilibrium flows through the piece so that the sighting or meeting, when it at last occurs through the mirror, does not amount to a gaze, removed and objective from audience to performer. Rather, it is a *search* for and between both parties. It is not one detached from the other, but a merger of both.

Does the moment in the mirror, when the performer and audience member are visible to each other, create an intimacy between the two faces, layered one upon the other, reflecting the one and the other, holding one in the image of the other with a closeness and an intimacy intensified by the proximity? Such questions reformed and reasked themselves with each performance, with each image shaped on the glass. For me, they remained as questions, coaxing further performance enquiry into the levels of intimacy possible in performance. Similarly, audience feedback to the piece posited an intense and intimate relationship between performer and audience, which further encouraged me to continue with this quest of closeness:

The mirror, the mirror, the mirror I need to go through again NOW.

I experienced something so special, the focus on me was shuddering and unusually strange but beautiful.

Your voice made me feel very secure despite the potentials of great insecurity, it was fundamentally a moving moment in life.

I felt so connected, so guided, so cherished and so much as if I belonged in each moment of, I would say journey, but I feel as if

I have been immersed in the same moment wherever you led me. And now I feel bereft, now you have sent me away.

Funny, shocking, humiliating, sexy, intimate, scary, touching, heart-breaking. How do you *know*?[6]

The simplicity of the flame belies the complexities of the representations. Far from the 'limelight' that separates audience from performer, this flame is what enables them to meet; it is the heart of the piece. Yet, they meet only to say goodbye.[7] Once more the closeness holds within it a separation. The flame is blown out, the face of the performer disappears and the audience member is left staring at her own reflection once more. The journey is over.

On the Scent

On the Scent explored the relationship between smell and memory. The performances took place in homes, as domestic spaces provided a meaningful and familiar setting for work, laden with personal memories and a sense of place and identity. The performances were set in the rooms of a house where visitors are received, working in from the semi-public nature of the living room to the cozy familiarity of sitting round the kitchen table to the intimate inner sanctum of the bedside for visitors to the sick room. One performer occupied each of the three rooms, creating a smell-scape and a related narrative of personal memories and emotions for their room. Audience members experience the piece in discreet groups of no more than four at a time, to preserve the intimacy of the design and the feel of being guests in the home. The small audience numbers meant that we, as performers, maintained the ability to work in a highly personal way.

The audience group are handed the key to the house and let themselves in. They hear a voice coming from the living room. They follow the voice and enter the room. A glamorous woman in black evening dress, Lois Weaver, is in mid-flow, speaking to a camera set on record. Her impossible, compulsive project is to capture the 'essences' of moments and save them to enjoy again and again. The audience have interrupted this moment and Lois takes a moment out from her task to tell them to 'wait a moment, I have to finish this', before returning to the camera to finish recording her smell memory. This room, the space of greeting and farewell, is the scene of temptations and delayed gratifications. The smells in this room are heady with nostalgia – 'Evening in Paris', rose and violet cream chocolates, and vases dripping with heavy stems of lilies. Lois then turns her full attention on the audience, telling them that she has been waiting for them. She goes up very close to the audience and sniffs each of them, delighting in their scents.

The blurring of the borders is palpable from the start of the piece. There is no architectural distancing provided by a theatre or gallery space. The audience have entered, with their own key, someone's home and are instantly made to feel two contrasting feelings; that they have interrupted something and yet at the same time that they have been expected. The physical intimacy of Lois's greeting turns the tables again. Because of the intensely personal nature of smell a sniff can be more intimate than a kiss, it goes beyond the skin, delving deeper into the essence. It is more animal, more instinctive, distinctly primitive, and as Lois pushes her face into the neck of the audience member and takes a deep full draught of them, the feeling that things might be too close for comfort is definitely in the air:

> Sniffing and smelling, a predilection for powerful animal odours, the erotic effect of sexual odors – all become objects of suspicion. Such interests, thought to be essentially savage, attest to a proximity to animals, a lack of refinement, and ignorance of good manners.[8]

The kitchen is the next room the audience enters, where the comforting smells of home cooking begin to mix and mingle with the dangerous smells of burning. The performer, Leslie Hill, invites the audience to join her round the kitchen table and the cozy setting becomes more imbued with danger, as she talks about her native New Mexico, home of the atomic bomb, while all around them the temperature begins to rise. The audience performer borders seem as hazy as thick smoke pervades the room, so much so that when Leslie cuts five lines of red chilli powder and snorts one line through a rolled-up dollar bill, the audience members become extremely anxious as to whether they will be offered a line and how they will be able to politely refuse. From the kitchen, the audience makes their way into the most intimate room, the bedroom, where the performer, Helen Paris, lies in bed, home sick, steeped in the aroma of Dettol and Pepto Bismol. This is a room of limbo – where faintly unpleasant odours permeate and linger despite every attempt to freshen, to heal, to fend off ageing and death. The performer tosses and turns in the sheets, recounting different stories of homesickness, eventually collapsing back under the covers. When the audience enter this room, the stakes are at their highest. Chairs are positioned in a line right by the bedside of the performer. What will be expected of them in this room, the doors closed and the smells sealing the experience in?

Each performer in the piece remains in the smell-drenched environment of their own room as audience members arrive and leave to be replaced by the next group. There is no interaction between the performers either during the piece or in the moments between performances as the performances are tightly scheduled to follow on from each other. There is an isolation for the performers, each in their own room waiting for the audience members to come in. Their arrival does in a sense feel like an anticipated visit. In each room the audience are in close proximity to the performer, with the doors shut the strong smells enforcing a feeling of intimacy that is intense, almost claustrophobic. Herein lies the other side of border panic, not only is there a risk inherent in the path navigated by the audience member when borders are disrupted, but the performer is also presented with her own sense of fear. Affected by the inescapable sickening smell of Dettol that clung to the bed sheets, my clothes and my skin, the airlessness of the room there was a sense of comfort when the audience arrived and at the same time a sense of anxiety. The closeness of their presence to me in the bed was intense. This room that I inhabited all day, for large periods alone, felt very much like my own space, my own bedroom and the entrance of the audience into it distinctly personal.

It is interesting to note that in the early performances of *On the Scent* the audience numbers were restricted to two at a time, and then later during the tour increased to four which, in comparison, suddenly seemed like a big audience. Having just two people in the audience felt, at times, too close for comfort for the performers as well as for the audience members themselves. Increasing the number to four made the performance less intimidating which allowed for a more relaxed, open experience both for audience and performer.

In the final stage of their journey, the audience members return to the living room where the performer seems to have been expecting them: 'There you are. Come over here and sit down. Now you need to give me something before you go. A little something to keep me going. Something personal.' She asks them to tell her of a smell that makes them think about home, or makes them feel homesick, or just makes them feel sick and carefully records and labels each memory. Through these interviews, an archive of smell memories and associations is formed as the work tours, with each audience member contributing to the growing collection – imbuing it with something of their own essence. The audience members, although usually strangers to each other, form a kind of solidarity as they journey through the house and this is fully realized in this final part of the performance when they share their own smell memories not only with Lois, but also with each other. As they tell their stories, the audience members are performers to the camera and each other and their own 'smell memory' becomes a part of the show they have just experienced. As with *Vena Amoris* the audience member becomes the performer and their action is the action of the performance. Audiences to *On the Scent* described the experience as being very personal and intimate. After experiencing the journey through the house, taking in an intense variety of smells and hearing the various stories from the performers, audience members described how satisfying it was to be given the opportunity to share their own smell memories and hear those of their fellow audience members. Although unnerved by having to face the camera, audience members described a sense of relief in being able to respond to what they had witnessed and share their own memories.

As with *Vena Amoris* there was a desire on the part of the audience to be reassured that the experience in the house, the closeness they had felt to the performers and the stories they had shared with them had been unique and special, just for them. At the end of *On the Scent*, the audience leaves the house and hands over the key to the next waiting audience group, often triggering a certain anxiety. There was a need for reassurance that it was not too boring for the performers to repeat the performance so many times, the fear that they were perhaps the unwanted guest at the end of a long day of 'entertaining'. In reality the act of repeating the show eight times a day for eight different audience groups made for a very intense performance experience as each new audience group imbued the piece with their own different energies and dynamics.

The border crossings and levels of intimacy in *On the Scent* are not only to do with the proximity of the performers to the audience and the closeness of the domestic environment and personal nature of the stories shared, but by the elusive, emotive nature of smell itself. Smell is a dexterous border crosser, traversing and transgressing boundaries; 'Smells resist containment in discrete units, whether physical or linguistic; they cross boundary lines.'[9] Smell is placeless, ephemeral, unpindownable and at the same time, smell can transport us back to a moment in our past more vividly than any other of the senses. The confines and delineations of time are crossed, as it seems to play no role in odour memory. People, places and events from the past are relocated as clearly and vibrantly as if they existed in the present. The body is transported through time and space as moments are re-experienced and relived. Smell does not keep behind the lines and in this way is like one-to-one performance, wherein the codifications are gone and the barriers are down; 'you really had to be there' goes one step further to become 'you really had to breathe there'.

Deserter

The experience of the one-to-one audience – performer contact, its 'nearness', the mix of tension and intimacy it engendered was addictive. The question was: could this intimacy be integrated within the format of a 'regular' theatre piece? The artistic desire within *Deserter* was to maintain some of the intimacy of one-to-one performance within the structure of a theatre piece for a larger audience in a black box theatre space. *Deserter* was made for the studio theatre of the newly reopened Project Art Centre in Dublin. The piece was designed to play to an audience of 40 and to contain within it two moments of one-to-one interaction.

In *Deserter* the border panic was very deliberately orchestrated as exits and entrances were disguised, sealed, misleading. A large black door was built in the corridor through which the audience usually entered the theatre. The door did not open into the theatre, as all external appearances suggested it might, but instead into a confessional box. However this was a confessional box with a difference. The space the audience member stepped into was narrow, the walls bright pinewood like the inside of a sauna. There was a discernable heat, intensifying the sauna-like atmosphere. The floor was covered with white sand, evoking the landscape of the desert.

For a moment the audience member stands in this hot box, alone, disorientated by the light and the heat, a little claustrophobic, realizing the door that they entered from has shut automatically and does not open from the inside. Unable to see a way out, things start to feel very definitely too close for comfort. There is a sudden rasping sound as a discreet shutter in the wall of the box is slid to the side. The wire slats of a confessional grille criss-cross the opening and through them, ghostly and fragmented due to the sharp contrast of light and dark, the face of the performer can be seen, as if suspended in the blackness. It is the performer who confesses to the audience member, whispered, fast, intense, in an address that is personal, direct, and which presumes an expectation, a knowledge and an intimacy. Then, the confession over, the performer slowly slides the grille closed.

One by one the audience 'desert' each other and disappear through the black door through which they do not return. The audience members witness this gradual disappearance of their fellow spectators. In this way each audience member has a slightly different experience of the piece, depending on when they entered the performance. The first audience member enters the auditorium from the confessional box. A red running track stretches the length of the space and ends in a long jump pit. Two microphone stands are positioned diagonally across the space. At one of them is the other performer, Leslie Hill. As soon as the audience member enters the auditorium Leslie walks towards a stack of chairs, removes one and carries it into the space, positioning it facing the running track. On the chair is a card with a question. Leslie invites the audience member to sit, takes the paper, returns to the mike and reads out the question. The audience member is not sure as to whether they are supposed to answer the question and it hangs in the silence as performer and audience wait for the next audience member to exit the confessional box. There is a shift as the audience member slips into the safety of their role and watches the performance of the next audience member entering the space, a little unsure, blinking after the sharp light of the confessional, and sees them handed their seat and hears them being read their question. And then there are two . . . and so on.

Gradually the auditorium fills up, as the audience watches the process of the audience entering, seeing in each other that moment of transfer between being an audience and being a performer as they enter the auditorium from the confessional box. Each person is positioned at a distance from the next, either side of the running track, illuminated by tiny pinpricks of light. In this way the audience remain a little isolated from each other, like islands throughout the piece, echoing the moment of aloneness at the very start in the confessional. It is not clear to the audience members if they have each had the same experience in the confessional. The questions asked of each one of them by Leslie are all different, so potentially the private one-to-one experience has also been different. The text in the confessional is deliberately worded as if it were spoken just to them. Is the intimacy in *Deserter* less intimate because it is repeated verbatim to each audience member who passes through? Does the performer 'perform' intimacy? Are her words meaningless, or indeed her confessions true?

In *Vena Amoris* the mirror moment is simultaneously a moment of meeting and leaving and likewise in the confessional moment, the face behind the grille seems disembodied, placeless, intimate and distant at the same time. Close and distant. Placed and placeless. In both performances there is literally a border between audience and performer; the glass of the two-way mirror or the wooden panel and grille in the confessional box. And each time this border is made, for a moment, permeable to allow performer and audience to meet. There is a certain amount of trust that happens in this moment between audience member and performer. The performer needs to trust that the audience will stay with them in the moment, that they will not try and flee from the encounter, knowing that, despite the claustrophobia, heat and intimacy of the confessional box, the performer will protect them. After having had such an intimate moment with the performer, the audience member has to then share her with the rest of the audience for the duration of the performance. In turn, the performer has the very particular experience of coming out into the auditorium with the experience of having met with and spoken to each one of the audience who now watch her. It is not the usual circumstance of a sea of unfamiliar faces in the theatre; the performer now can recognize each of the audience members.

The end of *Deserter* mirrors the beginning of the piece as the audience members leave the auditorium one by one. This leaving also takes the form of a one-to-one interaction, this time not via confession but by a communion with the other performer. Leslie kneels at the edge of the long jump pit and brushes aside the white sand to reveal a bottle of Tequila, 40 shot glasses and a box of lime slices. The final ingredient for this cocktail is salt, which is revealed to be in the presumed sand of the long jump pit. The audience members come up one at a time, kneel facing Leslie and take the communion. As they do so their chair is removed and they are shown out through another door on the opposite side of the auditorium from which they entered. Slowly the chairs are removed and stacked as the audience members leave and finally the space is as it was when the audience first entered it, deserted.

In each of the performances described, the proximity and nature of the relationship between audience member and performer is challenged. The arc of the experience encompasses discomfort and comfort, nearness and isolation, vulnerability and a sense of being protected, cared for, loved. The intensity of experience in one-to-one performance is felt not just by the audience member but also by the performer. Negotiating the boundaries of how close is too close is a constantly shifting journey. In both *Vena Amoris* and *Deserter* there are screens that form some sort of barrier between performer and audience in the one-to-one encounter, the mirror, the grille. Ultimately the screens are revealed as permeable membranes that reveal performer to audience member. Unlike the one-to-one interactivity of digital technologies where the screen is both portal and partition, in the live encounter there is no way out.

The screens allow both a closeness and a distancing. In different ways each of these pieces experimented with different levels of closeness possible in live performance. Ultimately it is by maintaining a level of separation that a more tangible closeness can form. The distancing device of the phone in *Vena Amoris* actually made the connection between performer and audience member seem closer. Similarly the combination of the very intimate one-to-one confessional moment alongside the less specific, shared audience experience in *Deserter* accentuated different levels of performer/audience contact possible. Too close for comfort is when the gap between performer and audience is closed to such an extent that there is no longer any space left for possibility, for communication, for silence, for the unknown. Looking up at the overwhelming movement, colour and image on the ceiling of the Sistine Chapel the eye focuses itself on the tiny gap; the place wherein creation is possible, the fraction of space that lets the mind wander and wonder. The space in which anything, everything is possible and which draws the viewer in closer and closer.

Come closer. There is nowhere to hide. There is nowhere to hide, baby. Nowhere but in my arms.

Notes

1   A Curious production supported by Artsadmin, 1999.
2   A Curious production supported by the Wellcome Trust and ACE, 2004.
3   A Curious production commissioned by Project Arts Centre, Dublin 2000.
4   This situation can be seen in some ways to be reflective of the work and ideas formulated by Brazilian theatre director Augusto Boal, who used interactive techniques to transform theatre into a dialogue between audience and performer. Here, in Boalian terms, the audience member has become spect-actor, the single entity that embraces both functions within a single body.
5   P. Levinson, *Soft Edge: A Natural History and Future of the Information Revolution* (New York: Routledge, 1997), p.66.
6   Selection of audience members' comments left in comment book after performance of *Vena Amoris* at Toynbee Studios, London.
7   Luce Irigary writes: 'I see myself in the mirror as if I were an other.' Here the dynamic for the audience member is simultaneously one of difference *and* sameness: 'Between the other in the mirror and the other who inverts me, there is also the other of the same, at once closer and more distant.' L. Irigary, *An Ethics of Sexual Difference* (New York: Cornell University Press, 1993), pp.170–1
8   A. Corbin, *The Foul and The Fragrant: Odour and the Social Imagination* (London: Picador, 1997), p.7.
9   C. Classen, *Aroma: The Cultural History of Smell* (London: Routledge, 1995), p.204.

16
Parallel Power: Shakespeare, Gunfire and Silence

Paul Heritage

How many shantytowns – *favelas* – are there in Rio de Janeiro? It's the sort of question that defies the town planner as much as the tourist. Just one more mystery that Rio de Janeiro refuses to reveal. Recent estimates talk of more than 600 *favelas* on the hillsides and borderlands of the city. Over 600 places that are outside the official geography of the city. Over 600 communities improvised and named by their own inhabitants. Over 600 territories occupied illegally by 20 per cent of the urban population.

The forces and processes that make up Rio de Janeiro originate beyond the physical and political construction of the city. The *favelas* have for a long time formed an influential part of the city's mythology as well as its reality. For the first half of the twentieth century, the hillside communities were often celebrated as a source of the poetry and musicality of the city, idealized for the dignity of a harmonious life. The unsustainability of such myths is ever apparent today in the face of the social exclusion and extreme poverty of so many of those who live there. The relationship between the *favela* and the rest of the city can no longer be characterized as a source of inspiration, but of fear.

In this chapter I will describe the making of a performance project, the staging of a Shakespeare play, within the context of not only the practical but also the emblematic difficulties of Rio de Janeiro's *favelas*. I will attempt to describe the processes by which cultural work negotiated a temporary and largely symbolic cessation of conflict in a place where the usual regulatory means and social structures have failed. Where the active participants, both the agents of the state and many of those who oppose them, have turned to violence as a discourse and a method.

There are certain dynamics of geography and history that seem to feed a vision of Rio de Janeiro both as Paradise and Inferno. In the early

1990s the Brazilian social commentator Zuenir Ventura used the term *Cidade Partida*, divided city, as a title for a book about Rio's racial, social, political and cultural exclusions, and it has become a persuasive paradigm to imagine the sometime capital and perpetual gateway to Brazil. Ventura's thesis is that the planning of the city in the twentieth century facilitated the urban elite's desire for separation following the disappearance of the absolute segregations made possible under slavery. The book was published in the wake of a series of violent acts in the early nineties that brought international attention to Rio's problems, precisely because they happened in the areas that the middle-class elite had reserved for itself. The book *Cidade Partida*, while conceptualizing the divided city, was borne out of a moment in which the separate worlds had collided and the concept itself was in danger of collapsing. The violence had come down from the hillsides and left blood on the pavements and beaches of those areas that thought themselves immune.

In the decade since the book was first published, events have served both to intensify the image of the *Cidade Partida*, but also to question its major assumptions. At the same time as it so distinctively marked out the division, the book reveals the inadequacy of the paradigm. The image effectively masks the social divisions and cultural diversity of the city that are also to be found within the *favelas*, and the extent to which the divisions of the *favela* are repeated across the city. The danger of the paradigm is that the complex fragmentation of Rio de Janeiro is subsumed into one overriding partition, and the *favelas* become the 'other' of the city itself. They are outside the city proper and become subject to a discourse whereby division can only be healed if the *favela* can be recuperated by the municipal authorities. Although little progress is made towards such an end, it remains a part of the rhetoric of successive political and civic actions, including those to which Ventura looks for the reconciliation of the two supposed halves of the city. At the point that he invokes the divide, Ventura must also imagine the city as a site of potential integration or incorporation. In announcing the staging of Shakespeare on the fissures of the fragmented city, we seemed to be caught in the same irresistible paradigm, proposing by implication that boundaries would be crossed and divisions might be healed.

The residents of Rio experience their city in what might be described as a hybrid condition, as both witnesses of the social divisions and daily collaborators in their maintenance. Individual and collective acts of resistance are difficult to register or to codify. Although not everyone may experience the effects in direct or brutal ways, it is difficult to conceive of a life lived in Rio without reference to the violence and divisions that have come to characterize the city. The project that I will discuss was just one more attempt to reject the assimilation into the state of siege that has become a way of living in Rio de Janeiro, even while acknowledging that it seems increasingly difficult to think and act outside the framing of the opposition between *asfalto* (the official paved city) and the *favela*.

If the *favela* is conceived as being outside the city, then any entry to it involves the crossing of a certain border. These frontiers to the city's extremities are maintained by both the official and unofficial forces and are as concrete as they are also conceptual: access roads are subject to stop and search 'blitzes' by the military police and the immediate points of entry to the *favelas* are at least monitored and often 'secured' by armed *soldados*, the soldiers of the drug gangs. The divided city is very visibly maintained by these rival powers, but the inadequacy of the bifurcation is experienced in the commonality of the experience of being subject to both the forces of law and disorder. Thus the *favela* is not so much outside the city of Rio de Janeiro, but the most powerful signifier of the experience of living there. And how can anyone in this city know which side they are on? The implication of the police in the violence of the *favelas* disturbs the sense of security that might be expected to accompany interactions with agents of the state. The arbitrary and excessive way in which the police force has exercised its power has been graphically shown by research from CESeC (Centre for the Study of Public Security and Citizenship), Julita Lemgruber's research centre at the University of Candido Mendes. Meanwhile, the complicity in maintaining those boundaries for all those who live in the city, indicates the impossibility of a division based on innocence or guilt.

The image of the *cidade partida* – the divided city – is tied closely to another imagining: the notion of a 'parallel power' that frames the negotiations of the city. The abdication of civic responsibility for these excluded zones is overlaid by a strong sense that there is another power that rules on the other side of the divide: the drug gangs. While there has been a proliferation in the number of the *favelas*, there has been a concentration of the drug-trafficking into three main gangs: the *Comando Vermelho* (Red Command), the *Terceiro Comando* (Third Command) and *Amigos dos Amigos* (Friends of Friends). Rio has suffered two decades of territorial wars between the *Comando Vermelho* and the *Terceiro Comando* with the smaller and more recent ADA (Friends of

Friends) making inroads into traditional strongholds of the two more established factions. As a gang takes over the drug-trading within a *favela*, thus the supposition is that control of the *favela* itself passes to one or other of the gangs. The identity of the separate communities is therefore doubly lost. First of all an area with a distinct name and its own separate geographical and social features is categorized simply as a *favela*. Then it is subsumed into the identity of one of the drug factions. The residents are identified as being in allegiance to the faction that has taken control of the drug trade in their neighborhood, regardless of the absence of intention of the traffickers to assume any of the other aspects of the social infrastructure.

Myths abound about the beneficence of the drug barons: their distribution of basic food parcels, their support of leisure activities, their assistance in medical emergencies, their 'protection' of the community, and so on. But in no sense can they be seen to be providing alternative civic services, nor can their conflict with the forces of the state be characterized as a war in the traditional sense in which one side wants to replace the other. The gangs seek neither to represent their communities against the state nor to substitute the fragments of the legitimate authority within these communities, rather they simply and terrifyingly take any action necessary to protect their market in drugs.

While the history of those who live in the *favelas* is marked out by a refusal to accept the ways in which they are characterized by the places they inhabit, the strength of the stigmatization is pervasive. The last two decades have seen a rise in *favela*-based movements that challenge the notion that these communities are simply places of criminality, and offer positive identifications linked to these sites. However, it should not be a surprise that in the contemporary cultural manifestations that have emerged from the *favelas*, the emphasis is on partition and exclusion. Hip-Hop, Funk and Rap offer powerful reminders of unresolved urban conflicts and form part of what has been termed the 'sociability of violence' that characterizes Rio de Janeiro. The cultural forms that have emerged as part of that sociability are in turn denominated by their relation to the dominance of the *narco-cultura*. These contemporary musical forms – and the clothes, hair, attitude, tattoos, graffiti that accompany them – have become both a part of dialogue within these communities and also made their way down the hillsides, away from the peripheries and into the fabric of the 'official' city.

The music that had previously followed the route from the margins to the centre has for decades been seen as part of a homogenizing process by which potentially explosive urban divisions could be disguised or avoided. Thus samba is traditionally seen as emerging from the *favelas*, but it has found its place as part of the official cultural identity of the city of Rio and subsequently of the national patrimony. At some level, however fictional and retrospective, samba and the processes associated with the annual carnival allowed people from diverse socio-economic backgrounds to assume common cultural associations. In seeking proximity to the site of production and the authenticity of the cultural experience, those who lived in the 'official city' found a reason to enter the *favela* and visit the samba schools which were in turn increasingly situated at the edges of their own communities for easy access for those from outside.

In contrast, the musical forms and cultural production of the last two decades have been divisive rather than homogenizing. Rather than simply marking out a supposed duality of the Divided City, contemporary cultural production within the *favelas* reflects the fragmentation of the communities themselves and marks out new urban divisions that the old paradigms do not contain. Whereas samba and its related art form of carnival was a cultural and social process that might be seen to unite, funk, hip-hop and rap are potentially divisive within families, local communities and the city itself. At the same time as such forms potentially create disassociations within the *favela*, they open up new allegiances across other urban partitions through the familiar mechanisms of youth culture.

Narco-cultura, and the transit it establishes between *favela* and the formal fabric of urban life, has as important a role to play in the breaking of the duality of the Divided City as the marketing and consumption of the drugs themselves. Almost inevitably the products of *narco-cultura* blur the relationship between the licit and the illicit so that the song, the film, the t-shirt, the street talk, the physical attitude each mark out an undefined relationship to the drug-trafficking where it is impossible to identify the extent of the contamination. Indeed, it is often the allure of the illicit that marks the potency of the cultural manifestation. These cultural products form part of a continuum that includes funk songs banned from city radios because of the promotion of particular gangs, through to an international success such as the film *Cidade de Deus*.

City of God might be described as the best-known product of Rio's *narco-cultura*. It is a film that has no financial or ideological link to the drug trade or the gangs, but its visual and aural aesthetic is deeply rooted in the *favela*. It is marketable because it is an extremely well made film made by a talented artistic team and promoted by some of

Brazil's leading media players. But it is also a successful commodity because of its declared intention to bring its audience into contact with the hidden worlds of the drug gangs and the *favelas*. The identification of the author and some of the young cast with the communities that are dominated by the narco-traffic was an important mark of the film's 'authenticity'. It depended on its own emergence from, and links to, that *narco-cultura* as much as it needed to mark its legitimacy through its distance from it.

Growing alongside and in response to the same sources as the *narco-cultura* has been the development of cultural initiatives that are almost exclusively generated by NGOs (non-governmental organizations). Such cultural production is constantly marked as being outside the normal arts framework and sometimes negatively characterized as being part of the fashion for art at the service of a social agenda. It frequently remains marginalized as much by its origin within non-governmental initiatives as it does by its emergence from, and links to, the world of the *favela*. As its existence is defined at those margins, there is no obvious imperative to bring the work to an imaginary centre. The challenge that remains is how to create art that rearticulates the margins and the centre within new dynamic social and cultural practices.

The Brazilian sociologist Candido Grzybowski has asked if it is possible that the city of Rio de Janeiro can be a 'sphere in which the differences function as an engine of democratic transformation, and not as a form of exclusion of some people and the domination of the few over the rest?'. Is it possible that cultural mechanisms can find ways to answer that call? Is it possible to create moments of resistance to the seemingly persistent ways in which Rio de Janeiro and its diverse communities are imagined? How can we negotiate the real and imagined borders and at the same time challenge their existence?

From April to July 2004, I directed a project called *Amor em tempos de guerra – Love in Time of War –* across four contrasting neighborhoods of Rio de Janeiro. I worked with the Cultural Group Afroreggae and several of Brazil's most popular television stars to produce two Shakespeare plays which have almost never been performed in Brazil: *Measure for Measure* and *Antony and Cleopatra*. In reflecting now on the process of staging the plays, it is not so much the productions that I am interested in talking about as the negotiations around place, access and borders that arose through the practical concerns of making artistic work in these locations. Negotiations with those who control and secure spaces and people: drug-traffickers and military policemen, city officials and TV directors, politicians and preachers, film stars and community artists. The project was an attempt to create a sphere in which the differences could function as a means of transformation, albeit in the temporal and phantasmic realm of performance.

In naming the project *Love in Time of War*, I was aware that I entered a polemical debate about the characteristics of the violence that dominates Rio de Janeiro. For some commentators the ethnic and economic origins of this conflict mark it out as civil war in all but name, for others the term is not helpful as it does not adequately reflect the reality of the situation. What is undeniable is that the levels of firearm-related mortality rates are characteristic of conflicts that elsewhere we recognize as territorial warfare. Every year Brazil loses almost the same number of citizens to death by small-arms, as the number of American soldiers who died in all the years of the Vietnam War. Silvia Ramos from CESeC has shown that

> Comparative analyses with countries that are at war or in situations of intense conflict conclude that over the same time periods there were more firearm-related deaths in the city of Rio de Janeiro than in the armed conflicts in Angola (1998–2000), Sierra Leone (1991–1999), Yugoslavia (1998–2000), Afghanistan (1991–1999) or Israel (1991–1999).

As in any 'real' war, children figure high in the number of fatalities. In the conflict between Israel and Palestine, 467 under-18-year-olds were shot dead between 1987 and 2001. Research undertaken by the NGO Viva Rio, shows that during the same period in the city of Rio de Janeiro, 3937 under 18-year-olds were killed as a result of small-arms combat.

Seventy per cent of Brazilian murder victims are aged between 15 and 24. These young people are not evenly distributed amongst the general population. They are usually young men who have not completed first-grade education, live in marginal urban areas, and are of Afro-Brazilian descendency. While public discussion of the incidence of the violence is clearly important to the way in which the war or non-war is prosecuted, neither the discourses nor the data are literal reproductions of real events, but a series of social practices. The cultural interventions that we as artists propose are just another such social practice. In the project *Love in Time of War*, the 'war' announced in the title is ambivalently poised between the Shakespeare play of *Antony and Cleopatra* and the contexts in which it was performed in Rio de Janeiro. The legitimacy of the declaration of war by us as artists required neither sociological data, anthropological analysis nor political contingency. The power of art to model and modulate our vision of ourselves was the justification taken, and forms part of the inversion of the discourse of power that is at the heart of such projects. To speak about love in time of war and conflict was the aim of the project. To define the act of performance as an act of love and to take it on to the battlegrounds of Rio was intended both to invert the social practices of theatre and its confinements as well as the discourses that control the ways in which we negotiate the city and its violence. The perverse processes by which the performance was able to take place, the negotiations and their consequences, the success and the failure of the project, all in different ways contributed to those inversions.

Rocinha, Vigário Geral, Parada de Lucas and Leblon. Three *favelas* plus one of the iconic neighborhoods in the rich Southern Zone. Rocinha – the largest *favela* in Latin America with over 200,000 inhabitants – follows the classic pattern of the intricate and high-density communities that cling to the mountainsides in the Southern Zone. Vigário Geral and Parada de Lucas emerged in the bleak Northern suburbs in the 1950s between a railway line and a mango swamp, and unlike the hillside *favelas* they are both entirely flat. And Leblon? Well, it's a neighbourhood that borders the beach of Ipanema where that Girl went walking and all the men went 'aaaagh!'. It is home to some of Brazil's richest inhabitants, a narrow strip of very expensive real estate between the lake and the sea, where theatre takes place in shopping malls with air-conditioning and security guards.

Crossings were built into the structure of the project. Both the plays were to be presented in each of the neighbourhoods across a three-month period, with performances on Monday nights in the *favelas* and Tuesday/Wednesday nights in Teatro Leblon. Free buses and tickets were arranged for residents from five different *favelas* to see the plays in the Southern Zone instead of inside one of their own communities. Thus we attempted to disrupt the ghettoizing that occurs with attempts to launch cultural activities in marginal spaces. Although the actors all lived in the official city neighbourhoods, the musicians came from the *favela* of Vigário Geral. For three months, artists, technicians, producers, critics and audience were making contrasting journeys that cut through the sharply defined and often treacherous landscape of Rio de Janeiro.

This was never more clearly articulated than on the opening night, which took place on 8 June 2004 on the border between Vigário Geral and Parada de Lucas. These two communities are distinctive in the social geography of Rio because they are one of the key sites where neighboring *favelas* are dominated by rival gang factions. Of all the many borders that divide this city – social, economic, racial, political, religious, geographic – this is a frontier that is recognized as one of the most explosive and violent and ultimately uncrossable. The enmity between the two communities arose before the emergence of the current gang formations. They had not been good neighbours at the best of times, and this has been exploited and defined by the drug-traffickers since the 1980s. The story that everyone indicates as the catalyst of outright warfare between the two sides starts with a football match 22 years ago in which teams from both communities were playing against each other. A drawn game on the scrubland pitch at the border was being decided by a penalty shoot-out. Vigário's goalkeeper saved the final penalty, securing victory for his team, but with the ball still clasped in his hands he was shot dead by someone from Lucas. Residents from both sides point to this moment as the beginning of their 'state of war'.

These two *favelas* are linked and also divided by one narrow track of about 200 metres, guarded at each end by adolescents with semi-automatic rifles and a variety of hand pistols. On one side of the border track is a row of houses and in the middle of these, a police station. On the other side is a school that young people from both communities attend, with entrances at different points in the fence. The frontier is known locally as the Gaza Strip. Gunfire during the day is not common, but at night this border zone becomes a shooting gallery. As I was informed on my first visit, if a dog ventured there at night, it would be shot by both sides.

I was taken to the border for the first time one night in April 2004 by Vitor, the 24-year-old community co-ordinator of the Cultural Group Afroreggae. Formed in 1993, after 21 residents of Vigário Geral were massacred by the police, Afroreggae has achieved national recognition for their inspirational work in taking young people out of the drug-trafficking. Gilberto Gil, Brazilian music icon and currently Minister of Culture, is just one of the many international music stars who make regular appearances with Afroreggae not only in *favelas*, but also on stages in New York, Paris, London and later this year in Haiti.

It is difficult to describe Afroreggae without romanticizing them as heroes within this war. Perhaps one should not even try to resist. They are acknowledged as such within their own communities and also in certain segments of civil society that looks to them as an indicator that we could dare to hope for a different outcome to the conflict. The heroism that I locate in the artists of Afroreggae belongs perhaps to the nature of the territory in which these conflicts are fought. Luiz Eduardo Soares, former State Secretary for Public Security in Rio de Janeiro, has written of life in the *favelas* as being reminiscent of feudal warfare:

The masculine hegemony is affirmed in the supremacy of courage and loyalty, which has always been restricted to the arts of war, and to a hierarchized environment exclusive to the group itself, which enforces an explosive situation of fratricidal factionalism.

These values are precisely those that modern society has supposedly abandoned in favour of a world which recognizes, at a certain level, the equality of human beings. Elsewhere the war-lord's authority has been replaced by that of the individual and the citizen, a world in which politics, civic administration and psychology govern lives. But these Brazilian urban borderlands still belong to a pre-modern world, where control is exercised according to violent suppression and the rule of the gun.

If anyone should doubt the mortal conflicts between the law-enforcer and the bandits at these borderlands, the homicide rates for Rio de Janeiro will give the brutal picture. Rio de Janeiro registered 6624 homicides in the year 2003. Of those, over 1195 were killed by the police. That is 18 people a day killed in the State, eight people per day killed in the city, over three people a day killed by the police. I noted above that it is important to take note of who is dying, but it is equally important to remember where these deaths take place. Almost none of those deaths are registered in the middle-class areas such as Copacabana or Ipanema. Despite the panic felt at times by tourists visiting the city, the Southern Zone – with its world-famous beaches – has a homicide rate equivalent to Sweden or Norway. It is on the frontier lands – beyond the boundaries of the city itself and yet deep within it – that young men are dying. Carlos Calchi, a workshop leader for People's Palace Projects and artistic collaborator with Afroreggae, was just one of those 6624 people to be murdered in that year of 2003. In running a project in a youth detention centre in the northern Rio suburbs, Carlos crossed those frontiers and was shot dead in the borderlands.

As both the personal and public responsibility for the excess of violence and death in Rio de Janeiro has been so impossibly blurred, and the villains have become irredeemably confused, we can surely be forgiven for wanting to look for heroes. Mythical figures of a pre-modern world.

What secured my safety as I stood that night with Vitor on the frontier, and through the next three months of the Shakespeare project, was the respect that the rival gangs hold for the daily work that is done by Afroreggae with young people in the *favelas*. As I was to discover on the nights and days spent at the frontier during the preparations for the production, the artists of Afroreggae have created from within their frame a means of being warriors for peace. In terms perhaps more familiar in a British context, they are the principal mediators within their communities. They have established clear ways of talking to the highest levels of the drug factions and of negotiating from a position of strength with the 'soldiers' on the ground. Those brief minutes on the frontline in April were to develop across the weeks into a full cease-fire for seven days to allow our company to set up a stage for the opening performance on that very borderline that had been for so long a total no-go zone.

In creating a project in which we would mount two Shakespeare productions in three different *favelas*, I had failed to make some basic calculations about the lack of public space in such communities. There is none. Public space is not created when communities emerge in a haphazard manner based on individual need within collective territorial development. It was only in the frustration of not finding an indoor public space that Junior, the director of Afroreggae, raised the idea of staging the opening production on the no-man's land between the two *favelas*. The fact that no one ever went there would, he argued, give us a clear goal for the project. Junior set the challenge: if ten people went out on to that frontier to watch Shakespeare then we would be successful.

The rest followed according to the impossible logic of Rio de Janeiro. Despite the city authorities' historic absence from any regular commitment to civic services in these communities, the Mayor's office agreed to build a stage more appropriate to a rock concert for a one-off performance. They replaced the shot-out lights in the lamp-posts, provided chemical toilets and seating and, under careful instructions from Afroreggae, invented the necessary infrastructure for the staging of *Antony and Cleopatra* on the border.

None of this would have been possible without a series of negotiations, including nightly meetings in different and secret locations with the local leaders of the drug gangs. From within the communities, the image of the 'parallel powers' that supposedly govern the city began to seem inadequate. A fundamental property of parallel lines is that they never converge, whereas Rio has complex networks involving the civic powers and these who hold the AK-47s. Working with Afroreggae I learnt to interweave and cross a world in which nothing was parallel and everything was delicately intersected and interdependent. In official *carioca* terms, all the conversations we had in order to facilitate the project were regarded as 'impossible' – conversations that could never and would never happen. No one talks about talking to drug-traffickers.

Our night-time conversations with the gangs were mostly about practicalities. They control an immense and highly profitable movement of guns and drugs on a daily basis and they needed to work out how they could guarantee protection for their business within the context of a cease-fire. How would they know who was coming into their community? What if the other side used the opportunity to launch an attack? In another part of the equation, there were different business interests to be protected. I was called to meetings with Luis Erlanger, executive director of TV Globo, the fourth largest commercial television company in the world. Some of Globo's most important stars were acting in these two plays, and Erlanger wanted guarantees about the cast's safety. His investment.

But who could give security assurances in an area in which the civic authorities have so little legitimacy? Thomas Hobbes argument in the seventeenth century that civic order depends on a mutual relation between protection and obedience would indicate the potential fragility of our proposal. Erlanger was well aware that the area in which our project was to take place is given no protection by the state, and therefore we could expect no obedience to the norms of citizenship and order. The city and state authorities are at political war with each other, and at a meeting called by Globo they showed there was little prospect of a co-ordinated response. The most that could be extracted from the forces of 'order' was a promise that there would be no police presence in the vicinity of either community on the night of the play. Once police action was removed as a potential threat to security, Globo produced free television advertisements for the project and airtime for coverage of the performance. The combination of these actors and William Shakespeare at this particular frontier was news.

Despite the low-level goal that we had originally set ourselves – success judged on the presence of 10 people in the audience – we put out 400 chairs for the opening night. There was no way of knowing who, if anyone, would come. Using the established promotional strategies of the *favela*, we hired a car with a sound-system to drive through the tight streets of both communities for six hours per day for a week before the performance, broadcasting the title, the all-star cast list and a one-minute sound-bite version of *Antony and Cleopatra*. Everyone in Vigário and Lucas knew of the loss of an empire for the love of a woman.

Over 2000 people from both communities came to the opening night, putting their faith on the line in ways that I could never have imagined. As Afroreggae fired out the final drumming sequence that completed their live musical accompaniment to the performance, the cheering echoed across the frontier where gunfire had for so long been the only sound.

For some of the cast, the night was a triumph. For many of them, the performance was a disaster. The audience walked around, talked to each other, laughed and pointed noisily at everything that took place. Feeling cut off from direct contact with the audience by their radio-microphones and the brutalities of a stage more appropriate for rock concerts, the actors found it impossible to gauge reactions. For the audience, the evening was unlike anything that had happened before – a unique, bewildering, fantastical event. Both collectively and individually members of both *favelas* showed their enjoyment graphically during the performance and in the following days when I returned. What the actors feared to be inattention on the part of the audience could be read in many ways, not least as a profound excitement to be part of the event and a consequent desire to participate. The photographs and video shot from the stage on the night show rapt but never silent attention of the audience.

When the performance finished, the Third Command, who control Parada de Lucas, launched a blazing and unexpected fireworks display that shot through the night sky. A tribute and an appreciation of the event, but which led to panic in the cast. The Red Command from Vigário Geral had no fireworks on hand, so they replied by shooting their pistols and semi-automatic rifles into the air, which intensified the fear and sent actors and guests diving to the floor. The Reuters news report for that night which was headlined 'Shakespeare Silences the Guns' could not have been less accurate. Shakespeare set them a-blazing. As ever, Afroreggae negotiated the safe exit of the cast as the audience split back festively to their separate spaces in each community.

When did our story finish? The performance launched a project called PARADA GERAL in which People's Palace Projects runs daily drama and animation workshops for adolescents in both communities. The city council initiated a series of weekly play activities on the frontier, with team sports, bouncy castles, music and organized games. Afroreggae moved the rehearsals for two of their bands to the frontier and have continued to act as mediators between the two gangs.

And the cease-fire? It held for 18 days in total: seven days before and 11 days after that single performance. No one was prepared for such a result. We were kept informed by both sides about when the cease-fire would break, and it did so with a shot from one of the young men across the frontier, catching the leg of another adolescent on the opposite side. The battle recommenced. It was not reported anywhere in the news. There was no story.

Love in Time of War was just one passing project in the growing catalogue of arts activities that are being orientated towards social problems in Brazil and beyond. As state expenditures on the non-commercial arts are reduced, artists and arts managers have looked to other areas of financial support, most noticeably the funds that are available for addressing social issues. Whether it is in the fight against racism, the resolution of conflict, the renewal of the urban landscape, the reverse of economic decline, the rescue of lives lost to crime and delinquency, the arts internationally are being directly harnessed and indirectly celebrated in ways that challenge many of the notions on which our western cultural landscape has been based. In doing so, a power is invoked that runs in parallel to the economic and aesthetic factors that have been marked out as determining artistic success. What the arts can *do* has moved from the implicit to the explicit, as the management of social crises is increasingly seen as a validating purpose for artists in the new millennium.

The arts have found a new means of productivity that can be formalized into a social practice within the so-called Third Sector. Theatre companies, galleries, orchestras, and artist collectives have been reconstituted as NGOs. This has created a new cultural economy, where value has shifted from what the art work *is* to what the art work *does*. Despite the difficulties of agreeing the indicators of success within areas of social justice, the performativity of the arts is being measured in a borrowed vocabulary that in turn remodels artistic practices and our perceptions of them. The cast of *Antony and Cleopatra* felt the tensions at play in this new matrix, as each of us struggled to understand the significance of what we had done on one night in June last year. By certain criteria, using respectable qualitative and quantitative data, the performance could have been described as an unparalleled success. And yet the actors' sense of frustration and anxiety in terms of their artistic goals produced shock waves in processing the event. What we achieved 'socially, politically, discursively' was never going to be equal to their disappointment about what they might have reached artistically. Performativity it seems is still an uncertain accomplishment for performance.

Yet the doubts and uncertainties are as powerful in the social domain as the artistic. How can we talk about the success of this project when the breakdown of the cease-fire was followed by a dramatic intensification of the war or non-war? Even though in the 11 months following the performance, the frontier has continued to be used for a variety of cultural events during the day, only last month two young girls were shot playing in that space we had sought to make safe. Victoria suffered bullet wounds to her stomach, while her 5-year-old friend Eslyn da Silva Pires was killed by a single shot to her head.

It is as vital as ever to remember that NGOs of any formation are not a substitution for government action or state responsibility. At best they act at the interface between individuals and society, creating and articulating links that have broken down or failed. At times they may be able to open up space for partial, illustrative transformations of what might be achieved if new alliances can be forged between citizens and the various manifestations of the state. They offer a temporary shift in social relations, but no permanent change in the concrete means of production or control.

No parallel powers, then, for what Shakespeare or the actors who came hither that night were able to perform. Rather a crossing and weaving between worlds that have become fragmented in such ways that the intersections and converges have become lost. If the staging of *Antony and Cleopatra* was a performative act of any significance, it was because it was an invented practice for that one night only. It was multiple and mutable. For all the noise that could be heard as the play finished, from the drumming to the gunfire, it is the silence that remains. We can each hear different failures and absences in that silence. The failure of the cease-fire to hold beyond the 18 days, or the State's failure to negotiate even one day of peace in over 20 years. The absence of a sustained civic programme to address the multiple needs of these residents, or our own absence from those communities tonight. Perhaps in the silence we can hear the echo of the work that was done, the processes that were established, the relationships that were forged, the promises that were made. I like to think we can hear the call to build each day the new practices on which social justice depends.

Bibliography

Barcelos, Caco. *Abusados*, São Paulo: Companhia das Letras, 2003.

Dowdney, Luke. *Children of the Drug Trade*, Rio de Janeiro: 7 Letras, 2003.

Junior, José. *Da Favela para o Mundo*, Rio de Janeiro: Aeroplano Editora, 2004.

Mir, Luís. *Guerra Civil*, São Paulo: Geração Editorial, 2004.

Itamar, Silva. ed., *Rio: a democracia vista de baixo*, Rio de Janeir: Ibase, 2004.

Ventura, Zuenir. *A Cidade Partida*, Rio de Janeiro: Companhia das Letras, 1994.

Yúdice, George. *The Expediency of Culture: Issues of Culture in the Global Era*, Durham, NC, and London: Duke University Press, 2003.

Zaluar, Alba. *Integração perversa: pobreza e tráfico de drogas*, Rio de Janeiro: Editora FGV, 2004.

Part V
Theatre in a Crowded Fire

Theatre in a Crowded Fire: Introduction

Leslie Hill

> The primitive hut and the primitive fire are revealed to be
> inseparable. The protoarchitectural fire of the treatise writers,
> the sacred flame of the city and the house, and the smokey
> chimney of the child's drawing all show the close identity of
> house and fire in the luminous furnace that is the origin, the
> singular and unrepeatable moment, in which architecture is
> born in myth, in rite, or in consciousness. The warm hut of the
> imagination manifests this in the even more far-reaching
> moment in which architecture is reborn into dream.
>
> (Luis Fernández-Galiano[1])

In the years just before theatres extinguished their fires and switched
from gaslight and limelight to electricity, nearly every aspect of
theatre design was influenced by the fear of fire. Wood, the beloved
material ideally suited both to building and burning, was replaced
piece by piece in nearly all London theatre buildings with iron, metal
and asbestos. City authorities began to require theatres to crown their
roofs with iron smoke flues so that in the event of a fire, the theatre
would quickly devour itself in flame without spreading to other
buildings. City councils called for theatres to be separated from other
buildings, ideally on open sites, but if not, then at a distance of no less
than 20 to 30 feet. Brick walls were constructed to enforce segregation.
Some theatres were sunk into the ground to make them shorter from
street level, taking into consideration that the water pressure of
average Victorian fire-hose could only reach 30 or 35 feet. Sunken
theatre stalls were favoured by city planners, who reasoned that in the
event of a fire in a crowded theatre, people were less likely to be
trampled to death running up the stairs than down. From the city

council's point of view, the ideal theatre design at the beginning of the twentieth century would have looked something like a military bunker, and would preferably have been about as far away from populous areas.

After long enjoying status as one of the A-list in the world of civic architecture, the theatre building was suddenly an architectural leper, moved out, cordoned off, walled in and buried into the earth. Appropriately enough for an art form which has been considered particularly 'inflammatory', the real danger in the theatre was perceived as coming directly from the stage. In the event of fire it was the stage and the audience that had to be separated. The proscenium arch was redesigned so that it could be completely sealed off from the auditorium; water curtains, solid iron shutters and asbestos curtains were proposed; a fire curtain was designed with water sprinklers immediately behind, which would automatically discharge a continuous stream of water down the back of the curtain to keep it cool. In addition to a sprinkler system, a huge tank of water was suspended in the ceiling above the stage. Performances were strictly quarantined behind the proscenium arch. What danger – what suspense; the Promethean flames of the limelight hissing and licking at the actors' feet.

So even before the architectural puritanism of post-war modernism, the theatre was being gradually paired down to a black box, an altogether more placeless space. Performance art and Live Art are often described as postmodern, but the dedicated spaces they happen in have a distinctly modernist feel to them – the cement floor, black box studio theatres and the stark, minimal white cube gallery spaces. You wouldn't call them fiery, would you? Architecturally scorching? Sizzling? Blistering? You wouldn't even call them dramatic or atmospheric, would you? They are made, like so many modernist spaces, to be voids, to be shells: they are purposefully made not to set the world on fire.

A hundred years distant from the limelight, biological human memory no longer preserves the experience of fire in theatres. The material memory, too, is gone as theatres themselves, gutted and wired, suffer a structural amnesia about their old flames. In our domestic spaces, too, the fire has gone out for many of us who have traded our hearths for televisions, arranged mantel-like in the centre of living rooms with the chairs huddled round. When we do have fireplaces, they are often no more than decorative features, sometimes simply mantels without functional hearths or working chimneys. Frank Lloyd Wright despaired of this trend early in the twentieth century and sought to reinstate working hearths into American design: 'The "mantel" was an insult to comfort, but the integral fireplace became an important part of the building itself in the houses I got to build on the prairie. I found it refreshing to see a fire burning deep in the masonry of the house itself'[2] (Frank Lloyd Wright's house burned down.)

The extinguishing of living flames, and the inherent threat associated with them, from civic buildings and homes has corresponded with unsettling civil engineering trends in which cities themselves were designed to act as giant flues. In the 1950s when the American government continued to massively subsidize highways and ignore public transportation, they justified their environmentally disastrous policies by reasoning that nice wide roads would ease traffic congestion out of cities during nuclear strikes and make it easier to clean up the Armageddon. Comforting? It's as if humankind has been scaling up right from the very beginning and as we remove the local fires from our dwellings and civic spaces, we design our cities for the larger catastrophes of warfare and terrorism that our civilization now enables. So now the city itself is the civic space that just might burn down. The toothless old theatre building holds no fear, or if it does, as in Moscow, the danger certainly isn't coming from the stage. It's the architecture of the tube tunnels, the bridges, the skyscrapers and the airports that now whisper *inferno*.

So, if theatre buildings themselves are no longer incendiary public spaces for the meeting of art and ideas, then where are they? Where are the contemporary spaces that offer the heat and the friction, the danger and excitement the theatre tendered back in the days when it was the most combustible building in the city? Where can you go these days to see a performance that might burn down the house? Where are the artist/alchemists now? Are they out chasing the city's flammable shirt-tails? Mixing Molotov cocktails in the form of public happenings? Or maybe, just maybe, they are busy working on their laptops, their portable electronic tinderboxes.

The final section of this book is an exploration of architecture and performance from artists' perspectives. In Chapter 20 writer and performer Matthew Goulish considers a meeting of extraordinary architecture in the work of the Chicago-based performance artist, Lawrence Steger. Lin Hixson, director of Goat Island, in Chapter 17 considers the places where performance begins; in Chapter 18 Julian Maynard Smith, director of Station House Opera, offers a glimpse into their multi-site work in progress, *Live From Paradise*; and in Chapter 19 filmmaker Andrew Kötting gives us pulses of thought, framed by the flickering of the faint electric current powering his laptop in a remote farmhouse in the Pyrenees – an artist's retreat heated only by logs thrown on the fire.

Notes

1   Luis Fernández-Galiano, trans. Gina Cariño, *Fire and Memory: On Architecture and Energy* (Cambridge, MA: MIT Press, 2000), p.17.
2   Frank Lloyd Wright, fourth Princeton Lecture, 1930, in *The Future of Architecture* (New York: Mentor, 1963), p.150, quoted in Fernández-Galiano, *Fire and Memory*, p.9.

17
Starry Night Sky

Lin Hixson

I perceive the world as vast and overwhelming; each moment stands under an enormous vertical and horizontal pressure of information, potent with ambiguity, meaning-ful, unfixed, and certainly incomplete. What saves this from becoming a vast undifferentiated mass of data and situation is one's ability to lay down a line. For me there is no place of performance until taped lines go down on the floor.

In this marked off space, I discover what I might know. I discover the place of roses:

1 The place of roses beginning:

> Wann,
> wann blühen, wann
> wann blühen . . . ja sie, die September-
> rosen?
>
> When do they flower, when
> yes they, the Septembers
> the Seven ambers
> Roses, when when

This text, written by Paul Celan, is said in German and then translated into English near the beginning of our most recent performance, *When Will the September Roses Bloom? Last Night Was Only a Comedy.* We begin the performance in a four-sided rectangle that is 17 feet by 36 feet. Two taped lines delineate two walls of audience sitting opposite one another. Two opposite walls delineate the other two sides. We begin in the location of roses in a room we construct. For this writing, let's say we begin with roses in an Italian Renaissance garden. Here the beginnings of landscape architecture take place. Here the beginnings of a performance unfold.

Gardeners turn over earth with a shovel in a 17 foot by 36 foot plot of land:

THEY dig canals –
sculpt surrounding bushes
build artificial mounds
simulate rain
hammer foliage
intermix box-trees and cypresses
mold ivy
fake façades
build water staircases
order still water
fork paths
slope terrain

Experiments begin according to meteorological and astrological conditions, geographic placement, and seasonal growth:

THEY study locality –
ponder particularity
make secret laboratories
twist growth
crossbreed rare plants
breed hybridity
imitate surfaces
combine philosophy and hydraulics
join botany and theatrics
merge artifice and poetry
turn geography and fantasy
cloister a habitat
and join it beyond
sky meets ground
incomprehensibility meets thought
THEY exclaim,

> As in a single moment did I see
> Ice and the rose, great cold and burning heat
> A wondrous thing, indeed . . .

On 5 October 2004, at 8:15 p.m. in London, five performers run in a 17 foot by 36 foot rectangle. THEY cascade over one another. THEY pile up dance steps. THEY zigzag and rush forward:

THEY scratch their innocent behinds on a tree –
kill a man in justice
die of it
tighten a nut
tighten a bolt
rotate the earth
have a party
eat soup with their feet
think they're dead
tell Tommy Cooper jokes and become dogs
THEY make pigeons disappear –
count to 13
count to eight
count to five, three, two, one, one, one, one, two, three
sing a song
go through a tunnel in the noonday hour
cover an eye
sip water
try little experiments
enter blind spots
grumble like bears
escape through a hole
THEY are one-eighty long with legs
THEY are eighty-one without legs
It's a tragedy

THEY rest on artificial, cardboard limbs and adorn the space as: Simone Weil, the French philosopher; Paul Celan, the Romanian poet; and Lillian Gish, the American silent-film star. There is a surprise, astrological effect when a video of the performers' heads, without their bodies, projects on a cardboard screen. Five heads float in a starry night sky.

THEY exclaim:

May God grant that I become a dog.

2   The Demon of Time

On All Saint's day at the Mirogoj cemetery in Zagreb on 1 November 2004, it looked like the earth had turned upside down and the night sky shone at our feet. Matthew and I travelled to Zagreb to teach a workshop on 1 November. Then our hosts realized 1 November was a holiday. Because it was a holiday we postponed the workshop until the next day. We attended instead the yearly event at the Mirogoj graveyard and saw the lights.

It was dusk when we entered the cemetery. The graves lit by candlelight formed galaxies and constellations on the ground. There are approximately 270,000 graves in the Mirogoj cemetery. Some graves remained dark. Others shone strong like the tomb of Franjo Tudjman, first president of the newly proclaimed state of Croatia. Light-years of light burned from the red, blue and white candles on his tomb, the colours he chose for the flag of his independent state, the same flag used by the fascist Ustasha during World War II.

'If there was no Tudjman there would be no Croatia. I just do not understand why people do not respect him', said 65-year-old Danica Seme as she bent to light a candle on the black-marble tomb, a ritual she repeats every time she goes to Mirogoj.

Drazen Petrovic also burned bright. The 29-year-old Croatian basketball star died in an automobile accident when a truck driver fell asleep at the wheel, leaving the wheel and truck to travel on its own.

Few lights hung on the partisans who fought in World War II.

But lines of light formed rows and rows in another part of the cemetery. They marked the ground where young men were buried. They were born in 1970. They were born in 1969. They were born in 1974. They were born in 1972. They were born in 1973. They were born in 1975. They all died in 1995 during another war at the age of 25. 19. 21. 23. 22. 20.

My father was cremated and scattered in Kentucky. My mother was cremated and left in an urn. I saw Adrianne Gonzalez in an open casket in a Catholic funeral home when I was 17. I did not look at George in his casket. I did not go to the graveyard for Adrianne's and George's burial. I have seen the graves of Karl Marx, Jean-Paul Sartre, Simone de Beauvoir, Franjo Tudjman, Drazen Petrovic and William Butler Yeats. I have seen Yew trees in graveyards in Ireland and Britain. I have been to the graveyard for the burial of a person I loved once.

We stood around the hole. The hole had four sides. A tent without walls made a ceiling over the hole. We stood with others on three sides and made walls. The casket sat on the edge of the fourth. Astroturf surrounded the hole covering the grass. I did not see earth even though the hole was made from taking dirt out of it. I could only see the Astroturf surrounding an opening. I had seen the tent before in catalogues advertising shelter from the sun. Margo Leavin had them at her graduation party. The casket was lowered mechanically. A priest said a prayer. We left.

Place is where time, in its human modes, takes place.
What intervenes in natural time is human finitude.
Death claims our awareness before it claims our lives.
The mortalization of time gives place its articulated boundaries and locality.
Beneath our feet are millions of matter years.
Local time is based in geology, geography and particularity.

We begin the performance in London in local time – 8:15 p.m. We perform in local time in a locality that we carry from Chicago. We carry three trunks, a DVD player, and a portable record player and unload it in London. It is 2:15 p.m. in the afternoon in Chicago when we begin the performance in London. It takes 1 hour and 55 minutes to perform. Particular words, particular gestures, particular performers, a particular clock, a particular wall, a particular floor and particular people watching, make the locale of the performance. Worked through the demon of time, the local changes, grows, decays and dies. Time gathers around it and mortalizes itself.

I perceive the world as vast and overwhelming; each moment stands under an enormous vertical and horizontal pressure of information, potent with ambiguity, meaningful, unfixed and certainly incomplete. What saves this from becoming a vast undifferentiated mass of data and situation is one's ability to lay down a line in the night sky of the Night of the Hunter.

In this marked off space, I discover what I might know. I discover the place of the hunter.

3 The place of the hunter

A camera tracks a preacher driving down a country road in an open-topped Model T. He is black-cloaked, wearing a wide-brimmed hat, and eerily calm as he speaks to the Lord:

Well now, what's it to be Lord? Another widow? How many has it been? Six? Twelve? I disremember. (He tips his hat.) You say the word, Lord, I'm on my way... You always send me money to go forth and preach your Word. The widow with a little wad of bills hid away in a sugar bowl. Lord, I am tired. Sometimes I wonder if you really understand. Not that You mind the killing. Your Book is full of killing.

It is the *Night of the Hunter* and Robert Mitchum plays the preacher, who hunts and kills his prey in the Ohio River Valley, in the 1955 black and white film, directed by Charles Laughton. Rachel, a farm woman played by Lillian Gish, warns her foster children about the hunter. In the opening scene of the film, she materializes over a star-filled night sky in a plain dress with a shoulder shawl. To her five disembodied foster children suspended around her in the night sky, she tells a Bible story while a chorus sings behind her, 'Dream, Little One, Dream': 'Now, you remember children how I told you last Sunday about the good Lord going up into the mountain and talking to the people. And how he said, "Blessed are the pure in heart for they shall see God." ... And how the good Lord went on to say, "Beware of false prophets which come to

Figure 17.1   Lillian Gish as Rachel in *Night of the Hunter*. Still from *'The Night of the Hunter*, 1995, courtesy of MGM. Clip + Still

you in sheep's clothing, but inwardly, they are ravening wolves. Ye shall know them by their fruits." '

From the place of the sky at night, Lillian Gish sees with divine perspective the terrestrial hunter and his malicious intents. Her words, 'beware of false prophets which come to you in sheep clothing', become memory aids to guide two of her children to safety. By remembering her words from the sky, they escape the evil hand of the hunter, disguised as a priest, as he chases them across the valley.

The act of laying down lines between the stars also aids the memory and provides tools to navigate. By connecting with lines:

BETELGEUSE (Alpha Ori)
RIGEL (Beta Ori)
BELLATRIX (Gamma Ori)
MINTAKA (Delta Ori)
ALNILAM (Epsilon Ori)
ALNITAK (Zeta Ori)
Nair al Saif (Iota Ori)
SAIPH (Kappa Ori)
Meissa (Lambda Ori)
Tabit (Pi 3 Ori)
Tabit (Pi 2 Ori)
Tabit (Pi 4 Ori)
Tabit (Pi 1 Ori)
Thabit (Upsilon Ori)
M42 The Great Orion Nebula (diffuse nebula)
M43 part of the Orion Nebula, de Mairan's Nebula (diffuse nebula)
M78 (diffuse nebula)

one makes the constellation of another hunter, the celestial Orion.

The first thing you need to know is that constellations are not real! The constellations are totally imaginary things that poets, farmers and astronomers have made up over the past 6000 years (and probably even more!). The constellations help by breaking up the sky into more manageable bits. They are used as mnemonics, or memory aids. For example, if you spot three bright stars in a row in the winter evening, you might realize: 'Oh! That's part of Orion!' Suddenly, the rest of the constellation falls into place and you can declare: 'There's Betelgeuse in Orion's left shoulder and Rigel is his foot.' And once you recognize Orion, you can remember that Orion's Hunting Dogs are always nearby.

(from the website Constellations)

Five disembodied foster children hang in a starry night sky around Rachel, the farm woman. By connecting the lines between the heads surrounding Rachel, one makes a house with hunting dogs nearby. The house in the sky whispers to those below, looking up for guidance.

who in this shadow quadrant is gasping, who underneath glimmers up, glimmers up, glimmers up?

4   Falling upwards

Here are my notes from Paul Virilio's book, *Open Sky*, intermixed with notes on *When Will the September Roses Bloom? Last Night Was Only a Comedy*.

> *We can fall upwards.*
> *Today there is a way out up above.*
> *Man can shed telluric gravity.*

Five performers escape the performance. One of them guides the others on how to do it: 'All right now everybody. Quiet, and listen to me. There is a hole in the performance. We, the performers, must escape through this hole within the next 90 seconds. This is not a drill. Fetch the hole and fetch the escape equipment. Hurry – 75 seconds.' The performers stand around a hole. They cover their eyes. They turn. They leave the performance space. Mechanically, by making a video of themselves, they are lifted into the sky.

> *Everything is being turned on its head.*
> *Soon we will need to get used to the real time perspective of telecommunications.*
> *The old line of the horizon curls itself inside the frame of the computer screen.*

After exiting the space, the performers reappear on video as disembodied heads in a starry night sky. The video is projected on a large cardboard disc hanging on a wall of the performance space. The sky behind the performers on the video is the same sky as the celestial sky

Figure 17.2   Everything is being turned on its head

of Lillian Gish, in *Night of the Hunter*. We borrowed it and looped it behind the performers' heads. The performers' heads are in the sky on the video. Their bodies are on the ground behind the audience.

Everything is being turned on its head.

The performers' heads have a party in the night time sky. Then the video ends. The live performers return to the performance space to finish the performance.

Virilio continues into a future time and place.

> *Astrophysicists talk the emergence of a new conception of time.*
> *It is a time of chronoscopic exposure of the duration of events at the speed of light.*
> *Time is exposed instantaneously.*
> *If time is matter, what is space?*
> *It is not the geographic space of the golden hills of Tuscany.*
> *It is the night of spaceless time.*
> *The temporal day of our matter-years will be joined by a night of spaceless time years.*
> *Without weight or measure, there is no nature, or idea of nature, any more.*

The performance continues. Five performers run in a 17 foot by 36 foot rectangle. They cascade over one another. They pile up dance steps. They zigzag and rush forward. The cardboard disc hangs on the wall like a mirror, its reflection starry and incomprehensible. Seven points of light shine in the darkness of the mirror. They are the seven stars from Orion, the Giant Hunter. The seven stars of Orion are the reflection of the seven Saptarsis of Vedic astronomy, who keep watch over the cosmos and are its wakeful consciousness. The seven Saptarsis are the seven breaths that, uniting together, compose Prajapati, the Lord of Creatures. Prajapati, the guardian of animals, protects the seven sisters of Pleiades, the constellation. The seven sisters of Pleiades are the seven ambers of Paul Celan. The seven ambers of Paul Celan are the seven ambers of a performance in a 17 foot by 36 foot rectangle.

Without a distant horizon, there is no longer any possibility of glimpsing reality.

The performance begins to end.

> Wann,
> wann blühen, wann
> wann blühen . . . ja sie, die September-
> rosen?

> When do they flower, when
> yes they, the Septembers
> the Seven ambers
> Roses, when when

The text continues:

> In den Flüssen
> nördlich der Zukunft
> werf ich das Netz aus
> es sind
> noch Lieder zu singen . . .

> Cast the net in rivers
> north of the future
> there are
> still songs to be sung on the other side of humanity.

The performance ends. Two taped lines delineate two walls of audience sitting opposite one another. Two opposite walls delineate the other two sides. The taped lines on the ground define the stars up above and the stars up above define the taped lines below. *There are still songs to be sung on the other side of humanity* in this room.

The audience stands. They walk to the door. They leave.

It takes approximately 45 minutes to pack the three trunks full of the contents of *When Will the September Roses Bloom? Last Night Was Only a Comedy* after we finish the performance. All that remains in the space when we leave are the taped lines on the floor. Sometimes within minutes they vanish and the space becomes a disco. The party-goers dance on our grave and the disco-ball sky projects on the ground.

Cast the net in rivers north of the future where the end believes we're the beginning and where yes they, the Septembers, the seven ambers, roses, roses flower.

Bibliography

Calasso, Roberto. *Literature of the Gods*, New York, NY: Vintage International, 2002, pp.118–19.

Constellations (website) by the South Dakota Alliance for Distance Education.

Harrison, Robert Pogue. *The Dominion of the Dead*, Chicago, IL: The University of Chicago Press, 2003, pp.17–37.

Hejinian, Lyn. *Language of Inquiry*, Berkeley and Los Angeles: The University of California Press, 2000, pp.40–59.

Petrarch, Francesco. *The Triumphs of Petrarch*, Chicago, IL: The University of Chicago Press, 1962, p.97.

Virilio, Paul. *Open Sky*, London: Verso, 1997, pp.9–35.

Weiss, Allen. *Unnatural Horizons*, New York: Princeton Architectural Press, 1998, pp.8–44.

18
Live From Paradise: A Work in Progress

Julian Maynard Smith

Figure 18.1   Station House Opera

Begin with someone who knows exactly where he is, but it feels like nowhere and he can't understand why he took himself there.

It is dark most of the time, and very thin; or so it seems.

Travelling got him down; the idea was never to have to go anywhere again. Also, his memory, never very good, now left him with little internal geography to orient himself to.

The early work was enlivened by someone who had the unique knack of being able to, or being unable not to, disappear in full view of the audience. She would fade from the attention, and only some time later appear again, somewhere else, doing something else; or appear to appear.

On at least one occasion this arrangement was reciprocated – with the aid of a bottle of brandy she disappeared from herself in the middle of a performance; some time later she reappeared to herself to find herself still in performance.

One exercise involved trying to enact this deliberately – how to disappear and how to appear. One good way to appear to an audience was to go through their coats hanging on the wall, relieving them of the contents of the pockets.

The construction of another world, a kind of architecture through performance, has its roots in an adolescent desire to escape another unpleasant place, the home. Architecture is always part of the behaviour of the designer. (That is why architects refer to land assembly, as a way to achieve impartiality.)

Performance architecture can be reduced to the basics of perception, the turning on and off of a light. 'Limelight' consisted of being able to see, or not, by means of the incandescence of the material comprising the physical surroundings, piles of quicklime, heated by oxy-propane torches. Disappearance is the inevitable corollary of appearance, which are the two necessary elements of architecture.

The experience of space is like the experience of thinking. A corner turned is like an idea come about, a discovery of what is already there, Thence comes the earthworks, the engineering, the fine honing, the rewriting, if you are so inclined. It feels as if thinking has evolved in order to solve three-dimensional problems, so now three-dimensional events provoke thinking. Digital media are still in thrall to three-dimensional imagery. Why does nobody know what else there is?

To avoid the tyranny of the reactionary 3-D digitalization of space all schools should teach hyperbolic geometry and relativity from an early age. Maybe then we could understand and so think with space in its unobservable aspects.

We are caught between physics and biology. We perceive ourselves as individuals, and as a result as a body in space, and as part of a web of kinships and friendships, and as a result as information in flux, non-dimensional.

The universe is not finite, because it doesn't seem to have a convex curvature, and it seems to be equally full all through. It seems that anything you can imagine in three-dimensions exists, somewhere, because there are only so many ways a space can rearrange its protons. My perfectly identical *doppelgänger* exists a certain distance away. A lot further away exists the hell as envisaged by Bosch and now in the Doge's Palace, and at the same distance the paradise as painted by Tintoretto and hanging in the Louvre. The pain and joy are real, but they are not ours. This justifies nothing, but what does it do for our imagination?

As with the Copernican revolution, we have been displaced from the centre of things. Our imagination is no longer ours, radiating out to encompass the universe, but is merely a map somewhere in the universe of something which exists somewhere else.

My genes are standard English/Scottish. My father is Burmese, living in Rangoon, and my mother is Ghanaian, living in Lima. Or the other way round. I don't wish to travel any more.

The presence of somewhere else is a paradox of course. But is the somewhere else I bring, via eyesight, telephone, internet, to my own here under my control or not? I see what I want to see. In Buñuel's Phantom of Liberty a child is reported missing to the police. The police can get a good description of the child because she is right there, with her parents. Of course they continue to look after her while she is missing. Many months later, she reappears.

Family ties are strong. They straddle the world tighter than any other. They are non-dimensional.

The individual is separate because of space. The human being is bound because of family ties.

My Burmese father is still my father even though he has never met me or my mother. He is special also because he is exotic, just like I am exotic to him. We actors never meet. We operate from all around the world, meeting as images only. But we are all real, as real as our own family.

I tell a story about him; he tells a story about my mother; she tells a story about me. But we are all real.

Does she tell a story about my idea of him? Does he tell a story about her idea of my idea of him? Do I tell a story about his idea of her idea of me?

I also see the sun rise in Peru as it sets in Myanmar.

We are what we know. What we know is non-dimensional, but we perceive in dimensions. My daughter knows I am her father, and she will be cursed by this knowledge her whole life. But she doesn't have to see me. Out of sight is out of mind. I see this woman in Peru. By knowing that she is my mother, I am creating an information model of a spatial world too big for me to control or understand – a way of collapsing distance. An emotional colonization of the world.

A deliberate projection upon innocent others. An exploitation of distant human resources for one's own pleasure.

I can make my mother as mad as I like. As she makes me.

But she has her feet on the ground, I expect. Her table bears the same food as I would expect. If it is McDonald's I can duplicate it here. At least, here in nowhere I would have to drive to the town, whereas hers is on the next street corner. But replica meals, replica conversations, replica love-making, across the world, on replica beds from Ikea.

In my story of her I naturally appear – this is a recollection, a cine-matic flash-back. I am played by my *doppelgänger* in Lima. We have both bought our clothes from Gap. In my telling, of course, I am different from the way I really am, so my face being different is no problem. In my recounting of my life with her she tells me about meeting my father, portrayed in cinematic flash-back with herself in Rangoon, played by a Burmese *doppelgänger* dressed, as she is, in identical cheap Chinese imports. He is rather older than she is; he tells her, in flash-back, about his recent visit to Europe where his grown-up son now lives. He of course is played by a European, and his son by me.

Or suppose: if in place A, X tells a friend about meeting a young man Y in place B and having a passionate affair; and in this place B, Y tells X about meeting an older man Z at place C and killing him because he wouldn't get out of the way; and then Z appears at place A as the husband of X and father of Y; does this add up to the Oedipus story, or is it three unconnected tales? If the Xs Ys and Zs are the same, it does, and if they are not, it doesn't. It is what you know: knowledge of the connections destroyed Oedipus and Jocasta. But before the knowledge, the facts brought a plague to Thebes.

Geographical distance still usually protects us rich people from disease, war, disaster, poverty. We fly in, we fly out. We need to be fully engaged with distance. We need to stay off aeroplanes. On the one hand is the book of knowledge, on the other the street of space. How do we confront the people we are?

(*At this point the writer appears to have gone off for his lunch.*)

* * *

In this very dark and thin place he sits and starts again. He is in his mother's room, but she has forgotten that he is there.

Imagine a reception in a large room – in every corner is a different band. As the guests wander from place to place the dominant sound shifts from jazz, to classical, to salsa. This makes sense as drama, in the form of the guest's spatial journey through a soundscape. The event becomes tangible, as opposed to the composition, which remains intangible in the guest's mind. What kind of links are created? They are ones of form, of colour, of texture rather than of specific content.

This is an old idea in music, reaching back through people like Ornette Coleman and Stockhausen to prehistory. The enticements of chance, patterns set up and allowed to run. But being music, the commonalities of form, colour, timbre remain. At the reception it is not the music but the journey which makes the drama, actions and places in sequence, while the sound remains a field. But what are the commonalities of a drama whose elements are separated, spread out in different places in the world? None are narratives in themselves, but a collection, a sequence of the physicalities of relationships between people, and objects and space; a human sculpture. These are chosen to evoke the intangible when juxtaposed, an emotional life that is suggested into existence. This is a balance of order and accident, the sarawagi which teases the mind to discern exactly where nature ends and artifice begins.

Three independent physical presences in different places will doubtless each wish to spin its own global narrative from a shared stock of images. What is the common ground? Each narrative must depend upon making connections with the other places, and upon the same material. Suggestions are made for space, action, orientation, rules for behaviour, time. Within a flexible overall time structure, specific cues are allowed; the acceptance of cuing is one of the initial common conditions.

Put together there is a problem: the viewer is not confronted with a show so much as asked to occupy a space. The viewer, limited in space to one location, misses two-thirds of the show. It is not a single, coherent drama. The ideal of the comprehensible space is absent. This information gets past the technology: for the viewer it is like trying to read a book in a chaotic street, while aware that also looking at the same pages (though in a different order) are others, in other streets.

There are many places on earth called Paradise; in Portugal there is one to be found once you have passed through the town of Purgatory. Presumably the peoples of the earthly Paradises still have hope, unlike the eternal heavenly one where hope is impossible. Once time is removed from the equation so is so much else; once life is recorded our engagement in it changes to one of contemplation, reflection, judgment, appraisal, the emotions one has when at a safe distance. A live broadcast clings to its lifelikeness by a thread – hope is a rare emotion. Can one bring hope, fear, expectation, regret to something perceived only as a moving image?

Amsterdam

The pilot version of *Live From Paradise* was produced in collaboration with De Daders, Amsterdam in October 2004. Three places in Amsterdam (an apartment on Beethovenstraat in the old south, an empty shop in Bos en Lommer, an artist's salon on Prinseneiland) were linked by high-bandwidth Internet connections carrying continuous video and sound streams from a single, mobile camera in each location.

In 1998, Station House Opera, having seen the state it was in in contemporary theatre, began to work with video projection. The sequence of productions, including *Roadmetal Sweetbread*, *Snakes And Ladders*, *Mare's Nest* and *How To Behave*, consist generally speaking of a performance recorded (and edited cinematically) and projected in the same place the audience find themselves in, alongside a very similar live performance. The drama consists in the subtle differences between the two parallel events. These pieces crucially make use of the audience's own personal experience and memory of the spaces shown on the video (and its inhabitants, the performers) to present the video space and the actual space as equivalents. Only then can a conversation between the rivals for the audience's attention and trust be achieved.

Live From Paradise uses no recorded video. The elements are three simultaneous physical events separated by distance, while the intangible, live-broadcast narrative is built from images taken from each of these elements, sent via the Internet to the other places, where they are edited in real time and projected on the wall. (The further away the locations are the better, preferably at the corners of the largest stage, the world.)

Two images are projected edge to edge: connections can be spatial, as when a single object or event seems to carry through the dividing line, creating a panorama linking the continents. Connections can also be cinematic, as when each image shows a separate aspect of a complex space: a man at a window looking out, and his view from the window of the street below; or a conversation between people in neighbouring rooms joined by a doorway. And each projection can of course be edited linearly, in the traditional cinematic manner.

An audience in each place witnesses the local event and absorbs the images, becoming increasingly aware that the images it sees from distant locations originate in physical events of which it knows really very little. The equivalence is between the three physical locations, one experienced directly, the others virtually unknown, an echo of how one's own life is constructed, in which there is experience of only one who feels pain, one who experiences consciousness, and it is only by assuming equivalence with others that one joins the mass of sentient human beings. (This most wonderful illusion may indeed be only that, the evolutionary product of the search for a means to predict the behaviour of others...)

The equivalence of physical existence at a distance can only be indicated by a play of images. They would be like the shadows in Plato's cave, were we sure there was a single reality that they emanated from. The audience sees a cinematic event in which every image is live, but it remains a show, transforming the actual into the representational. What, then, is the relation of the cinematic space inhabited by human images on the wall, to the non-cinematic space occupied by the audience and the performers in their non-projective guise?

For an actor, it is exhilarating to work with a ghost. An absent player is a challenge. It accords with most people's sense of reality by evoking the invisible. But the invisible is not the distant; it has to be potentially visible, in the room. The invisible that surrounds us in the West used to be religious, but now it is as much the invisible presence of pollution, hidden cameras, carcinogens, mobile phone conversations, pollen, TV and radio signals, DNA and radiation. With these invisible presences added to the age-old population of characters invented by the infinite human capacity for projection, through paranoia, fear, obsession, racism, desire, love and death, the modern realm of the invisible is large.

When the actor responds or connects with another who is only an image, this is like an accident that has been allowed to happen: the reality is that the actor responds to what is there in the room but invisible, in his or her head, or in the air. The appearance of the image of the other actor is seemingly ignored; noted invisibly and used tactically, connections are made between the images while in the physical space the actor is responding to the visibly or invisibly present.

This might cause mental problems for the actor: the strange reliance actors have upon one another in the rehearsal space; the energy, inspiration and confidence which they give each other are all removed from the equation when they work together over the Internet. At a rehearsal's end there is the sense of having been with someone all day, while a terrible isolation and frustration also envelops you. Something crucial is missing. Is this a symptom of the future, close, intimate, emotional contact with an image alongside the sense of absence? In Amsterdam the actors were able to meet after work, or at least to phone one another for a personal reassurance of their togetherness, and they needed it. When the groups of actors can never meet, what will their feelings be? And will these feelings affect the piece, become part of the drama as perceived by the audience?

And talking of the audience – how does it even find itself at the place of performance? Sometimes it has to find its way to the abode of the artist. This is often best. Sometimes the artist occupies another space and attempts to make a home from home. The idea of the actor walking on to a strange stage and re-creating a somewhere else is obviously abhorrent. But even the ritual and circumstance of attending a theatre in a prime location and which boasts both architectural form and effective décor sometimes pays dividends. There are exceptions to every rule, but in this instance the space dictates, and so the audience has to find it. It has to wander the streets.

This helps it observe the surroundings, to realize that the here is a player.

The found spaces were located in the usual fabric of the city, domestic or at least feasibly inhabitable spaces, with doors and windows, some opening on to the street, with access to other rooms, stairwells, and so on. In the performance neighbours, passing traffic, casual intruders played their part. The audience's own experience of the spaces immediately adjacent played a role in understanding the sarawagi, the *frisson* of the intended and the random interaction, and the borrowing of their urban landscape for private dramas to be played out at a distance. Certain rooms and spaces were decked out so as to seem to belong to one of the other places, and elaborate plots between performers elaborated to re-enforce this illusion. Fictitious composite places and hence dramas were invented. Everything was borne and sustained upon the bubble of illusory connections. In the hysteria of the attempt to maintain paradise all else was forgotten, made irrelevant.

In practice, in our search for *Live From Paradise*, the found spaces were usually unloved, and even in those which were not, once we had moved ourselves in and moved out everything that was not useful to our needs, a patina of unlovedness had descended upon the place. What is this place in which the audience has gathered?

An air of compromise permeates the room, for it is no longer properly derelict, nor decorated in the true height of bourgeois fashion, but is in fact a film set. It is well known that a film crew will destroy a house.

And with the paraphernalia of seating units, video projectors, lighting equipment, computers everywhere, the attempt at an uncanny reconstruction of place does not work.

My sense of place largely derives from alienation which takes a physical form rather than a biological one – hence I think in terms of space rather than emotions, or rather I convert impressions into ideas about space rather than into ideas about emotion. So my thought about place in relation to *Live From Paradise* is primarily incomprehension about the space of the world – we can theorize about technological extensions to our senses, but we are still very limited in our immersive capabilities (and is this the point?) – and what it is like to be with a person who is very far away. Over a few feet our senses operate in conjunction, but with video or telephone they pick up information from unconnected objects. I don't really like this. I wondered if you can get a sense of place from a live feed from across the world, and/or if this sense is always highly constructed. I remember a film by Jean Marie Straub consisting of two takes – one a static view of the outskirts of a rural village in France which lasted about 40 minutes while the voice-over gave a political view of the social statistics, the other a shot through a windscreen of a car travelling a rural road in Egypt, with similar commentary. The first shot was better, because the camera didn't move. I felt like I was there. Most people (including me) were bored rigid. But this was the point. Is this what a sense of place is? Or is this like those early Warhol films?

Live from Paradise was meant to create a sense of there-ness for a place far away, by means of a fictional diversion, a there-ness which is essentially invisible because of the fictional load placed upon the images. I wanted to see if an essence would exist behind the surface – and apparently it didn't. The power of images is not enough when treated so cursorily. Is this a point for durational performances?

I found it quite easy to work with people I never met. Many people found it maddening. Maybe they had the saner response. I found it difficult adjusting afterwards to real people again. Perhaps my treatment of the performers on-line was not engaged enough in the ordinary needs of most human beings. Maybe when working like this, you need to maintain a heightened sense of human interaction and contact in order to overcome the alienating effect of the technology and the distance.

In the United Kingdom *Live from Paradise* spanned London, Birmingham and Colchester with no daily physical contact between sites, resulting in a strange disconnection between experience and feedback. I was in Colchester while most people went to London or Birmingham. It is clear I have engaged in making a piece which other people have seen and responded to, but which I myself have never seen. It is like doing a painting with your hands behind your back on a canvas you never look at and which is carted off unseen to a gallery you never visit. What can you learn from such an experience?

These remarks concerning the aftermath of *Live from Paradise* were written after the first phase of the project in Amsterdam. They bring together some impressions and enthusiasms about space – the company has primarily always been architectural, trying to sequence space into a narrative, space which obviously contains objects – inevitably mundane/everyday/'found' objects in order to foreground their use, their position in space, their physical presence rather than their design or style – which is then used as the performance world. At times, instead of a physical object or material, a means of presenting space is used – light or video in one of its forms.

If the audience wanders the streets to find a space no one it cares about has ever been to before – and in this it shares its feeling with the artists who have found it, prepared it for performance, but likewise treat it with disdain – how can this unloved place become a place for a performance? Is it only energy, hysteria, magic, narrative that transforms a place? Or is it that it has to be here that the artist truly works, lives and possibly dies?

Figure 18.2 Station House Opera

19
Hidy-Hole and Inner Sanctum

Andrew Kötting

A Byway of Explanation

The bundle of approximations and inconsistencies that sits down for breakfast is later reborn as the work intended.

Or is it?

I've set about trying to commit to paper in one day, an unmediated-mediated everything-there-is-to-say about *On Location* within the context of *Placelessness*. I had to go to ground, to get away to a place of deepest remoteness, *my inner sanctum*. The rains turned to drizzle and then sleet, and eventually the morning. I wanted to be transported by the endurance of an unbroken meditative prose outpouring. My points of reference had little interference as they all lined up with their own particular significance.

(And possibly because of Emma Kay and her *World View*.)

Maps are useful
They tell you where you are and help with plotting the journey.
Where are you?
Are you sitting comfortably?
Then let us begin.
There was a time when meanings were fixed
When beliefs would stick
Nowadays round some parts

(not these, the Pyrenees),

they are open for interpretation.

Figure 19.1   Points of reference
2247 Ouest
Lavelanet
Serie Bleu 1:25000
Through the forest from Montségur
Grid reference D4
Louyre
I'm there

The rain batters down and I gather wood for the fire and worry that the electricity might stop and thus this, my sentencing.

Mediated unmediated
Me as cipher to the stream of think.
I watch
As it makes its way from this mountain location to sea level
And off into the eversoBigbeyond.

The bundle of approximations and inconsistencies that sits down for breakfast
   is later reborn as the work intended.
Or is it?

Place your bets.
Placeless place or coordinated zone?
See I remember he said,
He said:
I'm going to take you to a place that you have not been before.
I remember his words most distinctly, most clearly, most enjoyably.
There was a time,
Way back when,
People didn't have the *knowing*.
It was either one thing or the other.

Not the in between,
Not the un-scene.

Beckett's place.
Notathome:
Vladimir and Estragon.
A country road.
A tree and evening.
The wait and the wait and the wait.
Moves in their yesteryears.
Metaphor for metaphysical.
Headspace.
Indoors outdoors and in your neighbour's garden.

It's in the unlikeliest of places that you're likely to find things.

Bus Station Train Station or Airport Lounge?
Perfect the picture
This image now abounds.
Alfred Merhan
Refuge e or con?

Twelve years in the waiting,
Never alone?
Toothbrush and newspaper his companion
All else is gone.
Neither heimlich nor home.
Berczeller tells him
I've found a place for you in Paris.
And then again
It looks so much like Tarkovsky *it's unbelievable.*
But Mehran is happy in transit, never-always alone.
His zone.

Stalker's zone.
Post-apocalyptic placeless zone
The Stalker, now he's *never* at home.
He's roaming
Into a
Bleak unknowable future
Wish granter and wanderer.
The site, not non-site but site
Approached with trepidation and fear.

The poet the artist and the candlestick maker.
And Everyone else that might have been there.
The trick and the treater.
Tattered and torn,
Rags his nuts and bolts.
He leads them their merry dance.
They're waiting to be told.
We're waiting to find out.

Let things conceived come true.

A make-believe thing.
Same as it ever was.

Ridley Walker.
Talker, walker, assimilator and regurgitator.
Court jester, meanderer, hitherer and ditherer.
Intothefuture conveyor and reporter of things no longer.
Where was that place?
In-between place, in-between states.
The State of Elgaland Vargaland.

On and on and on until we come to KonungRikena Elgaland-Vargaland
The Kingdoms of Elgaland Vargaland.
Physically the largest nation on Earth.
Incorporating all boundaries between other nations as well as the Home
   Island and Digital Territories.
Every time you travel somewhere, you visit Elgaland Vargaland.
Where is it, what's in it and how do you get there?
(Is it Alun Rowlands World War II Sea Fort? Is it Sealand?)
Is it www.haven.com?

All right hold on tight here we go again.

Beuys
He's there
With his Dead Hare
Showman and *Sureman*
Explaining pictures
Explaining the meaning of things.
A way with the fairies to somewhere not been
He sets about invoking a transportation
From *his* place therein to thereout.
Then there's that bloke that lived under the floorboards of a gullery

Someone would enter
They're walking on top of me
He's wanking underneath them.
Seedbed
It was
Vito Accionci
Hidden in his Hole or
John Bristow in Nick Gordon Smith's
Hole.
That place between
States.
Flux
or
Lived-in-habited.

Out there-here, in the back of beyond, (and the shadow of the Gorges de la Frau), from babbling brook versus the whirr of the computer, to the tap of the finger and the happy-ever-after.

Property and propriety, we've lost the key.
Dada as the great grandfather of misbehaviour and saviour of anti-
    settledown.
Neither one thing nor the other.

Sets and subsets: tn38 0he is me
Backthere
Apparently.
But birthplace is home place
Home wins and away games count double.
The codification the decodifaction
Of this my meaning.
Configuration reconfiguration.
Fundamental existence in the worldfusion of human and natural order.
Us as *significant centres of immediate experiences*.
Consequently
Order prevails.
It's the knowing where things are
Where to put them and everything in its place.
Once this stateofplace has been experienced then the vagabondic begins.
Metaphysical wanderlust and of no fixed abode.
The long and winding road.

Peripatetic en route ists
Itinerant place to placeist.
The getting there and not the arriving.
How much longer? How much further? And are we there yet?
The irritation of not knowing versus the wonders and delights of not
   knowing.
The unfamiliar now familiar in this age of fun.
Make culture to consume culture.
Did you see her?

**Carving this out in the wilderness with woodworm my companion
and anti-homemaker.**

Vicinity
And Whereabouts.
Stelarc's place.
Aloof from and raised far above the ordinary.
Sublime.
In one glorious moment on a bright Copenhagen morning he trans-
   ports us to the void between.
The heaven's above you and the earth's below *him*.
Place of suspended disbelief.
A Suspension.
Suspension as suspended disbelief.
The spurious artistic intention as celebration of body-conquers-all-
   contemplation.
There he is, flesh pierced
Meat hooks gleaming
Crane dangling and him swinging
Thirty metres up.
Displaced and travelling.
Home is where the head is.
Home is for some: *couldn't-care-less*.
Has to be
Romany.
Pikeyjopeddler and Diddykoy.
No Fixed position entailed and
To be born is to be born in a place and that place becomes a home of
   sorts
Mobile home or home alone, home is where the placenta is
Was.

Italy, Sicily, France and Spain all round Elgaaland and back again.

Nationhood or Brother.

Which is home?

That sense of where, to whom and what we belong.

Honing in or escaped

Under the perimeter fence and out the other side.

Always an invisible barrier.

It extends along the line of frontiers: A no-man's land to die for, to leave the trench, get up early and play football with the enemy on Christmas day for.

Was it worth fighting for?

Sure.

Are you sure?

Occupation

Retaliation and

Un-bridled reiteration of rights.

The Resistance

And violation upon violation.

Homeland – Motherland – Fatherland

According to the declaration

Nationality is the preservation of our lives as human beings, where belonging is a foregone conclusion of freedom at any price.

Which is nice

Ius soli

(nationality based on place of birth)

Ius sanguinis

(nationality based on place of blood)

Unless you happen to be in the wrong place at the wrong time or of the wrong type or the wrong caste in which case you might be asked to pay the price.

Homewardbound and Homecoming?

Home.

Take off and Land.

Time-space compression.

On

And

On

And

On.

Space melts like sand

Running through the fingers.

Perec and his Species of Spaces.
My list of non-places;
Lifts
Staircases
Cupboards
Motorways
Shopping Centres
Casinos
Aeroplanes
And
Escalators

Up here hidden in my trees untouched and untouchable from the outside world. The fire exudes a warm glow and I have doubts.

Stylistic affectation can be compared to pulling faces.
Arthur Schopenhauer
Suffering for the world.

Video conferencing instant messaging online banking blogging and televisual vegging.
Virtual conversing streaming mass media communicating understanding and misunderstanding.
Stand ins
For?
Truth?

Walk talk and pay as you go.
Bounced around up there
On us down here below.
Phenomena of space and time are inseparable
Near – far
Located – Dislocated
Steadyreal – Everchangingvirtualspace
As
Is the examination of place and 'lessness
or
Artyfact – Blather
Stuck – Notallthere
Subjection – Agency

Take me off in ignorance at half time or keep me on as paradox until the end of the game.

One of the worst enemies of placefishing, especially in the days before
radio, was fog; obfuscator and deceiver.

Place grounds are zones where warm (new) and cold (old) currents
meet, mist is commonplace. It can be thick, so thick that the bow is
obscured by midship.

Skating on thin ice.

Plaice and chips?

Thus

The displaced peoples of Plaicelessness are enigmatic. They live christ-
knowswhere and not only is the origin of their language unknown,
but the origins of the people themselves remains a mystery. Dictators
Communists Fascists and even some New Ageists have all tried to
either subdue or assimilate them.

All have failed.

In the late twentieth century, at a time when their embryonic dialectic
was about to be whispered, (having been outlawed by some Stuckist
Gulleries), they secretly dispersed it through the use of technology.
Today anyone might speak it given half an inkling. Not only are the
Plaicelessnessae good at blather, but they are also a cyberfaring
people noted for their success in limited dissemination.

My plaice or yours?

That the folly of verbage as soundscape.

Here I am again.
Some *where* from which to make these forays.
Back to my continuing inventory of effort:

Marina Abramovic and her
The House with the Ocean View
Brings you indoors to then throw you out
There
With her
Up there
Performer spectator divide.
Not hidden but open wide.
Rooted reminder of those places we travel to.
To hide.

We're crossing waters to get to the other side, don't ask me why the Ocean's so wide.

Matthew Barney
Blimey

Where's he taking me?

Sergei Paradjanov mentor and founder member of this Poeticsymbolic
    reality?

Place is the place dwelled within,

Placelessnes is the place dwelt upon.

Place is home

Safe and sound

Non-place is no longer terra firma but on dodgy ground.

This Filthy Earth – as a mucking around

Sometimes familiar neither here nor there

The exact 'spot ' has gone to ground.

Spot-lessness.

Displacement through migration or exile has meant that 'homeland' is
    no longer given as

Found

Stable.

Hewn from the wilderness and settled upon.
Heidegger
I think.

Tomorrow we're going somewhere else are you coming?
Janek Schaefer's Recorded Delivery.

A voice activated tape recorder

Collects the sounds of the city,

As it is makes its way overnight through the system.

Pillar to post.

Messenger, harbinger and survivor of the British Postal System.

Witness to the place of non-place.

The things you hear nowadays.

Belkell, Oilyn, Crizzle and Bruke: A constantly updated catalogue to the
    portals of beyond.

www.entrances2hell.com

Imagination creates these places.

Here I am, here I am; journey-man-typer-confabulator
Sat here.
The drizzle outside.
Me the mister middle-aged lifer
Limited knowledge.

Piet Moget the painter?
And whirlwind performer

Again and again,
Up against the Mediterranean weather,
Year after year.
Canvas strapped to the side of a van,
Brush in hand
And
Intent on attaining
The depiction of the nothing as represented by the merging of the
    region that is land, sea and sky.
A Trinity (of sorts) achieved through his, as yet, elusive epiphany.
Don't ask me why the river's not wide but *he's* crossing it to get to the
    other side.
Collapsed foundational certainties in association with place.
Where are they?
What is it?
This psyche and its geography.
Inner space outside location.

Exterior
Day
The Elephant and Castle
Robbie Coltrane drums along to the shipping forecast.
Down below
Stuart Brisley drags his sodden body onwards in remembrance of things
    Marx and times endured.
What a place!
A Ghost Dance of a place.
Ken McMullen; Creator and Facilitator.
Lighterman and Ferryman.

You just need to find the right boat going in the right direction.
Mark Twain

Latitudes, attitudes and longitudes.
Fastnet fishing zone.

Back again, tap-tapping on this thing as proof of my whereabouts.

Commonal garden fantasy:
Alone in a zone neither here nor there,
Travel the world from your own armchair.
Reality tv for you and me.
Tv tv and no longer the stable sexuality.

Out there.
Far out.
Posited place of the non-settled.
Not in your own home town,
Not on your nelly
But
On the telly.
No Familiars to beat the path.
Nothing similar.
Uniquely, unlike nothing on earth.

Has this become a discontinous and fragmented temporal gadabout idea retrieval? Cerebral flotsam and jet sum?

Spit on my eyes someone and wake me up.

Close the eyes and indulge therein, blindness
Muscae Volitantes.
This is *new* territory?
It's Blue.
Radio Tele communication Blue.
Audio Visionary far sighted Blue.
Dying, with a dense veil of Yves Klein prevailing Derek Jarman all
    pervading invading.
Transports you to *that place that you have not been before.*
Precious and all consuming spot s.
Growing.
Somewhere, but not there.
Wherever.
His nook and cranny.
Then
Disintegration.
Reposition
and
Stopping

Place.

Edgelands of Contemporary Phenomenon.
Mixed messages.

Write it Big.
Write it Jennifer Holzer.

Or show it like Herzog in
Land Of Silence and Darkness.
Land Of Deaf Blind.
Where do they go?
Where do they live?
Solitude as *home*.
Locked into the castle of the however many senses.
Touching Tasting Smelling their only means of knowing
And as for the telling
Amazed they're not forever yelling,
But through the tap tap tapping, beating and stroking of hands eventually
    they come to the communicating and understanding?
This place, their place.
Sense of Place.

House of Leaves
Vortex and void
Not
To avoid
at all cost
else
Lost
Therein
Maze like
Of no fixed coordinates and permanently on the move.
With words Mark L. Danielwski plots a precarious foray deep into an
    Indoorabyss.
His place is a state of mind
It reflects the psychology of anyone that enters it – you can become
    yourself when you're there – Beware!
Collapsing
Expanding
Tilting
And Closing.
Disharmonious reflection of the consciousness therein.

The rain has stopped. The hunters are out with the dogs.

Arrive at a clearing and ease yourself down into the well of peacefulness.
It's all welling up.

Placelessness as anti iconic
Not a dense chunk of experiential information or stuff but
Mellifluous and flowing
Free-thinking.
Fickle?
And
Out there
One minute
Gone the next
Signifier to nothing but the desire to keep looking.
Channel hopping
Wife swapping
Dissolution
Devolution and
Supposed cultural erosion?
Mennonites, Hudderites or Bauman acolytes?
The tenuousness of this place at which we're at, shapelessness, point-
     lessness, directionless.

And me sat here, still, at the table of my immediate experience.

Felt not grasped, touched not held.
Post modern late modern latest modern post mortem Morton Feldman
     minimal hip modern hyper modern hyped modern.
Deservedly modern with all its mod cons modern.
Self accredited acumen as sole remaining passport to netherparts.

Hold on tight here we go again.

We approach it and then it disappears in the chaotic journey that is an
     attempt at understanding.
The Beuys man.
This time talking to his coyote whilst all around him New York sets
     about doing its very own version of an American Beauty.
Energy Plan for the Western Man, Old time German Expressionist or
     Original New Man?
Where is he at?
Where's he from?

Dispense with the logical structure of drama and making sense.
Hardware = Yoke

Software = Velcro
Reason = Home
Unconscious impulse = Nothome.

Floating piece of space and outoftheway place.
Steep hills and *Nowherevilles*.
Men resembling their times more than their fathers.
Is this as pure as it gets?
Dan Graham's present continuous past (s) in front of me
The Art Gallery
An eight-second tape delay
To play
With
And his infinite degrees of time continuums within time continuums
    reminding me of the possibility
Of a quest
For the void manifest.

**Reading back waiting for the kettle to heat and I'm all-a-fluster
with just my cryptic scattergun spewout missive.**

So not really landscape at all, but more of Manley Hopkins' *Inscape*.
Consciousness as it might look if it were dimensioned and therefore
    words
And
Soundscape to the Celluloidic.
And
Filmspace is a contemplative space not just a representative space.
Not just a peaking troughing car chasing place.
More Bergmanesque, existential experimental homestead.
Can you believe it?

**A knock at the door; the hunter has lost four dogs, I tell him I heard
    them in the night barking at the north star.**
Which is ever so far
Away.
He leaves, no smile on his face
And

Beckett is back.
Expanse of scorched grass rising centre to low mound.

Maximum of simplicity and symmetry.
Not often found.
The extinction of a body and a mind.
There there never mind.
Oh Happy Days, oh joyful days.
Evanesces.
Gone.
Bermuda Triangle gone.

(This place can take you prisoner – never let you go, never let you out.)

Engelbert sings: *Place release me let me go because I don't love you anymore.*
Ian Curtis sings: *This is the place come inside.*
Back to the headland
Danger!
Keep away from the cliff's edge.
Lands End.
Hear-me-now attending to what I half know.
Yi-Fu Tuan is the man with a plan for the Westernworld.

From too 'G' (heavy place) to zero 'G' (light-as-a-feather-floaty-place).
Between there and a hard rock.
Place is underpinned by the psyche and its geographies.
The smidgeons and the traces we leave behind.
(The *nature* of a space depends on who you are.)
Thus to the politics of placelessness and the real solution to
An Occupation.
Now there's a proper conversation.
Factions, enclaves and hierarchies.
I don't like that because I like that, I don't read that because I like
    reading that, I kowtow to this instead of that: thus the gulags become
    and the interloper is born.

It's often in the most unlikeliest of places that you are likely to find things.

Paradox of place as self-ish and social.
Place is what went on in the place in the first place.
And
The moment of definition is the moment of loss.
Definition is an approximation less we forget
So

We live in the lives we live in and these lives transpire within their own
    particular space,
Neither one thing nor the other
Yet both at once.
Ripe for a deciphering.

Dial 999 and tell the police: *As far as the mobile phone is concerned every place
is exactly the same as every other place. Telecommunication may have wanted
to disrupt the meanings and values of contemporary culture but these are no
longer grounded in the foundational certainties associated with 'modernist'
living. There has been too much 'seepage' and there is not a 'given' or 'self-
evident' context. Electro-magnetism travels quickly.* Fluids travel easily.

**I don't know what's going on. Alone in this workshop, disparity the
glue. This is the room from which it comes. Cold damp mountain
hidy-hole.**

And all along Music plays host to the aspirants of placelessness.
Jem Finer's
Longplayer
Soundtrack to a future from present and past
His message to others
And inscribed to last.
Penetrating the barricades of the Waybeyond.
Or
Early morning
Shanghai,
The pavement painters painting their prayers in water
To welcome the new day begun
There one minute
Then devoured by the sun.
The day is blessed and the backofbeyond touched:
Connection and reveal makes tangible the contact with the other side.

**As luck would have it the front door was open and the dogs are
    drying out in the cellar.**
They rest
From all their splendorous mucking about in the river.
The roof is not leaking and a new day is yawning.

Placetime – specific.
Elsewherelateron – non-specific.

If it's not one thing it's another.
Never the closure.
Never
The End

For confirmation on any of the aforementioned please visit: www.entrances2hell.co.uk.

20

The Ordering of the Fantastic: Architecture and Place in the Work of Lawrence Steger

Matthew Goulish

1 Landmark

You will know you have arrived at the location of what was once Lawrence Steger's apartment when you recognize the landmark directly across the street: a highly visible private residence known as the Cross House.

2 The fourth fragment

In an attempt to come to terms with the materials Douglas Grew gave me at our first meeting, on 1 April 2004, at Lutz's café, to start me on the project, I began by writing an inventory:

> *Excerpt from Sarajevo Journal Entry, 27 April 1998.*
>
> Photograph taken through a window of LS writing, in Ljubljana (Douglas thinks), Slovenia.
>
> The five pages of *No. 9*.
>
> Last letter, written to Karen and Michael in Ohio (college professors), dated 24.11.98.
>
> Film canister full of LS ashes.

At that time – the evening of 1 April and the morning hours of 2 April – I merely tried to absorb the contents of this list: the epilogue of a creative life. With the exception of the *Sarajevo Journal Entry*, which I had read when *P-form Journal* published it in the fall 1998 issue, this small collection was entirely new to me. It proposed a significant addendum to my understanding of Lawrence's work, and at first I saw it as proof of how that work had been trunated, the collection's fragmentation the result of a thought process interrupted. It was only later, after repeated cross-reading and rearranging, that I would begin to discern the intricate logic of the linkages between the five items on the list. I would start to consider the collection a work in itself, incomplete only in its lack of an overt decoding strategy. I would see the fragments as whole fragments, each bearing Lawrence's signature control, and the collection as paratactic; like a still life of five ornate objects displayed on a broad field, a dotted line leading from *Draft* (the last completed performance) into the next logical landscape, extending the ultimate series of landscapes each of which, the artist understood, might have been the last. Perhaps sensing this probable finality after all the possible finalities, he composed, with minimum effort, this collection in the form of a stepping-stone path leading into a terrain that I pictured as one of pre-dawn shadows on still water. Despite Iris Moore's mention of *No. 9* in her 8/4/99 letter to *P-form Journal*, I had forgotten about the existence of this unfinished script that Lawrence had been writing for Douglas and Steven Thompson. Now Douglas had given me this final text in the form of five separate pages, arranged apparently chronologically according to the dates of their composition: a title page, a short second page, and three pages dated respectively Sept. 5 1998, 12.9.98 and 16.9.98. Douglas emphasized that Lawrence 'was sick when he wrote *No. 9*'. Still, I resisted the inclination to see in its details, such as the differently rendered dates, the workings of a diminished mind, and became instead absorbed by its precision, rereading the five pages of *No. 9*, and beginning to think of them as akin to the microludes of the composer Gyorgy Kurtag – hyper-distilled music, all exposition and no development. Soon the text began to appear self-sufficient, containing all the internal clues necessary for understanding. Before coming to these realizations, however, I puzzled over the density of the *No. 9* fragments; a density not of the writing, rendered as it is in language with a transparent, instructional quality, but rather a density of associative thought. I began with the fragment that most intrigued me.

12.12.98

Film of cross house (finally) as is, with crosses removed, doing the reading of the names. Drone piece.

Film of Linda Pate talking about Mitchell and how he kept his house so clean. She points out that he referred to them as his 'doo-dads'.

Film of Dorothy Rosenthal talking about Mies Van Der Rohe in her apartment at New Year's Eve. Other reminiscences about various other Mies associates, i.e. Myron.

This fragment's architectural focus and presentational, documentarian restraint, stood out in the otherwise edgy collection. Furthermore, it existed apparently for the sole purpose of juxtaposing the minimal internationalist style of Mies van der Rohe, the legendary Chicago modernist, with the explosive local folk art of the Chestnut Street Cross House across from Larry's apartment. Without yet attempting to grasp this fragment's place within *No. 9*, I contemplated it instead as a piece in itself, and an indication of architecture as a form of expression in Lawrence's work. He had apparently been more involved with the Cross House than I had realized, and the 12.9.98 fragment linked it and Mies through the mode of filmed first-hand testimony. What logic could have lead to the composition of this micro-meeting-place, only six sentences long, of these two aesthetics?

2   Miraculous copy

The most remarkable of the buildings at Linderhof is the artificial Grotto of Venus, situated on the hillside above the palace and intended to represent the interior of the Hörselberg, where the first act of *Tannhäser* is set. The grotto was built in 1876–7 under the direction of the 'landscape sculptor' A. Dirigl.... A basic framework of iron girders and pillars was skilfully covered with cement, sometimes laid over canvas, which was sculpted to give a convincing impression of a natural grotto, complete with stalactites. The grotto was also given a lake, an artificial waterfall and mechanically created waves. On the waters floated a boat shaped like a cockleshell, in which Ludwig sometimes sailed dressed as Lohengrin. In addition the grotto was equipped with a device which could produce a programmed sequence of five different lighting effects, lasting for ten minutes each and concluding with the appearance of a rainbow over the painted tableau from *Tannhäser* which formed the backdrop for a small stage set into the wall. The electrical machinery that produced these effects consisted of 24 dynamos... The light with its changing colours was produced by 24 arc lamps which shone through rotating sheets of tinted glass, and the place was heated by seven furnaces to keep it at a temperature of exactly 20° Centigrade.[1]

I found this passage on page 135 of *The Swan King – Ludwig II of Bavaria* by Christopher McIntosh. I had begun reading the biography as background research for *The Swans*, Lawrence Steger's largest scale theatrical perform-ance, which he wrote, directed and starred in. *The Swans* took as its starting point an imaginary theatrical production, commissioned by King Ludwig, depicting the horrific occultist obsessions of the medieval Marshal of France Gilles de Rais, and starring Ludwig's favourite actor Josef Kainz as de Rais's Florentine conjurer Prelati. I had seen the piece twice at different venues in Chicago, and I knew that it had toured to Glasgow and Ljubljana. As I read the passage from McIntosh's chapter on King Ludwig's castles, I remembered a scene from *The Swans*, set in the Grotto of Venus, in which King Ludwig (Lawrence) shares a boat ride with Josef Kainz (Douglas). They sit in a replica of the cockleshell boat that Mary Brogger designed for the production: two life-sized swan cut-outs bracketing two metal folding chairs. Three stagehands manipulate painted cardboard waves, also Mary's design, on the stage floor in front of the boat.

The final pages of Wolfram von Eschenbach's thirteenth-century epic *Parzival*, a continuation of the Arthurian romance left unfinished by Chrétien de Troyes, contains the following brief mention of Lohengrin (here named Loherangrin).

> And indeed he was very loth to go. But his friend the Swan brought back a small and handy skiff.... Then Loherangrin went away. If we are going to do right by this story he was Parzival's son. He travelled over paths and water back to the keeping of the Gral.[2]

Eschenbach's *Parzival* had been the basis for Richard Wagner's opera *Parsifal*, which King Ludwig II had commissioned. The King viewed many of Wagner's operas in performances at which he was the sole audience member, and it was in this command-performance mode that Lawrence had imagined the Gilles de Rais production around which he constructed *The Swans*. In the performance, Lawrence often mediated the (re-enacted) action, either as Ludwig-as-audience on stage, or as Lawrence in Ludwig dress, officiating the sequence of the scenes. Wagner, the chosen composer, was one of many craftsmen, architects and engineers of Ludwig's grandiose and unfinished regal project: the construction of a complete mythology to both express and transform the national character of Bavaria. The operas and the castles functioned as two branches of this project, their designs guided by Ludwig's belief in reincarnation and desire to reframe the story of Parzival's quest for the Holy Grail. In 1868, he began the planning of a Grail castle, inspired by Wagner's operas *Lohengrin* and *Tannhäser*. Siting the structure on a hilltop where the ruins of the old Hohenschwangau castle stood, Ludwig named his castle New Hohenschwangau – it was renamed Neuschwanstein after his death, and, like the Grotto of Venus, remains a popular tourist attraction today – and conceived it according to Wolfram von Eschenbach's descriptions of Monsalvat, the castle of the wounded King Amfortas, building it entirely of white stone, apart from the red gatehouse, possibly in reference to Parzival the Red Knight. 'Clusters of towers and numerous palaces stood there marvelously embattled', wrote Eschenbach. Parzival, the hero predestined to succeed to Grail kingship, finds the castle by accident, having first encountered King Amfortas, who bears a diseased and festering wound that nothing will heal, that curses Amfortas to a state of misery, and reduces his kingdom to the condition of wasteland. Because Amfortas rests on a boat on a lake with restorative waters to ease his pain, he is known as the Fisher King. Parzival participates in a ritualized feast, a guest at Amfortas's table, on his first night at Monsalvat. He witnesses a presentation of the Grail, ignorant of its significance:

> whatever one stretched out one's hand for in the presence of the Gral, it was waiting, one found it all ready and to hand – dishes warm, dishes cold, new-fangled dishes and old favourites, the meat of beasts both tame and wild...for the Gral was the very fruit of bliss, a cornucopia of the sweets of this world and such that it scarcely fell short of what they tell us of the Heavenly Kingdom....For whichever liquor a man held out his cup, whatever drink a man could name, be it mulberry wine, wine or ruby, by virtue of the Gral he could see it there in his cup....Parzival well observed the magnificence and wonder of it all, yet, true to the dictates of good breeding, he refrained from asking any questions.[3]

He awakes the next morning, and the castle, now desolate and abandoned, bears no trace of the previous night's assembly. Parzival departs, only to learn that he has been in the presence of the Holy Grail and its King, and that his failure to ask a question has denied him his birthright and left the King and the kingdom in its limbo of suffering. For years he seeks to relocate to the castle and enact his redemption. At last, Parzival re-enters Monsalvat and repeats the scene. This time he asks King Amfortas, 'Dear Uncle, what ails you?' With this question, Parzival removes the curse, heals the King and his kingdom, and becomes himself recognized as the new Grail King and lord of Monsalvat. Just as Parzival obeyed the dictates of his birthright, so King Ludwig II of Bavaria obeyed the divine imperative in his soul; thus believed Richard Wagner, who referred to Ludwig as 'my Parzival', and shared with him the secret knowledge of his reincarnation, as heir to the Grail King lineage extending to Amfortas, Parzival and Lohengrin. The operas and castles simultaneously re-enact and actualize the mythology, as the Grotto of Venus both contains a theatre and is itself one, and King Ludwig II of Bavaria, reunited with his ancestors in a place outside of time, floating on the cockleshell boat in the costume of Lohengrin, no more nor less acts the part of Lohengrin than he acts the part when in the costume of King Ludwig II of Bavaria. The Gilles de Rais theatrical hallucination of *The Swans* makes explicit an implicit element embedded in Ludwig's mythology; a demonic flipside to the angelic cosmology, a visualization that history's hindsight enables, proposed as an endpoint to Ludwig's (retroactively proto-fascist) utopia. As one line from *The Swans* simply states: *He builds castles.*

The Grail, in addition to food and drink, provides oracular guidance in the form of words projected on its surface from within. In this regard it resembles the Decalogue – the stone tablets that Moses received upon which the ten commandments of the law appeared in writing. Moses stored the Decalogue in the Ark of the Covenant, and the dying King David dictated to Solomon the plans for the Temple to house the Ark. Once in the Temple, its permanent home, the Ark of the Covenant required a new container: the Tabernacle. The transubstantiated word made concrete enfolded itself within a multiplicity of containers, each consecutive layer acquiring more of the qualities of the treasure at its nucleus. In the Christianizing retellings of the Grail myth, the castle Monsalvat echoes the Tabernacle prototype. Ludwig's Neuschwanstein, a Monsalvat replica, consequently becomes tabernacular. In his essay *The Idea of the Golem*, Kabbalah scholar Gershom Scholem writes about the Tabernacle construction:

> It seemed likely – and so it was always assumed in the Jewish tradition – that this creation involved magic, though in a perfectly permissible form. The letters of the alphabet – and how much more so those of the divine name or of the entire Torah, which was God's instrument

of Creation – have secret, magical power. The initiate knows how to make use of them. Bezalel, who built the Tabernacle, 'knew the combinations of letters with which heaven and earth were made' – so we read in the name of a Babylonian scholar of the early third century, the most prominent representative of the esoteric tradition in his generation. The letters in question were unquestionably those of the name of God, for it was generally held by the esoteric Jewish thinkers of the time that heaven and earth had been created by the great name of God. In building the Tabernacle, Bezalel had been able to imitate the Creation on a small scale. For the Tabernacle is a complete microcosm, a miraculous copy of everything that is in heaven and on earth.[4]

In the light of this explication, the Chestnut Street Cross House appears as a structure of mythological/sacred theatricality, with naming as its mode of divine invocation in its proliferation of cruciform tributes. Here is a partial list of its hagiography:

Angel Gabriel
Don Juan
Saint James
Saint George
Zorro
Siam The King and I
Alligator Love
Rudolph Valentino
Chicago Queen Jane M. Byrne
Tyrone Power
Prince Valiant
Ivanhoe
Robert Taylor
Tarzan
Sabu

How does Mies van der Rohe's sublime transparency sit beside the overload of this baroque surface? With this question in mind, I remembered the many times I had ventured out of my way to visit the loop post office, waiting in line merely to talk with the attendant about what new stamps had become available. The wide structure seems low, wedged as it is between the towers of the Dirksen and Kluczynski Buildings, yet its ceiling floats above the usual single-storey level, and through its glass exterior walls one can, from the outside, see the line and assess the length of the wait, just as from the inside one watches the cars and busses go by, the bicycle messengers and pedestrians, or the people shopping at a Farmer's Market in summer and early fall. The broad plaza provides a stage for everything from those sedate markets to the chanting throngs of war protests. Its granite pavement continues uninterrupted into the post office's interior floor, an 'urban carpet' inviting entrance. Once inside, because of their subtlety, one may easily overlook the unbroken surfaces of materials such as the expansive panels of stone or wood behind the postal workers' marble counter, design gestures which can only be characterized as expressions of love for both the materials of nature and the mundane workings of the public sector; gestures dating from a time when their originator could scarcely have imagined the extent to which both of those spheres would one day become endangered. A nascent link between the Cross House and King Ludwig's castles had begun to form in my mind, with the Tabernacle as conduit; a link that had less to do with visionary qualities, and more to do with an understanding of architecture as that which accepts the impossible in order to organize it, anchoring itself firmly within the earthly confines of a place as a means of escaping those very limits. But Mies van der Rohe? How does his work relate to these improbable objectives? Of what universe could one say the Chicago loop post office presented a miraculous copy?

3 The tectonics of disappearance

The House That Made Mies
By Rem Koolhaas, 1993

My mother's friend's grandmother took a liking to her and always offered her tea and razor-thin sandwiches even though she was not her granddaughter. A very small woman with an immense fortune, she was feared by the girls...

There was one story which in the eyes of the children described the grandmother's power paradoxically more eloquently than the van Goghs and Mondrians that hung everywhere on the walls.

> Once she had asked an architect to design a house for her; she had built his project in canvas as a 1:1 model, then decided against it because a nearby train came too close to the theoretical house.

It was years later, in New York, that I understood that the (un)lucky architect had been the 'young' Mies. How and where had this rich older woman found such a young architect? He had not even been the first. Twenty-six at the time, he had been sent as a famous architect's assistant. After rejecting Behren's proposal – it too had been 'built' – she had asked Mies to do her house instead.... The catalogue that Philip Johnson produced for MoMA's first Mies exhibition in 1947 showed a picture of the 1:1 model placed in the landscape; there was no hint of the train.

The picture looked bizarre – as if a graft between two realities had not 'taken'.... Near the entrance stood a man. Was it Mies?

I suddenly saw him *inside* the colossal volume, a cubic tent vastly lighter and more suggestive than the somber and classical architecture it attempted to embody. I guessed – almost with envy – that this strange 'enactment' of a future house had drastically changed him; were its whiteness and weightlessness an overwhelming revelation of everything he did not *yet* believe in? An epiphany of anti-matter? Was this canvas cathedral an acute flash-forward to *another* architecture?

Then, coming out of nowhere, the ghastly surprise of the train erasing the mirage. Maybe this fiasco triggered the Mies who, from that moment on, would meticulously dismantle the traces and gravities that still clung to him from the nineteenth century and invent the tectonics of disappearance, dissolution, floating, with which he made history.

Did the canvas house lead to the curtain wall? All of Mies's later work used silk, velvet and leather as flexible counter-architectures. The most important love affair of this son of a stonemason would be with Lilly Reich, specialist in soft textures...

My mother ran over the ground where, 16 years earlier, hovered the house that Mies did not make; was it the house that made Mies?

4   Ablaze in each spectator

At our second meeting at Lutz's Café, on 8 September 2004, I outlined my thoughts to Douglas on how the fourth fragment of *No. 9* encapsulated the architectural motif in Lawrence's work. I proposed the Chestnut Street Cross House and the buildings of Mies van der Rohe as modern avatars of the spirit that guided King Ludwig's architectural project; a spirit that sought to externalize a thought system, with no corollary in the outside world, into an absolutely controlled environment. The buildings had in common an attempt to order the fantastic, and through ordering it to bring it into terrestrial existence – to materialize a bubble of another world in this one. In these structures, as Hélène

Cixous wrote of the novels of Jean Genet: 'A great multitude of signs, always very organized, prevails.' Douglas, in response, spoke of the concept of the 'monumental mausoleum', and pointed me to what he called the 'architectural text' of *The Swans*, which began with the words, 'He could be described...'. Later, impressed that he had recalled it so accurately after six years, I found the passage at the start of the second scene of *The Swans (remix)*, dated 3/98. The speech presents the script's first expositional passage. It sets the stage by describing a stage as a stand-in for the person who has conceived it. Lawrence wrote the speech for Laura Dame to deliver, as an introductory narration establishing both her voice and King Ludwig's presence, before she assumes the role of Gilles de Rais.

He's based on description. He can be described in many ways. Almost to a fault (*rolls back head to side, squints out of one eye, knowingly*) I've seen...(*changes her mind*)...nix that...never mind what I've seen. He's based on description. He's been delineated. Spoken of. Transmitted, translated and presented. (*pause*) Traced. (*pause*) Through transcripts, directions, contracts and alibis – I'm sure a line could be drawn that points (*thinks it over*) or better, illuminates a descriptive body of text. He would be there. He would be in a space. He would always be in a space, and be described there. (*smirk*) One would always have to mention that fact.

The space, (*quickly, coyly*) in-which-he-would-be-described is sometimes flat and sometimes vast. But always vague. But based on facts. Physical things. Like architecture for instance.

A church.
A crypt.

A hole.
A cavity.

A black box.
In the midst of nature.

Yes. He's in that space. Vague but true.

Space.

...

Well, this character King Ludwig, sets up enormous and elaborate structures to remove himself from the daily duties of the state. He doesn't want the responsibilities of a ruling monarch yet desires all the privilege. He builds castles.

Rarely in *The Swans'* 'architectural text' do we encounter the formulation of a complete descriptive sentence. Instead, we find description – in the form of starting and restarting, false starts and interruptions – approached via the nature of the impulse to describe; the encirclement of the object with unfinished gestures toward description, and through the common texture of those gestures, a rendering of definition. The description resembles a broken eggshell. We can read, in the gaps between evidentiary fragments, what the thing described must have been. That reading, however, recedes to the background, since the performance foregrounds the granular decisions and hesitations of the speaker, attempting a description at the moment of changing her mind. We see the performance of indecision. The objects of description – in the example of Laura's first speech, the coexistent entities of King Ludwig II and his castles – operate at the threshold of public decipherment. They resist description exactly because they deploy worldly materials for otherworldly constructions. The sentence as descriptive syntactic unit would fail to capture the exactitude of their position on the fissures of consciousness. For this reason, the pragmatic engineering of architectural drawings and plans (i.e., complete sentences) appears at best as a vain and grandiose exercise, and at worst as monstrous idealism. It can only falsify the fantastic animating spirit of the structure, which unlike the modernist spirit does not inhabit detail, but rather invokes detail to inhabit analogy. King Ludwig suddenly decides he wants 'a waterfall tumbling down one of the staircases' at Neuschwanstein. The architect employed to carry out technical planning, after great difficulty, dissuades him from the plan, and the literary historian enlisted as interior decorator records in his notes the King's 'very unclear conception of the limits of art'.

the feverish impatience of the King pressed ever forwards and allowed no single plan to come to proper maturity . . . [5]

Fantasy, methodically organized in a secondary nature, reverberates and reproduces itself *ad infinitum*, in echoes and repetitions: stairway/ waterfall; theater/mausoleum. We may consider the 'architectural text' of *The Swans* as one further generation of the transubstantiative act: the architecture *of* the speech incarnates the architecture *in* the speech, which in turn has materialized the sacred word. Jean Genet, in an essay from 1967 titled 'That Strange Word...', crystallized his thoughts on a manifestation of theatre that would never succumb to routine, but distil into a single incendiary performance. He could be describing the private spectacles that King Ludwig II alone witnessed:

> That strange word 'urbanism,' whether it comes from a Pope Urban or from the City, will maybe no longer be concerned with the dead. The living will get rid of their corpses, slyly or not, as one rids oneself of a shameful thought. By hurrying them to the crematorium furnace, the urban world will rid itself of a great theatrical aid, and perhaps of theatre itself.

§

> Among other aims, the theatre has that of letting us escape time, which we call historical, but which is theological. From the beginning of the theatrical event, the time that unfolds does not belong to any identifiable calendar.

§

> Drama, that is to say, the theatrical act at the instant of its presentation, this theatrical act cannot be just anything, but inside anything it can find its pretext. It seems to me in fact that any event, visible or not, if it is isolated, I mean fragmented in the continuum, can, if it is well directed, serve as pretext or even be the point of departure and arrival for the theatrical act. That is, any event lived by us, in one way or another, but whose burning we have felt, caused by a fire that can be extinguished only if it is stirred up.

§

> But drama itself? With the author, it has its dazzling beginning, so it is up to him to capture this lightning and organize, starting from the illumination that shows the void, a verbal architecture – that's to say grammatical and ceremonial – cunningly showing that from this void an appearance that shows the void rips itself free.

§

Monumental theatre – whose style is yet to be discovered – must have as much importance as the Palace of Justice, as the monuments to the dead, as the cathedral, as the Chamber of Deputies, as the War College, as government headquarters, as the clandestine venues of the black market or for drugs, as the Observatory – and its function must be all those at once, but in a certain way: in a cemetery, or quite close to the crematorium furnace...

§

Without becoming too preoccupied with the theatre, it seems to me that the important thing is not to multiply the number of performances so that a large number of spectators can profit from them (?) but to arrange it so that the trials – which they call rehearsals – end up in one single performance, whose intensity and brilliance would be so great that, by what it will have set ablaze in each spectator, it would be enough to illuminate those who aren't able to be present and stir up trouble in them.

5   *Esplumoir*

Genet's manifesto lights a fire in the theatre. In a liminal time outside of time, it inaugurates a series of destabilizations, between: cemetery and stage; performance and crematorium; cremation and animation; presence and absence. It speaks from a position squarely within the ephemeral moment that the designs of Ludwig of Bavaria and Ludwig Mies van der Rohe sought to eradicate. Genet's warp of the discourse aligns it with the concerns I detected in the fourth fragment of *No. 9*. Lawrence, I suspected, recomposed these architectural elements according to a rationale altogether different from their inherently utopian conceits, and at odds with the belief of their master planners, whether romantic or modernist, that their designs' realization would transform and restructure society. Lawrence's concerns struck me as more molecular and corporeal, not at all grandiose, and reminiscent of Genet's method of retaining but inverting the vocabulary of the castle. Genet states toward the end of *Our Lady of the Flowers*: 'I have made myself a soul to fit my dwelling.' Lawrence embraced and continued the work of this statement's implication: the work of an architecture configured of the subject's collected and organized *disjecta*, whether physical, psychological or mythical; the conformation of the subject to this miraculous self-produced enclosure; the work of the manufacture of the soul, and of its eventual disappearance. His approach forefronts the sacrilegious question: what becomes of the fantastic and monumental spires, the infinitely detailed chapels, the tabernacles reflecting the very structure of the stars, when the generative entity at the core – the word made concrete in grail or tablet – has vaporized? This reverse transubstantiation leaves the ceremonial and multi-layered enclosures enucleated, encircling a lacuna where a soul once burned. Exiting the library late at night, I walk the extra two blocks south to pass by Mies's loop post office. After hours, on a clear dark night, one could think of the structure as the world's most beautiful shell, ethereal, enclosing a void.

The *No. 9* fragments form 'a kind of organized mobile that takes off from a very precise and coded architecture' (Cixous), and I had to come to terms with them alongside the other items in the collection I received from Douglas at our first meeting: *Sarajevo Journal Entry*, photograph, last letter, ashes. The second half of Lawrence's last letter detailed a conceptual project loosely titled 'evidence':

But it's got me thinking, this whole disability thing, though. I've been busy for the past three years, getting my life in order (well, some modicum of order) and the little Virgo in me wants to document all of it. I've been saving bits of it (my life) and filing it away under 'evidence'; evidence of my health, evidence of my non-health....

I am documenting what is 'wrong' with my body. The disease has manifested itself in odd ways – wounds are a long time in healing, i.e. saving bandages from a wound on my shin that won't heal. Taking Polaroids of the wound in various stages of duress...And that's coupled with video-tapes of me looking outside my front window, documenting this guy who sits in his semi-cop car, documenting me. Eventually, he goes away. Pulling his car away as I repeatedly film him, filming me. All of this is part of a larger project.

The main part of this project is the documenting of my household. The aesthetic concerns that I have. Taking photographs, Polaroids, of the 'flaws' in the renovations that I have done. All of this is the work of Sisyphus, since the renovations are done on a *rental* property. Not owned, never to be owned. Molds (dental molds, to be exact) are taken of these 'flaws' re-cast in plaster (to be eventually done in bronze, – but 'never realized', painted the same white as my interior) and are of simple drips of paint (where the gloss paint has dripped), evidence of in-exactitude in the molding (where the molding gives evidence of a door once on a frame, etc.) and other such mundane household observations.

This project is driving me crazy. Compelling me to 'finish' the renovations, compelling me to 'finish' the 'finishing' and all with a slight sense of dark humor (as always) in the macabre sense of it, documenting, or trying to document what is happening to my body, but never going far enough into detail as to give t-cell counts, blood counts, etc. DNA also figures heavily into it, but an incomplete picture of DNA – I've been saving my finger-nail and toe-nail clippings for a year now, dating, as it were, all of the 'evidence' of drugs in my system. . . .

I'm not sure what I'm going to do with all this mess. I've never written anyone about this project – but I figure you would understand the need to document the ongoing changes, the changes in the landscape, my landscape, and the need to aestheticize them in order for them to make sense.

The final lines of the Parzival retelling attributed to Robert de Boron mention a dwelling so briefly that one could easily overlook it. Yet the quest for the majestic Grail Castle, in whose shadow this peculiar hut sits, could not have been fulfilled without it:

Then Merlin came to Perceval and to his master Blaise and took his leave of them. He said that Our Lord did not want him to appear to people again, but he would not die until the end of the world.

But then I shall live in eternal joy. Meanwhile I shall make my dwelling-place outside your house, where I shall live and prophesy as Our Lord shall instruct me. And all who see my dwelling-place will call it Merlin's *esplumoir*.[6]

Merlin constructs his house around a wordplay, an untranslatable invention reflecting the doubleness of his name, which he shares with the merlin, a small but powerful falcon of the north. Merlin builds his house as an *esplumoir*, 'a shedding of feathers'. Unlike the Grail Castle, invisible to the non-believer since 'a fence has been raised before it' for the heathen 'without benefit of Baptism', Merlin's house appears as a conspicuous sign, a wonder humbly available to all travellers, and it is

they who will give it its name. In that naming, they will identify the
house not as word made flesh, but the exact opposite, as word made the
shedding of flesh, the molting of feathers. The sublime lightness of Mies
and the ecstatic proliferation of the Cross House, Merlin has shown us,

Figure 20.1 The Cross House

present two diverging paths to the same end. Assign the materials of this world an other-worldly pattern. Designate a meeting place the grace of which defies the pull of gravity, and requires a new word for a name. Organize the remains to fabricate a fantastic house of evidence – of a life lived alongside its own death – a house as catalyst, to allow the body's disappearance and the soul's departure; a house of escape.

> With that Merlin departed; and he made his *esplumoir* and entered in, and was never seen again in this world.[7]

Acknowledgement

Thanks to Douglas Grew; Bryan Wildenthal Memorial Library, Sul Ross State University, Alpine, Texas; The School of the Art Institute of Chicago; The Lannan Foundation.

Notes

This essay grew out of a larger writing project: a response to the work of theatre/performance artist Lawrence Steger (1961–1999).

1   C. McIntosh and T. Parke, *The Swan King – Ludwig II of Bavaria* (London: Tauris Parke, 2003), p.135.
2   Wolfram von Eschenbach, *Parzival*, trans. A. T. Hatto (London: Penguin Books, 1980), p.410.
3   Eschenbach, *Parzival*, pp.126–7.
4   G. Scholem, *On the Kabbalah and Its Symbolism*, trans. R. Manheim (New York: Schocken Books, 1965), pp.166–7.
5   McIntosh and Parke, *The Swan King*, p.130.
6   Attributed to Robert de Boron, *Arthurian Studies*, XL VIII, and *Merlin and the Grail – Joseph of Arimethea, Merlin, Perceval*, trans. N. Bryant (Woodbridge: D. S. Brewer, 2001), pp.171–2.
7   De Boron, *Merlin*, p.172.

Bibliography

Attributed to Boron, Robert de. *Arthurian Studies*, XL VIII, *Merlin and the Grail – Joseph of Arimethea, Merlin, Perceval*, trans. N. Bryant, Woodbridge: D. S. Brewer, 2001.
Cixous H. *Readings – The Poetics of Blanchot, Joyce, Kafka, Kleist, Lispector, and Tsvetayeva*, trans. V. Andermatt Conley, Minneapolis: University of Minnesota Press, 1991.
Deleuze, G. *Masochism, Coldness and Cruelty*, trans. Jean McNeil, New York: Zone Books, 1989.
Genet, J. *Our Lady of the Flowers*, trans. B. Frechtman, New York: Grove Press, 1963.

Genet, J. *Fragments of the Artwork*, trans. C. Mandell, Stanford, CA: Stanford University Press, 2003.

McIntosh, C. and T. Parke. *The Swan King – Ludwig II of Bavaria* London: Tauris Parke, 2003.

Koolhaas, R. and B. Mau, *S, M, L, XL by Office for Metropolitan Architecture*, ed. Jennifer Sigler, New York: The Monacelli Press, 1995.

Scholem, G. *On the Kabbalah and Its Symbolism*, trans. R. Manheim, New York: Schocken Books, 1965.

Steger, L. *No. 9* (unfinished manuscript in possession of the author, 1999).

Steger, L. *The Swans (remix)* (manuscript in possession of the author, 1998).

Index

Performance Interventions

Series Editors: **Elaine Aston**, University of Lancaster, and **Bryan Reynolds**, University of California, Irvine

Performance Interventions is a series of monographs and essay collections on theatre, performance, and visual culture that share an underlying commitment to the radical and political potential of the arts in our contemporary moment, or give consideration to performance and to visual culture from the past deemed crucial to a social and political present. *Performance Interventions* moves transversally across artistic and ideological boundaries to publish work that promotes dialogue between practitioners and academics, and interactions between performance communities, educational institutions, and academic disciplines.

Titles include:

Alan Ackerman and Martin Puchner (*editors*)
AGAINST THEATRE
Creative Destructions on the Modernist Stage

Elaine Aston and Geraldine Harris (*editors*)
FEMINIST FUTURES?
Theatre, Performance, Theory

Leslie Hill and Helen Paris (*editors*)
PERFORMANCE AND PLACE

Forthcoming titles:

Lynette Goddard
STAGING BLACK FEMINISMS
Identity, Politics, Performance

Amelia M. Kritzer
POLITICAL THEATRE IN POST-THATCHER BRITAIN

Performance Interventions
Series Standing Order ISBN 1–4039–4443–1 Hardback 1–4039–4444–X Paperback
(*outside North America only*)

You can receive future titles in this series as they are published by placing a standing order. Please contact your bookseller or, in case of difficulty, write to us at the address below with your name and address, the title of the series and the ISBN quoted above.

Customer Services Department, Macmillan Distribution Ltd, Houndmills, Basingstoke, Hampshire RG21 6XS, England

Performance and Place